Relanguaging Language from a South African Township School

NEW PERSPECTIVES ON LANGUAGE AND EDUCATION

Founding Editor: Viv Edwards, *University of Reading, UK*

Series Editors: Phan Le Ha, *University of Hawaii at Manoa, USA* and Joel Windle, *Monash University, Australia.*

Two decades of research and development in language and literacy education have yielded a broad, multidisciplinary focus. Yet, education systems face constant economic and technological change, with attendant issues of identity and power, community and culture. What are the implications for language education of new 'semiotic economies' and communications technologies? Of complex blendings of cultural and linguistic diversity in communities and institutions? Of new cultural, regional and national identities and practices? The New Perspectives on Language and Education series will feature critical and interpretive, disciplinary and multidisciplinary perspectives on teaching and learning, language and literacy in new times. New proposals, particularly for edited volumes, are expected to acknowledge and include perspectives from the Global South. Contributions from scholars from the Global South will be particularly sought out and welcomed, as well as those from marginalized communities within the Global North.

All books in this series are externally peer-reviewed.

Full details of all the books in this series and of all our other publications can be found on http://www.multilingual-matters.com, or by writing to Multilingual Matters, St Nicholas House, 31-34 High Street, Bristol BS1 2AW, UK.

NEW PERSPECTIVES ON LANGUAGE AND EDUCATION: 99

Relanguaging Language from a South African Township School

Lara-Stephanie Krause

MULTILINGUAL MATTERS
Bristol • Jackson

DOI https://doi.org/10.21832/KRAUSE2125
Library of Congress Cataloging in Publication Data
A catalog record for this book is available from the Library of Congress.
Names: Krause, Lara-Stephanie, 1989- author.
Title: Relanguaging Language from a South African Township School / Lara-Stephanie Krause.
Description: Bristol, UK; Blue Ridge Summit, PA: Multilingual Matters, 2021. | Series: New Perspectives on Language and Education: 99 | Includes bibliographical references and index. | Summary: "Using data from a long-term ethnographic study of English language classrooms in a South African township, this book conceptualises language teaching not as a progression from one fixed language to another, but as a circular sorting process between linguistic heterogeneity (languaging) and homogeneity (a standard language)"— Provided by publisher.
Identifiers: LCCN 2021037270 (print) | LCCN 2021037271 (ebook) | ISBN 9781800412118 (paperback) | ISBN 9781800412125 (hardback) | ISBN 9781800412132 (pdf) | ISBN 9781800412149 (epub)
Subjects: LCSH: English language—Study and teaching—South Africa. | Multilingualism—South Africa. | Translanguaging (Linguistics)
Classification: LCC PE1068.S58 K73 2021 (print) | LCC PE1068.S58 (ebook) | DDC 428.0071068—dc23 LC record available at https://lccn.loc.gov/2021037270
LC ebook record available at https://lccn.loc.gov/2021037271

British Library Cataloguing in Publication Data
A catalogue entry for this book is available from the British Library.

ISBN-13: 978-1-80041-212-5 (hbk)
ISBN-13: 978-1-80041-211-8 (pbk)

Multilingual Matters
UK: St Nicholas House, 31-34 High Street, Bristol BS1 2AW, UK.
USA: Ingram, Jackson, TN, USA.

Website: www.multilingual-matters.com
Twitter: Multi_Ling_Mat
Facebook: https://www.facebook.com/multilingualmatters
Blog: www.channelviewpublications.wordpress.com

Copyright © 2022 Lara-Stephanie Krause.

All rights reserved. No part of this work may be reproduced in any form or by any means without permission in writing from the publisher.

The policy of Multilingual Matters/Channel View Publications is to use papers that are natural, renewable and recyclable products, made from wood grown in sustainable forests. In the manufacturing process of our books, and to further support our policy, preference is given to printers that have FSC and PEFC Chain of Custody certification. The FSC and/or PEFC logos will appear on those books where full certification has been granted to the printer concerned.

Typeset by Deanta Global Publishing Services, Chennai, India

Contents

Acknowledgements	vii
1 Introduction	**1**
1.1 Tricked into Detours	1
1.2 The Languaging of the Township	5
1.3 The Nomolanguages of Schooling	7
1.4 The Testing via Nomolanguages	9
1.5 The English of Township Teachers	12
1.6 The Ethnographies of Township Classrooms	14
1.7 The Experiment of this Book	17
1.8 The Route through the Book	20
2 Relanguaging Language towards an Alternative Perspective	**23**
2.1 Seeing Language Like a (Colonial) State	23
2.2 Unsettling Linguistic Objects	26
2.3 Languaging Our Way from Individual to Spatial Repertoires	37
2.4 Relanguaging in Two Directions	43
3 A Linguistic Ethnography for Seeing More	**48**
3.1 From Taxis to Classrooms	48
3.2 An Experimental Linguistic Ethnography	55
4 An Eagle Learning to Fly and an Analyst Learning to See	**63**
4.1 Before the Story Begins	63
4.2 Looking for Interesting Birds and Interesting Linguistic Features	68
4.3 Seeing Morphemes Guide the Change into a Chicken	75
4.4 Relanguaging 'Train' while Training the Eagle	91
4.5 What the Story and the Spatial Lens Teaches Us	101
4.6 Chapter Discussion	118

5	Complexities around Uing and Testing in Khayelitsha	123
	5.1 Before Beginning to U and to Test	123
	5.2 What Can U Do?	129
	5.3 Assessment Relanguaged to Make the System Work	142
	5.4 Chapter Discussion	164
6	Rewriting Nomolanguages	168
	6.1 The Idea for a Writing Task	168
	6.2 Seeing Writing Differently: From Deficit to Potential	179
	6.3 Chapter Discussion	194
7	Conclusion: So What?	198
	7.1 Seeing More	198
	7.2 Seeing Like a Township Teacher	201
	7.3 Blind Spots Blocking Educational Change	203
	7.4 Some Recommended Rethinking	205
	7.5 Outlook	210

Notes	213
Appendix A Glossing Conventions	219
Appendix B Noun Class Agreement Morphology (Positive and Negative)	220
Appendix C Lists of Lesson Transcripts and Interviews	222
Appendix D Table of Relanguaging Circles	224
Appendix E Excerpt from Formal Assessment Task Grade 5	225
References	229
Index	239

Acknowledgements

Mama und Papa, mit eurem Mut habt ihr ein Zuhause gebaut, das Freiheit möglich gemacht hat. Für mich unter anderem die Freiheit, meinem Herzensinteresse nachzugehen – oder wohl eher nachzufliegen. Das Wissen darum, dass euer Stolz und eure Unterstützung mir zu jedem Zeitpunkt sicher waren, hat mich immer wieder beruhigt, stabilisiert und ermutigt. Hier ist jetzt das Resultat. Ein Buch. Mein Buch. Aber auch euer Buch. Danke.

Ndiphelelwe ngamagama when it comes to my supervisors and mentors who have guided me through this with so much oversight, goodwill and brilliant insights. Tessa, Rose Marie, Mastin – ndiyabulela. Evi und Michel, ohne eure Unterstützung this book wouldn't be close to what it is now. Ich danke euch. Und I thank my friends and active supporters in Cape Town and in Leipzig. Enkosi kakhulu.

Dear teachers at Khayelitsha Primary

Ekugqibeleni, phambi kokungena kule ncwadi, ndifuna ukuthi enkosi kootitshala baseKhayelitsha. Enkosi ngokundivulela iingcango zeeclassrooms zenu nangokukwabelana ngolwazi lwenu. I have never seen abantu abakhathalela ikamva labantwana ngendlela nina nilikhathalela ngayo. Ndikubonile ukufundisa kwenu – ndiyazi le nto yokuba nina you are changing things for the better.

Ngentlonipho
Chwayita

Englished version:

Finally, before entering into this book, I want to say thank you to the teachers in Khayelitsha. Thank you for opening the doors of your classrooms for me and for sharing your knowledge. I have never seen people who care about the children's future in the way your care about it. I have seen your teaching – I know that you are changing things for the better.

Respectfully
Chwayita

*For the teachers and learners in Khayelitsha
who have shown me how to language*

1 Introduction

1.1 Tricked into Detours

Author:	So do you think there is almost like a specific Xhosa – or language – that evolves in the township? In the...elokishini?
Teacher in Khayelitsha:	Yah but it's mixed with ilanguage yamaColoured, amaXhosa and the White.

Language teaching is built on the assumption that named languages – nomolanguages – exist as separate, homogeneous entities and is aimed at the mastery of standardised codes. In this view, English teaching in South African townships like Khayelitsha is failing. Learners (and teachers) underperform in standardised English tests and are repeatedly described as cut off from the standard linguistic norms needed for success beyond the township. In my view, this deficit perspective has exhausted its explanatory potential. I wish to develop an alternative perspective on township English classrooms, its theoretical point of departure being the heterogeneity, flexibility and creativity of day-to-day language practices in (South) African urban spaces that the teacher describes in the opening quote. The next step is to theorise – in close dialogue with the Khayelitshan case – the relationship in which such heterogeneous languaging stands to the production of a homogenised standard language as the target of the traditional language classroom. I therefore explore the field of tension between linguistic fluidity and fixity, between heterogeneity and homogeneity. A closer look at the opening quote illustrates this tension.

With regard to linguistic form, this short exchange displays the dimension of fluid, heterogeneous languaging. The teacher and I practice here what I call 'Khayelitshan languaging': the routinised but not officially codified language practices of residents of the township Khayelitsha (Cape Town, South Africa) and of those who know how to language[1] there. She refers to these language practices as 'mixed', while I describe them as heterogeneous throughout this work – as assembled from elements with various different histories, like *almost*, *elokishini*, *i-*, *language* or *ama-*, all present in this short exchange.

The way the teacher describes this languaging to me then exposes the dimension of homogenised nomolanguages: She says that the language of the township is 'mixed with ilanguage yamaColoured, amaXhosa and the White',[2] presupposing language as divided into separate, named entities associated with population groups. In this case, 'Afrikaans' would be the nomolanguage of amaColoured, 'Xhosa' that of amaXhosa and 'English' that of Whites.[3] Looked at closely this way, the quote shows how South African townships that are known for linguistic heterogeneity and fluidity (languaging) simultaneously co-constitute our wider social world where language is seen as split into homogeneous units: nomolanguages.

I use the prefix *nomo-*, inspired by 'nominalis' as 'pertaining to a name or names',[4] because we normally distinguish named language units from the phenomenon *language* only by an article ('a' or 'the' language) or an -s (languages). Our commonsensical languaging therefore ties *language* closely to 'a language'. Here, I want to foster a view that entangles language more closely with languaging and that positions nomolanguages as the outcome of linguistic, administrative and didactic sorting, writing and naming practices. The prefix continuously unsettles deeply entrenched ideas of separate nomolanguages as primordial entities and as necessarily and always definitive of the phenomenon language. With this terminology twist, I don't wish to deny the existence and the social significance of nomolanguages but rather draw attention to the processes of their production.

Scott's (1998) memorable phrase 'seeing like a state' helps to understand nomolanguages as products – and simultaneously producers – of a persistent vision of the social world as structured into simplified, homogeneous units that render the practices of populations legible, measurable and manipulable for state administrations and their agents. As Halberstam summarises:

> for Scott, to 'see like a state' means to accept the order of things and to internalize them; it means that we begin to deploy and think with the logic of the superiority of orderliness. (Halberstam, 2011: 9)

Here, this orderliness is the ordering of language into nomolanguages. While this order of things that is produced and sustained by the statist[5] vision clashes with the actual fluid languaging in places like Khayelitsha, it has nevertheless become so deeply internalised that every consideration of language, academic or not, tends to take it as its point of departure. That too we can read from the opening quote: the teacher describes the language of the township as 'mixed'. In her account, as in most people's, heterogeneous languaging emerges from the manipulation of nomolanguages. Accordingly, we can perceive linguistic heterogeneity because linguistically homogeneous units exist. Nomolanguages come first, languaging second. Homogeneity is the norm and heterogeneity the surprise.

The directionality of this gaze is what I understand here by 'seeing like a state' (explained more in Chapter 2). But what if we saw things from the other side?

What becomes visible if we systematically turn the tables by 'seeing' languaging as normal and nomolanguages as surprising? The space that has prompted me to develop this vision is the Khayelitshan English classroom. The project proves, however, much easier to undertake than to accomplish, because I am myself caught in seeing language like a state – always, even if in ever more subtle ways, beginning my considerations from named boxes like Xhosa[6] and English. Khayelitshan languaging strikes me as different, otherwise I would never have asked the question in the opening quote. That being said, my project here not only requires me to turn the tables but also literally to turn myself around, so that I walk – i.e. analyse and interpret the data – the other way. In the run-up to this book, however, I kept walking in circles, undermining my own project by reproducing the statist vision in my analyses.

I eventually figured out that it was the analytical terminology I used that kept implying things I didn't want to say. Terms like 'translation', 'non-standard language', 'mistake' and even 'translanguaging', combined with the categorisation of every morpheme I wished to analyse as belonging to a nomolanguage or a nomolanguage family, made me see the data again like a state. What kept me in this loop was a conceptual conflation of linguistic features and nomolanguages (Section 2.1.2) that such terminology carries with it as a more or less explicit conceptual stowaway.[7] In line with Sabino (2018: 114), who shows how our established analytical terminologies 'limit our insights into human language', I argue that this conceptual conflation makes us unable to reverse the statist gaze and to begin our theorisations from languaging as a baseline condition. Instead, the conflation between linguistic features and nomolanguages subtly forces us to accept nomolanguages as a starting point for any theorisation. Especially when using tools from classical linguistics (close morphological analysis for example), nomolanguages as an ordering principle of data are so enshrined in the discipline that it proves extremely hard not to accept them as analytical categories. How to get out then? I decided to trick myself into continuously walking the other way – even if that implied taking many detours when much more direct routes were available. The trick, the walk, the detours and what I got to see along the way constitute this book.

The trick was to actively constrain my thought-possibilities by not allowing myself to use in my analyses any of the linguistic terminology I identify as entangled in – and therefore reproductive of – the statist view of language. This thought experiment (details in Section 1.7) is the trick that helps me to keep walking the other way by forcing me into describing and analysing my empirical observations in Khayelitshan English classrooms differently. *Walking the other way* has itself to be read in two ways here: firstly, it means to walk *into the other direction*, and secondly, it means walking *another* way, another route that is constituted mainly by detours. These detours result from rigorously avoiding (or walking around) the terminology and conceptualisations that im- or explicitly carry with them the conflation of linguistic features and nomolanguages, i.e. the statist view of language.

Adopting a *heuristic of detours* (see Beck, 2015 for 'Heuristik des Umwegs') led me to search everywhere – not only in up-and-coming notions such as 'translanguaging' but also in ordinary and well-established terms such as 'translation' – for traces of seeing language like a state. This search is partly documented in this introduction but mostly in Chapter 2, where I argue which terms and concepts I will rigorously avoid in my data analyses and why. This approach inevitably leads me to detour from many existing conceptualisations of classroom language practices that rely on the terminology I here avoid. While this is certainly controversial and risky, I couldn't shake my researcher's intuition that the existing analytical lenses just weren't leading me to the core of what was being done with language in the Khayelitshan English classrooms. Therefore, this book is the pursuit of the hypothesis *that the phenomenon I observed could indeed not be described via the repertoire of existing theories*. While putting me at risk of being proven completely wrong, this hypothesis also allowed me – or forced me – to develop some new analytical vocabulary and concepts. The new analytical language I propose is in close dialogue with contemporary work in socio- and applied linguistics that tries to think language in terms of spatial repertoires (Baynham & Lee, 2019; Canagarajah, 2018; Pennycook & Otsuji, 2015) (Chapter 2).

This heuristic of detours is not meant to gainsay existing work on language practices in language classrooms. Rather, it allows me to take on a fresh perspective and to poke some taken-for-granted assumptions. I want to offer a competing set of ideas and concepts to those currently dominating discussions of homogenised linguistic fixity and heterogeneous fluidity in classrooms and beyond, such as code-switching or translanguaging. In Chapter 2, I will argue that the latter ultimately rely on the statist vision and make analysts look from nomolanguages to languaging.

After much talk about the walk, let's go! I start by walking with the reader into Khayelitsha and its heterogeneous languaging, through its schools and their homogenised nomolanguages, through accounts of township (English) teaching into conceptual and methodological considerations. There, we learn about the detours taken in this work and come to eclectically build a possibly more suitable analytical lens for the data from Khayelitshan English classrooms. We then walk into these classrooms where Khayelitshan languaging and nomolanguages such as Standard English and (sometimes) Standard Xhosa meet, and where this study's terrain between heterogeneous linguistic fluidity and homogenised fixity is constantly being constituted. We then walk back and forth between the classrooms and the conceptual considerations to test and adapt the analytical lens in light of the empirical findings. What we get to see along the way is the theory that I ultimately call *relanguaging*. This book is a constant oscillation between a concrete empirical example and theory building and I invite the reader to walk and see with me. For starters, we will see how the tension between languaging and nomolanguages plays out in South African township schools and how teaching and learning in these spaces is currently discussed in scholarship and beyond. Towards the end of this introduction, we return to a more detailed outline of the thought experiment I just sketched as the engine of this book.

1.2 The Languaging of the Township

The linguistic heterogeneity displayed in the opening quote is typical for Cape Town's urban working-class settlements (Banda, 2018; Deumert, 2013; Dowling, 2011; Mesthrie & Hurst, 2013). Khayelitsha (ikhaya – home; elitsha – new: 'New Home'), where this study is set, is the biggest of these townships, located approximately 30 km outside the city and founded in 1983. This explains its name 'New Home'. It is the newest of Cape Town's townships and the apartheid government's last attempt to keep the growing Black population living outside the inner city. Apartheid died, Khayelitsha lives on. Today, with an officially counted 400,000 population (Frith, n.d.), but an estimated 1.2–2 million inhabitants,[8] it remains a marker of Cape Town's persistent socioeconomic and racial residential segregation.

Regarding language, most Khayelitshan residents share a denotational norm and a common sentiment for speaking the same language (Silverstein, 2014: 4) – or the same nomolanguage – namely Xhosa. But people's languaging often differs significantly from its standardised, codified version, as the opening quote shows. The complex migratory dynamics that characterise Cape Town's townships help to understand the heterogeneity of language resources and practices in these settings. Due to its close remoteness to the city centre and the possibilities for low-cost informal housing, Khayelitsha sees a constant migrant influx from the rural Eastern Cape (Jacobs, 2014). Those migrants mostly self-identify as Xhosa speakers and contribute their particular linguistic resources, often shaped by rural life trajectories, to the languaging of the township. On the other hand, many Khayelitshan residents regularly commute to Cape Town to workplaces dominated by English (Banda, 2018; Dowling, 2011). These commuters, together with Khayelitshan youth who are often schooled in former Coloured or White areas (see Section 1.5), hold the township in suspense between linguistic connection to, and separation from, city spaces where English or Afrikaans dominates. Since the foundation of Khayelitsha in 1983, English has been the dominant language of learning and teaching (LoLT) in Khayelitshan schools after the initial years of primary school (Section 1.3). Children therefore begin to handle Standard English resources in teaching and testing material quite early on.

All of these dynamics combine with English TV, radio shows and smartphones, making available a multiplicity of language resources for take-up in the area (Banda, 2018; Deumert, 2010; Kreutzer, 2009; Velghe, 2014). In Khayelitsha, particular intersecting patterns of people's mobilities and language practices (Higgins, 2017) produce what urban language scholars have described, for example, as 'heteroglossic speech where rules and norms overlap traditional language boundaries' (Makalela, 2013: 112).[9] Some sociolinguists speak in this context of a 'language shift' towards English (Anthonissen, 2009), but Banda (2018: 6) counters that 'bits-and-pieces or entire chunks of African languages aren't entirely lost as they are dispersed and dispensed in various combinations with English (and Afrikaans) across space and time'. He also emphasises that this way of speaking is, in fact, the 'mother tongue' of Khayelitshan residents. This description of the linguistic situation is reminiscent of the opening quote from the Grade 4 teacher and aligns with what I refer to as Khayelitshan languaging throughout this work.

This heterogeneous languaging *in the Khayelitshan way* is prevalent in the geo-semiotic landscape of Cape Town and other South African townships – on signage, billboards, the walls of barber shops and restaurants – as well as in TV soaps and radio shows in South Africa (Dowling, 2010; Stroud & Mpendukana, 2009). Private advertising firms exploit such languaging in their campaigns. Here, it has its own aesthetics and currency (Dowling & Grier, 2015). In its heterogeneity and fluidity, it provides advertisers with a 'malleable semantic code' (Dowling & Grier, 2015: 18) to create up-to-date adverts that reach a growing urban population by taking its language practices seriously.

While this aesthetics of heterogeneity and fluidity is appealing to scholars of urban language practices as well as to radio stations and private advertising companies in South Africa, it doesn't appeal to state administrations that order education systems, as a look at the 2011 South African census shows. Here, an aesthetics of clean-cut, homogeneous categories rules. The linguistic profile of Khayelitsha shows a list of nomolanguages associated with the percentage of Khayelitshan residents said to speak them: Xhosa is spoken by 90.54%, English by 3.22%, Sesotho by 1.36%, Afrikaans by 1.06% and so on (Frith, n.d.). In the administrative logic of seeing like a state that underlies this census, nomolanguages are ordering devices assignable to individuals, population groups and, in turn, territories. In this view, most people in Khayelitsha speak Xhosa. The township is therefore bureaucratically constructed and made legible to state administrators as a Xhosa area. The same administrative logic underlies the South African education system with its language policies and curriculum.

1.3 The Nomolanguages of Schooling

The logic displayed in the census is clearly thwarted by the actual heterogeneity of Khayelitshan languaging. Nevertheless, the categorisations with which state administrations work don't consider it. Taking heterogeneity seriously would pose 'an impediment to administrative uniformity' (Scott, 1998: 25). Advertisers can open their vision for heterogeneous languaging, since it is in their commercial interest. Centralised education systems, however, are 'state projects of legibility and simplification' (Scott, 1998: 9) that aim at making the performance of learners and teachers measurable and comparable across the state's territory and beyond – even more so with the upsurge in international comparative studies of literacy and numeracy (see, for example, Smith, 2016). State schooling schemes require a radical reduction in the complexity of local practices into separable, standardised and measurable units. Standardised nomolanguages are units of central importance here, functioning 'as the "neutral" (!) top-and-centre variety of denotational code usage' (Silverstein, 2010: 354) that becomes a vehicle to roll out education systems via in themselves standardised curricula and standardised tests (Prinsloo & Krause, 2019a). Nomolanguages are also the codes through which knowledge acquired in schools has to be examined so that it becomes legible and measurable for educational administrators who see like a state (Scott, 1998).

The gaze of officials in institutionally regulated spaces like schooling is fundamentally structured by these homogenised codes. Education systems globally are, to date, hard to imagine without standard (mostly national) nomolanguages. The Khayelitshan case, therefore, points far beyond itself in the theorisations that can be developed with it, because fluid urban languaging is evident all across the fast-growing urban areas of the African continent (Beck, 2010; Kießling & Mous, 2004; Nassenstein, 2016) and, in fact, globally (Nortier & Svendsen, 2015; Pennycook & Otsuji, 2015). Makoni and Mashiri (2007: 82) argue that 'Africans are shifting away from indigenous languages to urban vernaculars' and call for scholarship to explore 'the consequences of such shifts on language planning projects'. My close focus on Khayelitsha is therefore not restrictive regarding the conceptual and theoretical considerations it produces. These can be tested – and/or used – in various classrooms settings where languaging meets the statist demand for standard nomolanguages, a scenario also affecting classrooms in the Global North (in this work meant more in the socioeconomic rather than in the strictly geographical sense) (García & Wei, 2014; Jaspers, 2015).

What makes the South African situation unique, however, is that here, 11 such national nomolanguages are involved in structuring the administrative space of education.[10] In their dividedness, they are arguably colonial constructs that poorly reflect contemporary sociolinguistic realities. But they did serve European Christianising missions and later the divide-and-rule tactics of the colonial and the apartheid state – other state projects of simplification and legibility (details in Section 2.1.1). *Whether related to people's languaging or not, being administratively entangled with individuals, population groups and territories, these 11 nomolanguages are relevant ordering principles of South African education.* In line with the widespread conviction that children learn best through their 'mother tongue' (Alexander, 2009; Brock-Utne et al., 2003), in areas where a dominant 'African' nomolanguage can be administratively identified – e.g. in Black townships such as Khayelitsha in greater Cape Town and in most rural areas – schools normally use that nomolanguage as the LoLT in the Foundation Phase[11] (from Grade R to Grade 3) in primary schools. In accordance with what can be simplified as the 'monolingual nation state ideal' (Section 2.1.1), in Grade 4 the LoLT then changes to English in most schools (Ouane & Glanz, 2011).

For Khayelitsha Primary, the school where I conducted the research for this book (details in Section 3.1), this early transition language policy model means that in the Foundation Phase learners acquire their initial literacy skills in Standard Written Xhosa (SWX) and the curriculum material for all other subjects – except for English – is in SWX. Standard Xhosa and Khayelitshan languaging do share certain characteristics like noun class agreement morphology that is described under the Bantu linguistics paradigm in an extensive noun class system (Nurse & Philippson, 2003). We saw this agreement at work, for example, in the opening quote with '*i*language *ya*maColoured' *(the language of the Coloured)*, where the noun class prefix 'i-' (class 9) produces agreement for the possessive construction through 'y-' (see Appendix B for a noun class table). The data analysis will give the reader more insight into the workings of noun class agreement. For now, it is important that, while this morphology is certainly a more stable part of Khayelitshan languaging, overall the 19th-century standardised version of Xhosa (Brereton Mathiesen, 2000) differs significantly from the heterogeneous day-to-day language practices shared by learners and teachers (see also Banda, 2018; Dowling, 2011; Sibanda, 2019). Nevertheless, Standard Xhosa is the set of linguistic resources that they have to orient towards and via which their performance is measured in the Foundation Phase. It is therefore an important ordering principle and a social reality in these schooling spaces that has to be taken seriously in analyses.

Linguistically, Standard English[12] as the next LoLT that learners are confronted with, shares less with Khayelitshan languaging than Standard Xhosa but is the dominant nomolanguage in South African education and the economy. It has been shown to index ethnic neutrality, upward social mobility and success beyond the township (Blommaert *et al.*, 2005), and access to this code significantly increases opportunities on the job market (Casale & Posel, 2011). Standard English is a high-prestige set of linguistic resources that most children at township primary schools, and often their teachers as well, are socially and spatially distant from and rarely exposed to outside of classrooms. Still, Standard English becomes the major linguistic ordering principle in Khayelitshan classrooms after Grade 3 and again learners' and teachers' performance is measured through it.

The linguistic space of Khayelitshan and other township primary schools[13] is therefore constituted by two administratively fixed, homogenised nomolanguages (Standard Xhosa and Standard English), together with local, non-codified, heterogeneous language practices (Khayelitshan languaging). The two dimensions of language – languaging and nomolanguages (Section 1.1) – therefore co-constitute Khayelitsha Primary linguistically. In the statist view, however, Khayelitshan languaging is invisible, while Standard Xhosa and Standard English are the same kinds of ordering regimes. Children who start school with a Khayelitshan languaging background have to learn Standard Xhosa first, some words of which are actually less familiar to them than their Standard English equivalents (Ditsele, 2014; Dowling, 2011; Krause & Prinsloo, 2016). Then, within their early schooling careers, they also have to acquire Standard English, while their familiar, flexible languaging skills remain unseen (Banda, 2009, 2018; Prinsloo & Krause, 2019b; Sibanda, 2019). Township learners, as I emphasise in this book, therefore constantly have to sort out their heterogeneous languaging reality into two boxes: Standard Xhosa and Standard English. The English teachers in this study demonstrate this sorting mechanism – which I will come to call *relanguaging* – in the classroom. But before we look at that, it is important to consider how these two standard nomolanguages, Standard Xhosa up to and including Grade 3 and Standard English thereafter, play out in a centralised testing system.

1.4 The Testing via Nomolanguages

The Department of Education emphasises the importance of teaching English intensively as a subject in the early grades of primary school when the LoLT is an 'African language' (Western Cape Government, 2017). Learners are supposed to get prepared for Grade 4 when they will have to read, write (exams) and learn via Standard English and no longer via Standard Xhosa. However, recent research suggests that the early transition language policy model, which relies on two standard nomolanguages combined with nationally standardised testing procedures (Systemic Evaluations), produces a situation where this preparatory

English teaching is compromised. Systemic Evaluations in South Africa are regular assessments meant to monitor

> whether learners are meeting national standards, especially in reading, listening, writing, numeracy and life skills at the Foundation Phase, and at key transitional stages in the learning ladder, namely Intermediate Phase and Senior Phase. (Department of Education, 2003: 5)

These major evaluations therefore first take place at the end of Grade 3 when the skills of 'reading, listening, writing, numeracy and life skills' are assessed via Standard (Written) Xhosa. Preparing learners for these national tests, the results of which reflect on teachers' performance as well, Foundation Phase teachers tend to focus on Standard Xhosa while the teaching of Standard English falls by the wayside. A Foundation Phase teacher I interviewed in 2014 (for an earlier project at Khayelitsha Primary) tells us about this. She said: 'We [Foundation Phase teachers] always stress Maths and Xhosa, then we are little in English' (Interview Khayelitsha Primary Teacher 2014).[14] The newly founded Bua-lit Collective[15] in South Africa also shares findings from a research project at a different Khayelitshan primary school, where teaching was observed in Grade 3 classrooms in the run-up to the change to English as the LoLT in Grade 4. This is simultaneously also the run-up to the Systemic Evaluations that focus on Xhosa. The authors write:

> In the third term of Grade 3 we were not able to observe a single English First Additional Language (EFAL) lesson in the two Grade 3 classrooms over a period of four weeks. When questioned about this Grade 3 teachers explained that the systemic assessments were only testing isiXhosa at Grade 3 level and thus it was not a priority to teach EFAL. (Bua-Lit Collective, 2018: 13)

It seems unlikely for learners under these circumstances to 'reach a high level of competence in English by the end of Grade 3' (Department of Basic Education, 2011: 11). Yet, such competence is presupposed by the South African English first additional language (EFAL) curriculum for the Intermediate Phase (Grades 4–6), the phase on which my research mostly focuses.

At several points in the curriculum document, it is emphasised that English teachers in the Intermediate Phase 'will build on the foundations set in Grades R to 3' (Department of Basic Education, 2011: 14). Learners in Intermediate Phase classrooms are expected to 'take more notice of words and grammatical structures they are already familiar with from the Foundation Phase' (Department of Basic Education, 2011: 17). The English teachers I interviewed emphasise that learners lack these very foundations that are presupposed by the EFAL curriculum for the Intermediate Phase. For example, the Grade 5 teacher in this study, when asked whether she finds the language required by the curriculum adequate or too difficult, says:

> If from Grade R the teachers in the school will try by all means to speak English during in the English period then I wouldn't complain but because the teachers speak English, I mean Xhosa even during the English period. They code-switch a lot even when it is not necessary. [...] Because of that problem I think sometimes the words that they use are much too difficult for them. [...] I would prefer them, or the writers of the book or the department to give us a book with easier words. (Interview Grade 5 Teacher)

While this teacher is referring to the way English is taught in the Foundation Phase as being inadequate, the aforementioned research suggests that it might not be taught very often at all. This is directly connected to the pressure of being tested in one nomolanguage (Standard Xhosa) while having to prepare to be taught through another (Standard English), keeping in mind that learners' and teachers' day-to-day languaging (Khayelitshan languaging) is not very close to either of these two homogenised codes (Banda, 2018). In summary, it seems that the statist project of centralised testing – directed at making learners' performance measurable and comparable – combined with the two nomolanguages of schooling under the early transition policy model, produces local pressures that make learners lag far behind the demands of the EFAL curriculum when entering Grade 4.

So how do Intermediate Phase English teachers handle the books with the 'much too difficult words'? How do they teach the advanced English skills demanded by the curriculum to learners who are largely unfamiliar with the linguistic resources that this same curriculum presupposes? My entry point towards answering these questions is a close and fine-grained linguistic analysis of the language resources that teachers (and to a lesser extent also learners) mobilise. This is combined with in-depth interviews with teachers (details in Chapter 3). Approaching these questions is part of this book's journey. What complicates the linguistic analyses that I present is my commitment to reversing the statist gaze by tricking myself into the heuristic of detours (see Section 1.1). Nevertheless, I am concerned not only with eliminating what I consider to be persistent theoretical blind spots due to the statist gaze, but also with responding to existing classroom research in South African township schools.

While plenty of studies engage with the change of LoLT between Grades 3 and 4 and the problem of learning all subjects through English while having limited access to that code (Chick, 1996; Probyn, 2015, 2001; Setati et al., 2002), there is little ethnographic research with a linguistic focus that looks specifically at language practices in English classrooms in township schools (exceptions are Banda, 2018; Kapp, 2004). This book contributes to filling this gap via the experimental linguistic ethnography (LE) that I have begun to describe. Since teachers are the main protagonists here, Section 1.5 provides some insight into how township teachers – and in particular their English skills – are constructed by scholars, the media, parents and the Department of Education in South Africa.

1.5 The English of Township Teachers

Listening to major stakeholders in South African education, we firstly don't hear anything about the above-described language and testing situation that complicates English teaching in township primary schools. Secondly, we get the impression that Standard English is unattainable or altogether absent from township (English) classrooms, because teachers lack the relevant language and teaching skills to provide access to this code. For example, Black South African parents' distrust in township teachers' English competencies is displayed in what Fataar (2009) has called 'displaced school-choice'. If finances allow, parents send their children to schools as far away from their home township as possible, in search of better educational resources in general and 'better English' in particular (Fataar, 2009; Maile, 2004; Ndimande, 2012). A parent interviewed by Ndimande summarises:

> The main thing we want is to have our children be able to speak English fluently. They get to learn English in formerly White-only schools. Here in township schools you find teachers who speak broken English. (Parent interviewed in Ndimande, 2012: 536)

These 'formerly White-only schools' are ex-Model C schools – schools that received special government support before the end of apartheid in 1994 under certain conditions. Their student body had to be kept majority White and 'mother tongue instruction' would have to be provided for English- and Afrikaans-speaking children (for a detailed discussion, see Christie, 1995). Today, these schools are open to all population groups but mostly charge fees and 'remain the best resourced, highest achieving public schools in the country' (Christie & McKinney, 2017: 170). It follows, as Christie and McKinney (2017: 168) note, that '"Model C" schools play an important hegemonic role in a narrative of progress. They are accorded the status of being the "ideal type" post-apartheid school', and are thereby discursively constructed as the opposite of rural and township schools, which are depicted as the worst possible ones. For example, comparing ex-Model C schools and township schools and constructing the former as spaces of linguistic possibilities (i.e. of 'proper' English) and the latter as linguistic dead-ends (with 'broken' English) is common not only in public discourse but also in some scholarly work.

Krugel and Fourie, for example, use the standardised English Literacy Skills Assessment (ELSA)[16] in a comparative study of the English literacy skills of teachers in township schools and teachers in ex-Model C schools, to then correlate them with learners' test results in the respective settings. They write:

> The average grade profile of the participating teachers of the ex-model C schools is that of Grade 12+[17] (English mother tongue users) that signifies that these teachers have a sound English literacy. (Krugel & Fourie, 2014: 224)

In contrast, they find that 'the average grade profile of the participating teachers of the township schools is that of Grade 9', which in turn indicates that 'teachers lack the English proficiency that is necessary for effective teaching and don't have the knowledge and skills to support English language learning' (Krugel & Fourie, 2014: 224). The authors then show a correlation between learners' and teachers' performance in the standardised tests and summarise that township teachers' lack of English proficiency is reflected in the test results of their learners who perform significantly worse than their peers from ex-Model C schools (Krugel & Fourie, 2014).

It is commonly known in South Africa that learners in rural and township schools perform much worse than their peers from more affluent ex-Model C institutions that are mostly in the inner city or in suburbia (Department of Education, 2017). In the media (Nkosi, 2016; van der Berg & Spaull, 2011), in some other scholarly work on township teaching (Nel & Müller, 2010) and on parents' school choice in South Africa (Lombard, 2007; Maile, 2004; Msila, 2009), there is an implication that teachers are directly responsible for the often poor academic performance of their learners.

A *Mail & Guardian* piece from 2011 titled 'SA education: The poorest choice' says that many South African teachers in poor schools 'set extremely low levels of cognitive demand for their pupils' (van der Berg & Spaull, 2011). In a 2016 BBC Africa News piece, Nkosi writes:

> There are many schools in the townships and the government has built more schools in these areas since the advent of democracy, but quality teaching and a proper structured learning process is lacking. (Nkosi, 2016)

I argue here that, in fact, a highly structured mechanism of language teaching and learning – relanguaging – has so far been overlooked in research. In the same BBC piece, Professor John Volmik is quoted, saying that 'Teachers' knowledge of English has to be upgraded. Unless we [support them], results will continue to drop'. These voices are echoed by educational authorities. A recent evaluation report from the Department of Education (2017: 14) regarding the implementation of the Curriculum Assessment Policy Statements (CAPS)[18] curriculum finds that most Grade 2 teachers 'don't possess the subject knowledge required to teach English or Mathematics'. Similar results are presented for Grade 10 teachers with an emphasis on their

> poor writing ability in English [...] with the teachers achieving a mean score of 5.5 out of 10 on the simple descriptive writing task. These results suggest that fully half the Grade 10 English teachers tested aren't competent to teach English. (Department of Education, 2017: 15)

The conclusion of the same report states that while South African schooling remains profoundly inequitable throughout various curriculum reforms, 'this situation is not the fault of the curriculum, but the result of systemic non-curriculum causes' – one of these being 'weak educator knowledge capacity' (Department of Education, 2017: 22). This narrative of educational deficiency and the lack of English in poorly performing schools builds on comparing learners and teachers across different schooling contexts via standardised tests that rely on homogenised nomolanguages and produce numerically measurable results. From these neatly categorised results, conclusions about teachers' practices are drawn. Seeing like a state at its best. From this perspective, township learners and teachers are stuck without access to Standard English and even without the capacity to improve the situation. This prevalent bleak outlook is among the main motivations for this book, because it clashes with my experience of some committed township English teachers and their noteworthy language practices in the classroom. I show that teachers and learners are doing something – relanguaging – that has been overlooked so far. And instead of being deficient, practices at township schools emerge from this account as having something to offer in terms of didactic strategies and also regarding forms of resistance against hegemonic ideologies about language (and) teaching.

Two ethnographic studies of South African township schools have particularly pushed and inspired me to make this contribution: Blommaert *et al.* (2005) and Canagarajah (2015). Instantiating two ends of the spectrum of research on township classrooms – one producing a rather bleak account of linguistic lack and marginality and the other an agency-focused, optimistic account – I use these two studies to frame the following discussion of existing work on South African township schools.

1.6 The Ethnographies of Township Classrooms

In a detailed and influential ethnographic study of language and literacy practices in a Cape Town township school, Blommaert *et al.*

conclude that township teachers and learners lack access to standard linguistic norms and therefore remain stuck in the societal periphery. The authors analyse different types of learners' writing, where they find *'hetero-graphy*, the deployment of literacy techniques and instruments in ways that don't respond to institutional ortho-graphic norms' (Blommaert *et al.*, 2005: 388, emphasis in original). In their writing on the blackboard and in research questionnaires, teachers make similar 'errors' to those of learners in relation to Standard Written English (SWE) and teachers are also shown to often overlook many of the learners' spelling and grammar mistakes when marking tests.

Interviews show that, while teachers and learners aspire to an English that allows them translocal mobility and access to employment beyond the township, this English 'is not the "English" they articulate in their answers' (Blommaert *et al.*, 2005: 397) and display in their writing. The authors argue that schooling in this township is a case of 'peripheral normativity' (Blommaert *et al.*, 2005: 392) where teachers and learners are 'stuck' on a local-scale[19] level 'where access to elite (hyper-normative, homogenised) literacy is severely restricted'. Language and literacy norms that count in spaces of aspiration – the socioeconomic and political centres of power – are said not to reach learners and teachers in the township. Instead, what happens is 'the "downscaling" of education, bringing it down to the level of the local or regional community' (Blommaert *et al.*, 2005: 396). While the authors offer detailed insights into the language dynamics in the township school, the conclusions drawn are reminiscent of those produced by standardised language and literacy tests: township schools are sites of linguistic lack and deficit without much prospect for improvement.

While Blommaert *et al.*'s study mainly focuses on the writing of learners and the writing and marking practices of teachers, other studies describe the oral practices in classroom discourse as incompatible with what will be expected of learners in English-speaking spaces and with what is necessary to succeed in their immediate schooling context. In one of the few studies that comment specifically on English teaching in a township secondary school, Kapp writes:

> The discourse practices of the English classroom are incompatible with the need to use the language at cognitively demanding levels in other subjects, resulting in extensive code-switching and rote-learning in those classes. (Kapp, 2004: 260)

Such rote-learning or 'participation through rote-performance' (McKinney *et al.*, 2015: 116) is widely attested for township classrooms where the LoLT is far removed from learners' and teachers' out-of-school language practices. So is the 'class-chorus', where learners are trained to answer 'questions relating to self-evident general knowledge issues' (Kapp, 2004:

253) or to produce 'acceptable linguistic chunks' (McKinney *et al.*, 2015: 116) in a chorus that responds to particular intonation cues or tag-questions from teachers (see also Beck, 2016; Chick, 1996). Township classrooms emerge from these accounts as cognitively undemanding spaces marked by linguistically and pedagogically deficient teaching practices.

A response to such deficiency focused accounts comes from Canagarajah (2015). Specifically responding to Blommaert *et al.*'s study, he gives a different account of linguistic practices in a township school in Cape Town. He contests the notion of peripheral normativity and instead emphasises the ability of teachers and learners to 'shuttle across scales and norms' (Canagarajah, 2015: 49), demonstrating that they are well aware of which linguistic resources are to be employed in which contexts and are by no means clueless about external norms. He argues that it is misleading to treat local norms as isolated from the norms of other spaces and instead suggests a view in which 'the local is permeated by diverse other "locals"' where 'it is possible then for the local community to be not unaware of (and even not incompetent in) the indexical orders and literacy regimes of other places' (Canagarajah, 2015: 35–36). His analysis of a learner's essay shows this student approximating the norms of SWE as a homogenised repertoire. In their Facebook posts, on the other hand, learners are said to display heterogeneous literacy practices. Such varied writing in different schooling spaces shows their 'ability to adjust production to suit different scales and audiences' (Canagarajah, 2015: 44) rather than their confinement to peripheral normativity, Canagarajah argues. He cautions us that 'if we assume that township teachers and students are deficient and stuck in peripheral normativity, no amount of evidence will convince us of their agency' (Canagarajah, 2015: 39). But what exactly constitutes the lens that produces these deficit accounts and how can we look beyond it?

While Canagarajah focuses mostly on the presence of standard linguistic norms, not focusing in detail on heterogeneous languaging, there are other studies that bring forth potential-oriented rather than deficit-oriented accounts of township schooling by paying more attention to fluid linguistic practices (Banda, 2018; Guzula *et al.*, 2016; Guzula, 2018; Probyn, 2009, 2015). For example, in her analyses of language practices in science classrooms in township and rural schools, Probyn shows how teachers use code-switching as an efficient strategy to work towards learners' understanding. She writes that

> many teachers are able to utilise the linguistic resources of the classroom in a skilled and responsive way, to achieve a range of cognitive and affective teaching and learning goals. (Probyn, 2009: 124)

In a study on translingual practices in a Khayelitshan secondary school English classroom, Banda observes that by using the extended linguistic repertoire, the learners and the teacher have come up with a new classroom discourse quite unlike one you would find in monolingual educational contexts. (Banda, 2018: 214)

He argues that the inclusion of Xhosa, English and what he refers to as 'hybrid language' in classroom discourse doesn't contradict the goal of acquiring English. Rather, this inclusiveness produces a space where 'all learners participate in finding the solution to the task at hand, hence promoting collaborative learning' (Banda, 2018: 214).

Guzula *et al.* look at what they call 'languaging-for-learning' in an after-school literacy club in Khayelitsha and a mathematics holiday programme in the rural Eastern Cape. Here, children are encouraged to engage in oral as well as written heterogeneous languaging which is shown to be 'a practical and powerful way to draw on children's sociocultural resources, facilitating language and literacy learning' (Guzula *et al.*, 2016: 218). This research also finds that such practices unfold their potential better in the Khayelitshan literacy club – where the teachers or facilitators share the linguistic resources of the learners – than in the mathematics holiday programme, where there is a 'lack of shared resources' (Guzula *et al.*, 2016: 223) between teachers and learners.

These studies show two different perspectives on language dynamics in township schools that make us 'see' different things: linguistic and pedagogical lack or potential. Engaging with these different perspectives, I wonder if accounts of township schools as sites that trap teachers and learners in the periphery are productive in a quest to undermine existing structures of educational inequality. Township schools educate the majority of South Africa's urban youth, yet the dominant view of them is one of lack and deficit in relation to the norms of the so-called 'centre', where a minority of the population is schooled. It seems that this deficit perspective is reproductive of a status quo that relegates the majority to the educational margins and the minority to the centre. It also seems that studies which offer a different perspective are those that take linguistic heterogeneity seriously.

I attempt to take linguistic heterogeneity seriously and to put it in relation to the demand for nomolanguages in schooling. The spaces (i.e. English classrooms) I chose for my research forced me to think in terms of relationality, because here the tension between linguistic heterogeneity and homogeneity is ever present: one marks the routinised language practices shared by learners and teachers (Khayelitshan languaging) and the other the goal of teaching itself (Standard English).

1.7 The Experiment of this Book

Regardless of the particular languaging competencies that exist in Khayelitsha, linguistic homogeneity that fits a statist category remains the goal and the judge of how teachers teach and what learners learn in English classrooms. For schools like Khayelitsha Primary, the judgements this produces are clear: teachers speak 'broken English' and learners don't learn 'proper English'. Both parties produce a lot of 'errors' and learners do badly in standardised English tests. It seems that, when seeing like a state, the only thing we find here is linguistic deficit, a lack of Standard English.

Makoni and Pennycook (2007a: 36) push us towards developing a different perspective by asking 'What would language education look like if we no longer posited the existence of separate languages?'. My hypothesis is that Khayelitshan English teachers are already answering this question every day but that we are blind to the nature of their practices because our analytical concepts and theories entangle us in the statist vision. I therefore ask in this book not what language education *would* look like, but rather what it *does* look like in Khayelitsha, if we analyse it through a lens that is not *a priori* structured by nomolanguages. I therefore set out to find a lens that fulfils this requirement (see Chapter 2) and then to apply it to language practices in Khayelitshan English classrooms.

For me, a lens like this means that I aim at locating myself as an analyst on the languaging side in relation to the languaging and nomolanguages dimensions that both play a role in the English classrooms at Khayelitsha Primary. I then look out from that position at what linguistic dynamics are there to be found. This reverses the statist view that normalises nomolanguages and makes us see heterogeneity as the deviation. I therefore set out to walk the other way (Section 1.1), to take for granted the significance of linguistic heterogeneity while being open to finding the significance of nomolanguages without positing the latter *a priori*.

As mentioned earlier, I need to trick myself into walking the other way – with all the detours this entails – with constraints that make me stay clear of analytical terminology that reproduces the statist view. I therefore begin the experiment that is this book by *relanguaging* – that means by sorting out and reinventing – my own analytical language. I drop as many descriptors as possible that I see as entangled in the nomolanguage ideology.[20] This ideology and its vocabulary are deeply entrenched in the statist perspective on language, because it is centrally concerned with 'patterning that is economical and abstract – patterning whose primary purpose is to separate language from language, dialect from dialect, sociolect from sociolect' (Sabino, 2018: 9). My hope is that by refusing to describe language practices in such terms, I will be able to make those details of languaging in the Khayelitshan English classroom visible that are obscured by the statist vision. It then remains to be seen throughout this book where those details might take us not only with regard to rethinking linguistic analyses, but also with regard to reimagining South African language (in) education.

The list of terms I commit *not to use* will lengthen as I discuss my conceptual background in Chapter 2. However, I can already point to some descriptors that I will detour from, because they are rather obviously entangled in the nomolanguage ideology. The reader will therefore not encounter in this book (except in discussions of other scholars' work) the following terms:

First language (L1) and second language (L2): These terms suggest two separate linguistic objects co-existing in the language classroom. This view cannot be maintained if we take seriously the heterogeneity and fluidity of Khayelitshan languaging (Section 1.2).

Translation/to translate: This notion intimates the transportation of meaning from one bounded linguistic inventory to another. It is not a heterogenising process, because the nomolanguages involved remain pure and the complexity is to be found in the transportation between them. The notion therefore assumes and reifies homogeneous linguistic entities.

Non-standard language: In my view, speakers either try to approximate the standard – which is always an idealised, homogenised linguistic object that is rarely actualised (details in Chapter 2) – or they do something else that has nothing to do with the standard and should therefore not be described as a negation of, or a deviation from it, as the term 'non-standard' suggests.

Errors and mistakes: Descriptors like these indicate deviations from a norm that is positioned as 'correct' and this norm tends to be instantiated by a homogenised and standardised nomolanguage. Accordingly, I detour from these categories in my analyses as well.

Along the way, readers will discover how I deal with linguistic forms and practices that usually trigger the above terms. I cannot provide replacement descriptors at this stage, firstly because some of the categories these terms imply might become altogether irrelevant, and secondly, because detailed conceptual reflections and empirical findings drawn from my ethnographic inquiry are necessary before I can argue for alternative ways of describing classroom language practices.

Again, this experiment, which begins with turning down established analytical categories, is risky. It is not meant to negate the insights of scholars who did seminal work with the help of the descriptors I avoid in this study. I am indebted to them and will most certainly describe things they have long grappled with and discussed before me. Nevertheless, I have decided to take this leap, wondering whether there might still be more to discover and unable to come up with any other way to find out than to use the trick I described. I set out writing this book not knowing what I would get to see. Which questions would come up along the way? Where would I get stuck? What would tempt me to turn around and walk again into the more familiar direction on a much shorter and more direct route? Would my rigorous avoidance of certain categories silence me? Or rather: Would it make me go blind? Let's see.

1.8 The Route through the Book

Chapters 2 and 3 lay out the heuristic of detours that leads to an eclectic landscape of concepts and methods assembled for the experiment at hand. An LE emerges (Creese, 2010; Rampton *et al.*, 2004), that is tilted towards the linguistic and helps to see Khayelitshan English classrooms differently. First, I discuss the tendency of classical linguists to see like a state, due to a conceptual conflation of linguistic features and nomolanguages. I then trace the gradual unsettlement of this statist vision from ideas of verbal repertoires of speech communities and code-switching, via accounts of complex individual repertoires and translanguaging, to spatial repertoires and languaging as a spatial practice. I clarify which terms and concepts I detour from and why, to then introduce *relanguaging* as a descriptor for a linguistic sorting practice that emerges in the language classroom.

For a fine-grained analysis of the constituents of languaging as a spatial practice, the researcher must be very familiar with the ways of languaging at the research site. Chapter 3 shows how my long-term involvement at Khayelitsha Primary and my own linguistic biography make me able to dive into the intricacies of classroom languaging that are often overlooked. The spatialised analysis needs an agile methodology so that linguistic features can be traced through different spaces – classrooms, grammar books and townships for example. Actor Network Theory provides some inspiration here with its mantra 'follow the actors' (Latour, 2005: 29). Combined with elements of conversation analysis (Deppermann, 2001; Goodwin & Heritage, 1990; Psathas, 1994) and tools from (Bantu) linguistics (Nurse & Philippson, 2003; Pahl *et al.*, 1971), following linguistic features and asking teachers about their use of them in class allows *relanguaging* to become visible.

Chapter 4 is all about chickens and eagles as I take the reader through a Grade 5 English lesson from beginning to end. The lesson revolves around an eagle that is trained to be a chicken but eventually recovers its 'true self'. While the teacher nudges the learners into understanding the story, I face the challenges and potentials of the analytical lens I have crafted, which brings forth new questions that I direct at myself and/or at the teachers in the interviews. Showing plenty of examples of relanguaging, readers here become familiar with how I use the concepts discussed in Chapter 2 – *relanguaging*, *classroom languaging* and *classroom englishing* – and with some of the more technical linguistic terminology necessary to understand languaging in this specific space. Chapter 4 sets the tone for the rest of the book as it trains the spotlight on small pieces of language – often morphemes – which can tell us a lot about the local particularities in Khayelitshan English classrooms but are simultaneously also entry points into theoretical questions about language.

In Chapter 5, the attention to minute linguistic detail intensifies and the inspiration I draw from Actor Network Theory comes through. Starting in a Grade 4 classroom, I follow an actor – the morpheme 'u-' – from teacher to teacher and through different activities, classrooms, grammar books, city spaces and scholarly work. It turns out that 'u-' is a highly productive metalanguaging device, turning words into objects of analysis (e.g. 'uangry' = the word angry). Somewhat more counterintuitively, 'u-' can also act as an 'englishing device', marking urban language resources familiar to the learners (like 'because') as also belonging to Standard English.

Further into Chapter 5, I move to a relatively high-stakes classroom activity – the writing of a departmental test paper in Grade 5. From this testing activity, the analyses of empirical linguistic data provide insights into how township teachers negotiate their position in the wider system of South African education. I show how these negotiations are instantiated in their relanguaging. Going along with this lesson and integrating into the analysis the assessment-related statements that the teacher makes in interview, shows the influence that the demands, and the sometimes inaccessible texts of a centralised assessment system have on the linguistic strategies that teachers develop in the classroom.

In Chapter 6, learners become the protagonists. I show how, in order to cope at school, they have to be skilful relanguagers, good at ordering and *sorting out* heterogeneous spatial repertoires according to two nomolanguages: Standard Xhosa and Standard English. I begin with the hypothesis that a monolingual policy for writing hides part of learners' existing englishing competencies and test it by administering a writing task where learners are free to write using all language resources at their disposal in whichever combination. Based on my analyses of these heterogeneous writing practices, I strongly reject suggestions of a lack of standard linguistic norms in spaces such as Khayelitsha, which allegedly keep learners and teachers stuck in 'peripheral normativity' (Blommaert et al., 2005). Rather, learners' writing shows that there is an oversupply of standard linguistic norms that they have to navigate.

In the conclusion, I evaluate the thought experiment that drove this book. I discuss how far the concepts and methodology I applied made me *see* the data differently compared to accounts that rely on currently established linguistic descriptors. I summarise how my empirical findings and my conceptualisation of relanguaging allowed me to systematically unsettle a construction of linguistic heterogeneity and homogeneity as mutually exclusive and to conceptualise these two dimensions of language conjunctively. Seeing relanguaging instead of translanguaging makes it possible to propose, for example, ways of testing Standard English beyond its own confines, i.e. to test for increasingly sophisticated linguistic sorting skills. Such suggestions cater for children's fluid languaging backgrounds and linguistic sorting skills as well as for educational stakeholders' demand for more fixed codes and standardised testing procedures.

2 Relanguaging Language towards an Alternative Perspective

2.1 Seeing Language Like a (Colonial) State

2.1.1 Teasing out nomolanguages from languaging

What can constitute an analytical lens for language practices in the Khayelitshan English classroom that *is not a priori* structured by nomolanguages? This question guides the conceptual considerations in this chapter. Asking it implies that analytical lenses in linguistics *are* usually *a priori* structured by nomolanguages. I therefore first make the case that this is indeed so, by discussing continuing traditions in classical linguistics, before I move into concepts that grapple with heterogeneity and fluidity in language.

In Section 1.3, I discussed that nomolanguages co-constitute a system of simplified categories that are the basis for – and reproduce – what Scott has called seeing like a state. Nomolanguages themselves, as one set of 'categories that we most take for granted and with which we now routinely apprehend the social world had their origin in state projects of standardisation and legibility' (Scott, 1998: 64). The discipline of classical linguistics 'grew up', as Silverstein (2014: 23) puts it, within the order of the nation state, with linguists serving simplification and legibility projects. The discipline builds on the teasing out of nomolanguages from languaging through codifying and abstracting them into autonomous structures (Errington, 2008; Makoni & Pennycook, 2007b). Through standardisation, 'the imposition of uniformity upon a class of objects' (Milroy, 2001: 531), nomolanguages become codified sets of combinatory rules (grammatical and syntactical), tied to a delimited group of lexical and morphological features (Jørgensen *et al.*, 2011). Separable from each other, such homogenised packages of rules and features, codified in grammars and dictionaries, can be associated with population groups and territories. This way they become ordering principles that help state administrators to 'see'.

This resulting one-nomolanguage–one-territory–one-culture grid, rooted in more than a century of European epistemology (Beck, 2018), became extremely useful in the European nation state's imperial aspirations (Silverstein, 2014). The colonial expansion of Europe in Africa illustrates the role of nomolanguages in this imperial endeavour. As a consequence of their own disciplinary and cultural background, European missionary linguists simplified, homogenised and mapped out the complex and flexible languaging they were faced with in a foreign terrain. Resulting descriptions of African nomolanguages as grammar and lexicon produced linguistic objects in an idiom accessible via the European episteme. Regarding the descriptive terminology, the resulting nomolanguages are linguistic inventions that were, however, relied on by colonial administrations in their attempts to divide and rule, instruct and Christianise their colonial subjects (Beck, 2018; Errington, 2008; Harries, 1988; Makalela, 2016; Prinsloo & Krause, 2019b).

Harries (1988: 26) shows how, in South Africa, 'the delineation and codification of Tsonga as a written language was a product of nineteenth century European discourse rather than a reflection of local reality'. Tsonga today is one of South Africa's official nomolanguages and so is Xhosa, for which Brereton Mathiesen shows a similarly colonial history. It is in the 19th-century evangelical mission where, as she notes,

> we find beginnings of literacy in languages spoken in south-eastern Africa, and importantly, the systematisation and codification of what was to become standard Xhosa in terms of orthography, grammar and lexicography. (Brereton Mathiesen, 2000: 82)

Some of the missionary linguists' works laying this groundwork for what was to become Standard Xhosa are Bennie (1826), Ayliff (1846) and Kropf (1915). Colonial missionary linguists have certainly created a body of knowledge that continues to be helpful in analysing patterns in language practices. For example, I still revert to Kropf's dictionary at some points in this work. The language constructs they created, however, were also mapped onto populations as an effective means to help the colonial state – and later the apartheid state – to 'see'. These linguists therefore also, as Errington (2008: 3) put it, 'made languages objects of knowledge, so that their speakers could be made subjects of power'.

The political system of apartheid in South Africa, whose consequences the nation is continuously grappling with, is an extreme example of how divide-and-rule tactics can build on colonial linguists' sorting-out of complex ways of speaking into separate nomolanguages. A strategic political entanglement of these linguistic objects with ethnicity was 'used as a tool to separate and divide people, physically and socially (through geographic separation)' (Kapp, 2006: 30). Such colonial 'inventions' of nomolanguages still play out in (South) African education today (Errington, 2008; Makalela, 2018; Makoni & Pennycook, 2007b). Prinsloo and Krause (2019b: 6) note that the post-apartheid South African government has 'retained this earlier commitment to discrete languages and declared nine distinct "African languages" to all be "official languages"', alongside English and Afrikaans. The result is that a place like Khayelitsha, with high degrees of linguistic fluidity, is still administratively associated with one 'African language': Xhosa (Section 1.2). This association has direct influence on language policies in schooling. South African education therefore reflects the logic of seeing language like a state in two ways:

(1) Reminiscent of the colonial (and apartheid) state apparatus, distinct standardised 'African nomolanguages' are ascribed to distinct population groups and territories within the country.
(2) In line with one-nation–one-nomolanguage ideologies, beyond the initial years of primary school these standard African nomolanguages are abandoned in favour of another, supposedly ethnically neutral and national nomolanguage, Standard English, through which all learners eventually have to make their performance legible for state administrations.

This involvement of several nomolanguages in school language policies creates specific (linguistic) complexities in township English classrooms (also Section 1.4) that will continue to be relevant throughout this book. For now, let's turn to how the statist vision that relies on linguistic homogenisation is not only constitutive of such language-in-education policies but also underlies the discipline of linguistics itself.

2.1.2 Conflating linguistic features and nomolanguages

Silverstein alerts us that the seeing-in-nomolanguages of state administrators is also the dominant analytical perspective in linguistics. He argues that 'the linguistics and sociolinguistics of the state, especially the modern nation-state, have also tended to see things like a state, or, let us say, in conformity to how the state sees' (Silverstein, 2014: 18). Indeed, nomolanguages aren't only accepted, but in fact the default units of linguists' analysis. Otheguy et al. point out that, until today, linguists conventionally don't claim to analyse linguistic features, like articles or forms of past tenses, in their own right. Instead, their works' titles suggest that they write about 'the French tenses and the Spanish articles' (Otheguy et al., 2015: 289). They prefer to analyse morphemes as 'morphemes of a nomolanguage' rather than as 'morphemes'.

This practice displays a historically rooted conceptual conflation of linguistic features and nomolanguages. Words and grammatical morphemes are analysed as if they were in every situation associated with a standardised code or a describable bounded 'variety' of a nomolanguage (Milroy, 1999). Codification in a corpus of the relevant nomolanguage is therefore a sufficient condition to refer to a linguistic feature as 'Standard English' or 'English' in analyses. Accordingly, linguistic features are, per default and under all circumstances, linked to a codified nomolanguage.

This is whether or not the information that the features 'belong' to a certain nomolanguage adds anything to the analysis. This ordinariness of 'nomolanguage belonging' is also reflected in the idea of ownership that gets invoked whenever a linguistic feature regularly appears in a nomolanguage with which it is not officially associated. We then speak about nomolanguages 'borrowing' or 'loaning' words to each other (see, for example, Branford & Claughton, 2002; Bylund, 2014; Haspelmath, 2008), increasing the autonomy of these codes as bounded objects to a point where they and not their speakers are the central points of analytical reference and in fact become the central agents.

This conflation of linguistic features and nomolanguages is a result of the statist view of language and, so I argue, implicitly subscribes to one of the (colonial) state's most central ordering principles described above: the teasing out of different nomolanguages to then associate them with population groups and territories. Therefore, not only historically, but even today, many linguists indeed tend to see 'in conformity to how the state sees' (Silverstein, 2014: 18). This vision not only reproduces and stabilises nomolanguages as linguistic objects, but it also strengthens them as the categories that state projects like education are based on, stabilising these projects in return. Therefore, it is a matter of concern how far linguists' analyses of, for example, language in education can provide sometimes necessary correctives or alternatives to the status quo if their analytical apparatus is itself entangled in it.

Partly due to such concerns, throughout the last 60 years scholars of sociolinguistics have been increasingly problematising this statist, nomolanguage-centred linguistics and there have been continuous efforts to gradually unsettle homogenised linguistic objects as the default units of analysis. Herein lie the origins of a languaging rather than a nomolanguage perspective that is still in the making and to which I attend below. We are on the look out for an alternative perspective to the statist view of language, which will later allow us to see linguistic homogeneity as well as heterogeneity as constitutive elements of Khayelitshan English classrooms without systematically and *a priori* shutting out the latter.

2.2 Unsettling Linguistic Objects

2.2.1 From nomolanguages to verbal repertoires

Rampton (2017) also refers to the statist vision described by Scott when illustrating how the standardisation of nomolanguages has been one of the strategies of the modern state to make its population legible. In this context, Rampton comments on Gumperz' work from the 1960s on verbal repertoires and code-switching, which, as he suggests

> can be read as a critical response to institutionalised models promoting the linguistic legibility of populations, as a reassertion of the importance

of the 'complex, illegible and local' (ibid) [Scott 1998], and as the development of an analytic apparatus for demonstrating the limitations of prevailing institutional ideologies of language, encouraging us to 'listen in a new way' (cf McDermott 1988). (Rampton, 2017: 5).

I am particularly interested in the alternative 'analytic apparatus' that is here described as emerging from Gumperz' work. Its cornerstone is the introduction of the term 'verbal repertoire', defined by Gumperz (1964: 141) as 'the totality of linguistic forms regularly employed in the course of socially significant interaction'. Contrasting them with verbal repertoires, I define nomolanguages as 'statist repertoires', the totality of linguistic forms codified under 'one language' that exists in writing rather than in speech and that is abstractable from the realm of actual social interaction. Gumperz' verbal repertoires don't allow for this abstraction but urge us to investigate language in social interactions without jumping to separate nomolanguages as convenient, manageable categories.

He argues that, instead of the grammars of nomolanguages supposedly located in speakers' minds (Chomsky, 1965), it is the verbal repertoire shared in a speech community that 'provides the weapons of everyday communication' (Gumperz, 1964: 138) for speakers to choose from. The speech community shares these weapons and is defined as 'any human aggregate characterised by regular and frequent interaction over a significant span of time and set off from other such aggregates by differences in the frequency of interaction' (Gumperz, 1964: 137). The speech community then is the unit of analysis – such a community has a repertoire that it practices and whose constituents need to be studied, because they aren't synonymous with a statist repertoire (i.e. a nomolanguage).

The importance of studying linguistic features as constituents of practiced community repertoires, rather than as building blocks of predefined nomolanguages, is illustrated in Gumperz (1965), where he draws on the example of a Hindi language course at the University of Berkeley. This course regularly left students with a thorough knowledge of 'Hindi grammar' but unable to communicate with the actual Indian communities they went to live in. This inability of students to communicate after extensive study of Hindi illustrates how grammarians – and in turn many second language (L2) teachers – 'see like a state' and associate stable nomolanguages with distinct population groups. This means that students learn a statist repertoire that exists in writing but has little grounding in how people actually speak.

As suggested by Rampton (2017) above, Gumperz' work on verbal repertoires and the way it is being picked up by other scholars implies a critique of the statist view of language – one that was made quite explicit by Gumperz' contemporary Hymes in his discussion of communicative competence. Verbal repertoires can be seen as the toolkit to achieve communicative competence, which is the ability to have voice and make one's intentions understood in a community or the communities one lives in (Hymes, 1972 as cited in Blommaert & Backus, 2013: 17). Accordingly, knowledge of a speech community's verbal repertoire is essential for achieving communicative competence but the ability to have voice – i.e. 'people's ability to give an account of their lives' and have it listened to 'in a practice of mutual recognition' (Couldry, 2009: 580)[1] – also entails that one's language practices aren't stigmatised or devalued but count as competent ways of speaking. As noted in Beck (2015), voice is closely entangled with the ability to control a standardised national nomolanguage. In the same vein, Silverstein writes that

> when even laypersons ask 'What language(s) do you speak?' they mean what denotational code(s) – centrally, grammatically conforming words and expressions – for representing things and states-of-affairs in the world do you control. (Silverstein, 2014: 5)

It is then grammatically defined nomolanguages – statist repertoires – that count as the measure for communicative competence and other practices are silenced. In extra-institutional contexts in spaces like Khayelitsha, an ability for voice through heterogeneous language practices might well be there. The Grade 5 teacher in this study, for example, says in an interview that she likes to sometimes use four nomolanguages within one sentence and, asked if she feels speakers should keep those separate (also outside the classroom), she says:

> No. No you can mix the languages. I don't know whether it's because I like to do so. But with me, I like to mix the languages. I like to learn more languages. I can speak Swati, I can speak Ndebele, Sotho, Xhosa, Zulu, English. I would like to learn Afrikaans as well. I do say some words in Afrikaans when I speak to my daughter at home, because she do Afrikaans at school [...]. I wouldn't say that people should separate the languages. (Interview Grade 5 Teacher)

We might call hers a *languaging ideology*. Yet, in state institutions such as schools, competent ways of speaking aren't the heterogeneous practices the teacher describes but again those that fit into named boxes. As it stands, in the institutional context of the English classroom in focus here, only Standard English can be valued (for example in formal assessment) and part of the deficit-centred discourse around township schools and teachers is that township teachers don't (and cannot) adhere to these monoglossic ideologies (Section 1.5). This is reflected in parents complaining that

> teachers here in the township like to translate everything into native languages, instead of using English only. You also find teachers here

in the township 'mixing' (switching back and forth) languages. That is the reason we take our children to formerly White-only schools because they will learn proper English there. (Parent interviewed in Ndimande, 2012: 536)

The principal at Khayelitsha Primary also suggests that teachers 'like to teach English in Xhosa' (Interview Principal 2014)[2] and to code-switch in class and that this is why learners struggle with English. The Western Cape Education Department joins in by urging teachers

to reduce the amount of code switching and code mixing in order to ensure maximum exposure to the LoLT as the language of assessment. In the case of a large number of schools in this province, this would refer to English. (Western Cape Government, 2017)

Therefore, across stakeholders in South African education, township teachers' practices in (English) classrooms that are outside of homogenised Standard English are listened to not as competencies but as deficiencies. Township teachers' (and learners') ability to have voice then becomes very limited and stigma prevails over recognition of linguistic competencies (see also McKinney et al., 2015). This situation is reflected in accounts of teachers feeling bad for, or at least being apologetic about, their heterogeneous language practices in classrooms (Probyn, 2009; Setati et al., 2002, among others).

Hymes recognises the connection between the statist view of language and the conceptualisation of heterogeneous language practices as deficiencies rather than competencies. He writes that

we have to break with the tradition of thought which simply equates one language, one culture, and takes a set of functions for granted. In order to deal with the problems faced by disadvantaged children, and with education in much of the world, we have to begin with the conception of the speech habits, or competencies, of a community or population, and regard the place among them of the resources of historically-derived languages as an empirical question. (Hymes, 1972: 288)

The 'disadvantaged children' he speaks about are reminiscent of the teachers and learners in Khayelitsha whose 'speech habits' don't conform to either of the Standard nomolanguages valued in their education and whose competencies are therefore invisible and silenced (Beck, 2015; McKinney et al., 2015). Conceptualising their language practices in terms of competencies and questioning the role of 'historically derived nomolanguages' in Khayelitshan classrooms is part of my agenda in this book. This doesn't mean denying the reality of nomolanguages as possible – and in some spaces relevant – orienting principles, but it does mean seriously considering the possibility that nomolanguages don't always, i.e. per default, play a role in language practices. The analysis of language practices in terms of verbal repertoires is a major step towards making such a differentiation possible.

2.2.2 Code-switching

Theorisations of verbal repertoires and communicative competence also contribute to the increasing integration of those 'speech habits' into linguistic analyses that are reluctant to fit into nomolanguage boxes. Scholars who have looked at such heterogeneous languaging in education and beyond have done so mostly under the paradigm of code-switching (Ferguson, 2009; Gumperz, 1977; Myers-Scotton, 1997; Poplack, 1988; Slabbert & Finlayson, 2002). Code-switching studies achieved a great deal in promoting the inclusion of those language practices into linguistic analyses that don't fit statist linguistic boxes – by making use of these very boxes, as we will come to see.

After advancing his seminal work on verbal repertoires, Gumperz (1977: 1) also worked on language practices that are characterised by conversational code-switching, which he defines as 'the juxtaposition of passages of speech belonging to two different grammatical systems or sub-systems, within the same exchange'. From his study of such practices in different nomolanguage constellations, he developed a typology that includes six functions of code-switching in interactions: 'quotations', 'addressee specification', 'interjection', 'repetition', 'message qualification' and 'personalisation versus objectivisation' (Gumperz, 1977: 14–18). The details of these functions are not relevant here, but what is important is that heterogeneous language practices were seen as events associable with particular functions in the first place. This shows that they were perceived to be qualitatively different from other speech events – unsurprisingly so, given the hitherto dominant statist view of nomolanguages as homogeneous entities – and treated as *per se* interesting.

The analysis of the reasons for and the functions of language switches is still widespread in code-switching research. Reviewing studies of classroom code-switching, Lin (2013: 207) notes that scholars are often on a 'normalising mission' as they are concerned with showing that code-switching is a normal, functional linguistic practice. Many classroom studies 'have the effect of uncovering the good sense or the local rationality (or functions) of code-switching in the classroom' (Lin, 2013: 202). In the context of South African township classrooms, Ferguson, for example, observed that one of the functions of code-switching is to allow teachers to talk more meaningfully about texts. It is prevalent

> in teacher's commentary on, and annotation of, the meanings of these texts. The purpose clearly is to mediate textual meanings for pupils

who have limited control over the language of those texts. (Ferguson, 2003: 39)

Much of what I am concerned with in this study is also the analysis of teachers' talk around written texts and indeed heterogeneous language practices play a significant role there. However, I have committed to *walking the other way* and beginning my theorisations from the basic assumption of fluid linguistic heterogeneity. I cannot, therefore, accept the notion of a 'code' to describe that analytical starting point. This is not to say that scholars of code-switching generally equate codes with nomolanguages. Some studies are very differentiated in this regard and emphasise that it depends on what speakers identify as a code to orient towards in speech and not what linguists define as such (Auer, 1998, 1999; Meeuwis & Blommaert, 1998). Speaker orientation in defining what linguistic ordering principles might structure languaging is certainly important in my study as well and I here take inspiration from code-switching research.

Jaspers and Madsen make the convincing case that code-switching studies have indeed been very careful about seeing like a state – i.e. very careful about not equating 'code' with a nomolanguage – and have developed much more complex perspectives. There is the possibility of having codes that are in themselves code-switched or something that at first sight looks like one code but turns out to instantiate speakers' switching in orientation towards two or more closely related codes (Jaspers & Madsen, 2019: 6–7). I am not suggesting that such codes don't exist. They have certainly been shown to play a role in various interactions and there the notion of code-switching can be a very precise analytical tool. My point is that the linguistic practices in the English classrooms I look into would be distorted if I were to use the notion of code-switching. This is because there is one aspect that notion cannot be without: the grouping together of certain linguistic features into codes – codification that is – even if not along the traditional lines of nomolanguages. When using the code-switching lens,

> the goal for linguists is then to find when participants meaningfully orient to a juxtaposition between sets of co-occurring linguistic features, which must be done by investigating the possible conversational function of such a contrast and the social indexicality of the features in question. (Jaspers & Madsen, 2019: 6)

In Section 2.3, I discuss in more detail that classroom languaging in Khayelitshan English classrooms is not a code. It is not an analytically fixable 'set of co-occurring linguistic features' that speakers can orient towards. Instead, it is an *ad hoc, in situ* assemblage of linguistic resources that is heavily dependent on the languaging resources that teaching materials and tasks bring to the spatial repertoire of the classroom on a particular day, in each particular moment of a lesson (see also Canagarajah, 2018). I cannot stabilise such *in situ* assemblages into the notion of a code because that would give the linguistic resources used the fixed coherence of regular co-occurrence that they in fact don't have, as they change with every story the teacher reads from the textbook, with every task the teacher or the book formulates and with every test paper that arrives at the school from the departmental authorities.

The notion of a 'code' would also, in its last consequence, make the field of tension between linguistic fluidity and fixity disappear – or rather it would turn it into a tension between two or more fixities: codes. It demands some sort of grouping together and assumes coherence beyond the level of the individual linguistic feature. Because I am committed in this work to develop a perspective that doesn't fix fluidity but that grapples with the tension between fluidity and fixity, I cannot use the notion of code-switching for the purposes of this work – a decision that produces detours instantiated in elaborate explanations of classroom scenarios that might seem common and simple through a code-switching lens. It is these detours, however, that produce a different perspective on language in language classrooms that might be worth walking the additional miles. So where to from here?

2.2.3 Translanguaging

A new term that has been promoted in response to and as a critique of code-switching scholarship is translanguaging (Creese & Blackledge, 2010; García, 2009; García & Wei, 2014; Otheguy *et al.*, 2015). It is not the only term, however, that attempts to move beyond code-switching accounts of heterogeneous language practices. As Canagarajah (2011: 2) points out, 'the theorisation of this practice [translanguaging] is going on in different disciplines under different labels'. Some of these other labels are metrolingualism (Pennycook & Otsuji, 2015), polylingual languaging (Jørgensen, 2008; Jørgensen *et al.*, 2011) and code-meshing (Michael-Luna & Canagarajah, 2007), to name a few. The body of work dealing with the issue is growing fast, sometimes being summarised under a new research paradigm: translingualism. Canagarajah writes:

> Challenging traditional understandings of language relationships in multilingualism, which postulates languages maintaining their separate structures and identities even in contact, translingualism looks at verbal resources as interacting synergistically to generate new grammars and meanings, beyond their separate structures. According to this definition, the prefix 'trans' indexes a way of looking at communicative practices as transcending autonomous languages. (Canagarajah, 2018: 31)

From this perspective, speakers draw on mobile, adaptable language resources and language is reconceptualised as a dynamic social practice (Canagarajah, 2018; Creese & Blackledge, 2010; García, 2009; García & Wei, 2014; Heller, 2007; Pennycook, 2010, among others). Translanguaging, most significantly promoted in García's work on language in education since 2009, was first introduced in the 1980s in Wales to promote the role of Welsh in education, contesting the historic suppression of that nomolanguage as less prestigious than English in schooling. The term here stood for using English and Welsh additively in the classroom (Lewis *et al.*, 2012; Williams, 1996). As Williams puts it:

> Translanguaging means that you receive information through the medium of one language (e.g. English) and use it yourself through the medium of the other language (e.g. Welsh). Before you can use that information successfully, you must have fully understood it. (Williams, 1996)

In this early usage, the *trans-* in translanguaging tries to transcend the strict assignment of only one language per classroom activity. Nomolanguages themselves were not transcended but clearly divided along input and output lines and seen as existing as first language (L1) and L2 in the speakers' minds (Williams, 1996). Translanguaging was, at this point, a description – or prescription – of a didactic strategy, not a descriptor for language practices in general. This changes when García picks up the term in the context of Spanish–English bilingual education in the United States.

García's (2009) translanguaging unsettles the separation of mental grammars into linguistic systems like L1 and L2. She says that what bilinguals[3] do when they translanguage is 'to intermingle linguistic features that have hereto been administratively or linguistically assigned to a particular language or language variety' (García, 2009: 62). Here then, translanguaging is no longer exclusively reserved for certain didactic strategies but also comes to describe the day-to-day language practices of bilinguals. It is explicitly intended to offer an alternative to the statist view of language, foregrounding the linguistic repertoires and practices of speakers instead of nomolanguages.

Later, the linguistic definition of translanguaging becomes 'the deployment of a speaker's full linguistic repertoire without regard for watchful adherence to the socially and politically defined boundaries of named (and usually national and state) languages' (Otheguy *et al.*, 2015: 283). Here, the practice is no longer associated with a particular type of speaker (bilingual) and becomes *any use of language that is not watchfully oriented towards a nomolanguage* – even if it coincides with one. This definition becomes useful for crafting the analytical concepts needed for this project later on.

What complicates the picture when it comes to studies that apply translanguaging in educational settings is that the concept is not merely used as a descriptor for language practices that aren't oriented towards nomolanguages. It is also used to describe concrete didactic strategies and to summarise whole pedagogical approaches that are centrally concerned with treating the various languaging resources at the disposal of learners and teachers as affordances rather than as disturbances (Celic & Seltzer, 2011; Creese & Blackledge, 2010; García & Leiva, 2014; Makalela, 2018). Note how García and Wei (2014) talk about translanguaging as

> an approach to the use of language, bilingualism and the education of bilinguals that considers the language practices of bilinguals not as two autonomous language systems as has been traditionally the case, but as one linguistic repertoire with features that have been societally constructed as belonging to two separate languages. (García & Wei, 2014: 2)

Translanguaging turns from a descriptive to a potentially prescriptive concept that outlines how the education of bilinguals should be approached. Translanguaging is fast becoming a term with various meanings (see also Jaspers & Madsen, 2019 for a discussion): a linguistic descriptor for languaging that is 'unwatchful' to nomolanguages, a term for concrete didactic[4] strategies and for whole pedagogical approaches to education. An effect of (at least) a triple usage of the term is that scholars who describe or outline translingual pedagogies don't necessarily describe classroom language practices or didactic strategies in accordance with the principles of translanguaging as a linguistic descriptor.

For example, in the South African context, Probyn (2015) observes 'pedagogical translanguaging' in public rural and township schools. Her analytical tools for describing teachers' language practices that constitute this pedagogical translanguaging, however, are firmly grounded in code-switching research. For coding her data, she uses Ferguson's

> three broad pedagogic functions for classroom code-switching: (1) for constructing and transmitting knowledge; (2) for classroom management; (3) for interpersonal relations and to humanize the classroom climate. (Ferguson, 2009 as cited in Probyn, 2015: 224)

Probyn's study has great merit in that she shows how South African teachers often already treat their learners' languaging resources as useful assets, despite working in state schools where heterogeneous language practices aren't valued but rather frowned upon. Her study illustrates, however, how translanguaging, when used to refer to pedagogies and didactic strategies, is often used together with linguistic descriptors that imply the existence of separate nomolanguages (here: code-switching).

The triple use of translanguaging for the pedagogical approach, the didactic strategies and the description of language practices in a classroom becomes visible in García and Leiva (2014). They analyse a classroom dialogue in an English language arts classroom of a school for newly arrived Latino immigrant students in the United States. The material used is the lyrics of a song that features resources associated with Spanish and English and the contribution from teachers and learners are described as translingual. The authors assign general functions to instances of translanguaging, reminiscent of code-switching studies: 'The students' translanguaging serves three important discursive functions – to enable: 1. Participation, 2. Elaboration of ideas, 3. The raising of questions' (García & Leiva, 2014: 210). When the teacher translanguages, it is said to serve the following functions: '1. to involve and give voice, 2. to clarify, 3. to reinforce, 4. to manage the classroom, and 5. to extend and ask questions' (García & Leiva, 2014: 210).

Recalling Ferguson's (2009: 231–232) major functions of classroom code-switching: '(1) for constructing and transmitting knowledge [...] (2) for classroom management [...] (3) for interpersonal relations [...] and to humanize the classroom climate', it is not entirely clear where the difference or the additional merit lies in using translanguaging instead. The outcomes point to a similar analytical lens: general functions are assigned to language practices and/or didactic strategies that are *not monolingual*. Heterogeneous language practices under translanguaging are analysed as practices or strategies that are *per se* different from monolingual ones – otherwise they couldn't be assigned such general functions. An element of seeing like a state – of the conflation of linguistic features and nomolanguages (Sections 2.1.2 and 2.2.2) – seems to survive when applying translanguaging to classroom language practices.

Also, nomolanguages as analytical reference points are normally not abandoned in classroom studies that use translanguaging. Even though the theoretical backgrounds of those studies mostly suggest a break with a tradition that constructs nomolanguages as countable entities, the latter remain central points of analytical reference. Formulations like 'her utterance shows an overlap between isiZulu and English' (Makalela, 2018: 276) or 'both teacher and learners used more English than isiXhosa' (Probyn, 2015: 228) show that even though a critical stance towards such categories is asserted – Creese and Blackledge (2010: 108), for example, write that 'such classifications [into nomolanguages] are meaningless for the speaker' – alternative, potentially more meaningful classifications aren't provided and linguistic features continue to be attached to nomolanguages by default.

This then is one reason why the term 'translanguaging' prompts another detour for me. I do this again with an acute awareness of the achievements of translanguaging scholarship in unsettling the idea that education is necessarily a monolingual enterprise and in pointing out the disadvantages that speakers with heterogeneous language resources have compared to those whose repertoires are more homogeneous in the statist view. Translanguaging is a very successful language political term and also an emergent area of study that is disrupted and unsettled from different directions, foregrounding different functions of language beyond the referential and beyond what traditionally counts as language or linguistic (see, for example, Baynham & Lee, 2019; Blackledge & Creese, 2017). I am, however, on the look out for concepts that allow me very close *linguistic* descriptions without reverting to seeing like a state, and in its use as a linguistic descriptor translanguaging doesn't afford me that. As Otheguy *et al.* (2015: 282) write: 'As the term translanguaging gained adherents in sociolinguistics and education, it began to drift toward covering essentially the same conceptual terrain as code switching'. This means that analysts using the translanguaging lens have difficulties in distancing themselves from seeing 'in conformity to how the state sees' (Silverstein, 2014: 18) and remain distracted by nomolanguages or codes from looking at the minute details and functions of particular linguistic features in their own right – a point I will illustrate with empirical examples later.

The second concern I have with the term translanguaging is that, even if the *trans-* prefix does what it is supposed to do, namely encourage scholars to 'transcend' nomolanguages – or even language as such – in their analyses, this perspective is still different from the one I want to develop here. A translanguaging lens then leads from nomolanguages to a realm where nomolanguages don't matter. In order to 'see' translanguaging, we therefore need to first 'see' nomolanguages so they can then be transcended. This contradicts my project of walking the other way, starting from linguistic heterogeneity without assuming nomolanguages. Also, translanguaging then opens up a space where nomolanguages are irrelevant. Conceptually, this then would mean that nomolanguages and translanguaging are mutually exclusive and that any instance of translanguaging is an instance in which nomolanguages aren't relevant ordering principles. While there are certainly interactions where nomolanguages don't matter, in this study I am looking at English classrooms. Therefore, there is definitely one statist repertoire that matters as an ordering principle: Standard English.[5] A concept that implies the transcendence of nomolanguages altogether, systematically shutting out statist homogeneity in the manner in which classical linguistics has often systematically shut out heterogeneity (see also Jaspers, 2019), doesn't appear as an adequate descriptor for language practices in language classrooms. I prefer to use the term 'languaging', as I have already been doing throughout my writing, to designate day-to-day language practices that aren't limited by 'watchful adherence' (Otheguy *et al.*, 2015) to the boundaries of a nomolanguage. Languaging is therefore always potentially heterogeneous. I distance myself, however, from individualistic conceptualisations of languaging, seeing it as a spatial practice instead.

2.3 Languaging Our Way from Individual to Spatial Repertoires

2.3.1 Languaging as a spatial practice

For Jørgensen (2008: 169), languaging means that 'language users employ whatever linguistic features are at their disposal with the intention of achieving their communicative aims'. Comparing this to the above-introduced definition of translanguaging as 'the deployment of a speaker's full linguistic repertoire without regard for watchful adherence to the socially and politically defined boundaries of named (and usually national and state) nomolanguages' (Otheguy *et al.*, 2015: 283) shows that the two terms describe a similar phenomenon but with different emphases. While languaging underscores the goal-oriented nature of language practices for which *whatever* linguistic features can be mobilised, translanguaging puts more emphasis on the transcendence of administrative language boundaries.

Also, translanguaging emphasises linguistic features being actualised from the linguistic repertoire of a given individual. We find ourselves, therefore, somewhat away from the social sphere – for example, the speech community in Gumperz' definition of repertoires – in the mind of the individual, where linguistic features are said to be found (Canagarajah, 2011; Jaspers & Madsen, 2019). The retreat into the individual's mind connects to the anchor of a stable speech community being increasingly unearthed under conditions of globalisation and superdiversity (Blommaert & Backus, 2013; Busch, 2012). To capture contemporary language practices, Blommaert and Backus (2013: 15) argue that it is more helpful to define repertoires as 'individual, biographically organised complexes of resources', which 'follow the rhythms of actual human lives'. Individual repertoires are shaped by people's life trajectories and change constantly, influenced by the spaces individuals traverse and language in. While coming into being through social interaction, repertoires are seen as something that individuals then have – at least temporarily – and carry around with them. Translanguaging is then the actualisation of such individual repertoires.

While (bilingual) individuals are said to 'sort through the language features' (García & Wei, 2014: 15) in their repertoires in order to choose the appropriate resources for actualisation, these sorting processes allegedly take place in the minds of individuals. Accordingly, they remain invisible to the analyst who can only look at features actualised in interaction. Translanguaging, therefore, while it is sometimes *intended to describe this sorting process*, is applied in analyses to *the results of this process*, which are the language features that get actualised. This will later become an important distinction between what an individual, speaker-centred lens allows the analyst to see in contrast to what a spatial lens can do.

The idea of individual repertoires helps me to account for the resources that learners and teachers 'bring' into the English classroom but is not comprehensive enough to include all the linguistic resources used (Canagarajah, 2018). In the classroom, teachers and learners engage with linguistic resources they might not themselves *have* but that are distributed via centralised curricula and arrive in textbooks, etc. Those resources aren't necessarily part of the individuals' existing competencies but they are available and relevant in the classroom space during a particular activity. Thinking about linguistic resources as material elements 'externally "at one's disposal" rather than internally as part of one's competence' (Pennycook & Otsuji, 2015: 83) is helpful here. These resources are often not elements of an established code (see Section 2.2.2) but get 'assembled *in situ*' (Canagarajah, 2018: 37, emphasis in original) in languaging-in-space. The degree of stability that makes interaction possible is not the regular co-occurrence of linguistic features as forming a code, but the regular coming together of the teacher, the learners and the materials and activities in the English classroom. Linguistic features then don't have to be analysed as constituents of nomolanguages or other types of codes, but appear as material constituents of particular spaces. This analytical stance also allows for making linguistic sorting practices visible as they are no longer hidden in the minds of individuals – like much translanguaging scholarship has it (see Section 2.4.1).

Jørgensen's (2008: 169) definition of languaging as language users employing 'whatever linguistic features are at their disposal' in goal-oriented ways can accommodate this more material view of linguistic resources. It also makes room for nomolanguages to be potential – but not necessary – ordering principles. It remains possible to find homogeneity in heterogeneity without the either-or that the translanguaging perspective suggests. I work with Jørgensen's definition of languaging in this book, while defining it explicitly as a spatial practice.

Since the individual's repertoire no longer occupies centre stage, we have now languaged our way towards languaging as a spatial practice. This idea can be conceptualised by looking at how de Certeau described walking as a spatial practice in 'Walking in the City'. He writes that 'a spatial order organises an ensemble of possibilities (e.g., by a place in which one can move) and interdictions (e.g., by a wall that prevents one from going further)' (de Certeau, 1984: 96). It is the practitioner – in his example the walker in the city – who then

> actualises some of these possibilities. In that way, he makes them exist as well as emerge. But he also moves them about and he invents others, since the crossing, drifting away, or improvisation of walking privilege, transform or abandon spatial elements. (de Certeau, 1984: 96)

The spatial order,[6] in my case, is the physically and institutionally delimited space of the English classroom that organises an ensemble of linguistic possibilities – not merely by physical delimitation but also via institutional rules concerning what language practices are legitimate in a language classroom. The linguistic resources that are organised in this space reach there through institutional channels in textbooks and test papers and through the practices of teachers and learners. The walker becomes the languager[7] (here the English teacher or learner) and the practice of walking becomes the practice of languaging. Languaging no longer stands for the deployment of linguistic features from an individual's repertoire but for the actualisation of elements from a locally situated ensemble of linguistic possibilities. Languagers 'privilege, transform or abandon spatial elements' (de Certeau, 1984: 96) – here linguistic resources – and invent new ones as they go (or language) along. They always work from – and on – the ensemble of linguistic possibilities as space is 'handled and shaped by practices' (de Certeau, 1985: 137). English teachers in Khayelitsha handle and shape the ensemble of linguistic possibilities in the classroom by ordering it in ways that help them to teach English optimally, as we will come to see more clearly below.

2.3.2 From kitchen to classroom repertoires

The idea of situated ensembles of linguistic possibilities that are 'handled and shaped by practices' (de Certeau, 1985: 137) resembles what sociolinguists have recently been describing as 'spatial repertoires' when accounting for language practices in spaces such as restaurant kitchens, markets and gyms – mostly in urban settings of the Global North (Baynham & Lee, 2019; Blackledge & Creese, 2017; Pennycook & Otsuji, 2015). Less common so far are studies of spatial repertoires in educational spaces, with the exception of Canagarajah (2018), who studies a university class of Science, Technology, Engineering and Mathematics (STEM) scholars in the United States. These studies share a dynamic notion of space similar to that of de Certeau, where 'space transforms, and is in turn transformed by, action' (Baynham & Lee, 2019: 109). Spatial elements like linguistic features or other semiotic resources in this view constitute assemblages that form 'situated and emergent spatial repertoires' (Canagarajah, 2018: 48), which are performative and accommodate heterogeneity and unpredictability.

A good illustration of what can constitute a spatial repertoire comes from Pennycook and Otsuji when they investigate how staff members from diverse backgrounds in restaurant kitchens in urban Sydney get things done with language. They write:

> The repertoires of these kitchens are organisations of the totality of linguistic resources (including menus, the name of the restaurant, labels

on wine bottles and so on) brought to this place through the linguistic trajectories of the people and space. (Pennycook & Otsuji, 2015: 84)

Moving now from kitchens to classrooms, these organisations of the totality of linguistic resources – or ensembles of linguistic possibilities – consist of resources brought into the classroom not only through the linguistic trajectories of teachers and learners but also through the translocal, institutional channels of South African schooling. The language resources in school books and test papers, prescribed by centralised curricula and assessment systems, are somewhat like the language on the wine bottles in Sydney's restaurant kitchens. Just as kitchen and restaurant staff 'handle' the names of wines, dishes and the resources they themselves bring to the spatial repertoire, teachers and learners handle resources they themselves bring as well as those from the written material.

Regarding how the resources get there, however, an institutional space like the classroom and a commercial space like a restaurant differ. Restaurants aren't subject to centralised state planning. Wine can be ordered according to what is considered most appropriate for the clientele and dishes on the menu are likely (or hopefully) within the cooking expertise of the staff.

The resources that teachers and learners are confronted with in township English classrooms, however, are signs produced by various actors within and beyond the school that

> may include the state, national curriculum designers, schools and their boards, parents, school subject departments, individual teachers and students. Such processes of sign-making are never neutral, however. They are invested with unequal power relations, resource constraints and forms of coercion and resistance operating among different interest groups in the educational policy practice nexus. (Stein, 2008: 2)

These unequal power relations instantiated in the top-down implementation of language curricula bring particular choices of material containing linguistic resources that are sometimes to the frustration of teachers, who have different ideas of what would be locally appropriate for their learners. For example (see also Section 1.4), the Grade 5 English teacher says about the teaching materials prescribed by the curriculum:

> I think sometimes the words that they use are much too difficult for them [the learners]. […] I would prefer them, or the writers of the book, or the department to give us a book with easier words since English is their [the learners'] second language. (Interview Grade 5 Teacher)

As it stands, the 'book with easier words' remains the teacher's wish and the 'much too difficult' words are 'things' she *has to* handle. The 'books with much too difficult words' are instantiations of statist linguistic fixity in the form of Standard English resources that cannot be 'transcended' in Khayelitshan English classrooms, because their mastery is the very target of English teaching. So, if the spatial repertoire of the Khayelitshan English classroom (henceforth: 'classroom repertoire') is conceptualised, Standard English resources are part of its central elements.

But teachers and learners also routinely actualise the Khayelitshan repertoire and can enrol those resources into the classroom repertoire. Khayelitsha's ensemble of linguistic possibilities includes resources with various histories, some of which are quite sedimented[8] while others flow and transform due to the particular mobility patterns of residents and the suspense between connection and separation from the city that characterise the township (Section 1.2). The Khayelitshan repertoire, therefore, is a non-codified spatial repertoire, constantly transforming and being transformed by languaging. This is what makes it different from Standard Xhosa and Standard English. The latter are also spatial in that they structure the spatial order of state education. To allow for a more nuanced distinction, however, I prefer to refer to them as statist repertoires (nomolanguages), because they exist beyond the realm of languaging as comparably fixed linguistic codes and often also as aspirational ideologies. They aren't transformed by languaging but by the necessarily much slower written practices of standardising and codifying.

In this view, the Khayelitshan English classroom becomes a pivotal space where two linguistic spaces – instantiated via their associated repertoires – fold[9] into each other, forming together something new, a heterogeneous ensemble of linguistic possibilities:

(1) the space of state education instantiated by Standard English (and sometimes also Standard Xhosa)[10] as a statist repertoire constituted by practices of standardising, codifying, writing and testing;
(2) the space of Khayelitsha instantiated by a non-codified, heterogeneous repertoire dominated by oral languaging and subject to the social processes that Gumperz (among others) describes for speech communities.

Khayelitshan English teachers are pivotal figures in the classroom space, because, as fluent Khayelitshan languagers and trained English teachers, they have access to the full ensemble of linguistic possibilities. They can then order the classroom repertoire, sorting its constituents into heterogeneous languaging and homogenised Standard English, in the process teaching learners 'which resources go where' in the statist order, while making sure that they understand the content of the demanding material. This ordering of the classroom repertoire is done via a linguistic sorting practice I call *relanguaging* and that I will explain in Section 2.4, after discussing the notions of *classroom languaging* and *englishing* below.

2.3.3 Classroom languaging and classroom englishing

Teachers in Khayelitshan English classrooms have to work with and around the linguistic resources that come with the curriculum materials and establish Standard English – or their localised interpretation thereof – as a recognisable linguistic ordering principle in the classroom. They have to teach their learners how to sort out spatial repertoires so they can recognise and orient towards Standard English in their languaging – they have to teach them how to *english*.

If we take the heterogeneity – produced by the folding of the Khayelitshan and the statist repertoire into the classroom space – as the norm, then the heterogeneous classroom repertoire is always our analytical starting point for *walking the other way*. It is essential to note that the heterogeneity is not only produced by the Khayelitshan repertoire but also lies in the foldedness of Khayelitshan languaging and Standard English. What I will refer to as 'classroom languaging' is therefore not the equivalent of Khayelitshan languaging but describes the goal-oriented actualisation of this foldedness – i.e. of *whatever* linguistic features offered by the classroom repertoire, without restrictions on the boundaries of nomolanguages within that repertoire. Classroom languaging – that is often heterogeneous – is therefore also the generic term I use for teachers' and learners' language practices in class. In contrast, 'classroom englishing'[11] is the actualisation of *specific* resources from the classroom repertoire with a watchful orientation towards the boundaries of Standard English. 'Xhosing' expresses the same in relation to Standard Xhosa and along those lines a verb could be derived from whichever nomolanguage, indicating that the language itself – the statist repertoire – is not what people speak but whose norm is the written form. People's idea of what constitutes that nomolanguage, can, however, sometimes function as a major ordering principle in their languaging. Then, they 'english' or 'xhosa', actualising linguistic features while being watchful of – but not necessarily 100% in keeping with – the boundaries of a statist repertoire. One could speak here about 'nomolanguaging' as well. Englishing or xhosing can therefore also be instantiated in heterogeneous language practices that nevertheless display a strong orientation towards the rules and boundaries of a statist repertoire. My analysis of the morpheme 'u-' as an 'englishing device' in Section 5.2 will illustrate this point.

Below, I now turn to the much mentioned linguistic sorting practice that emerges between classroom languaging and englishing and that my heuristic of detours around established analytical lenses has allowed me to discover: *relanguaging*.

2.4 Relanguaging in Two Directions

2.4.1 Relanguaging as 'sorting out'

Remembering the folded condition of the Khayelitshan English classroom repertoire, the prerequisite for englishing is to order this repertoire so that homogenised Standard English can become recognisable and foregrounded. This implies a *sorting out* of the Khayelitshan resources in the classroom repertoire so that heterogeneity retreats into the background. This backgrounding of heterogeneity and foregrounding of homogeneity through *sorting out* is one intimation of the prefix *re-* in relanguaging.

In an extensive morphological analysis of the prefix *re-* as attached to different verbs, Saragih (2008: 25) finds that its most common meanings are 'back or again' and to 'redo something differently'. It always intimates that something is already there, which is then either worked on and emerges differently, or is reproduced ('again') or returned to ('back'). If we begin from the conceptualisation of the classroom repertoire as a linguistic space where both repertoires – Khayelitshan and statist – are folded into each other, forming a heterogeneous, unsorted ensemble of linguistic possibilities, then relanguaging is a *re*invention, a *re*doing of that linguistic space into one that appears more homogenised and makes englishing possible. In its homogenising direction, relanguaging is therefore the practice that systematically prepares englishing. It doesn't describe the actualisation of linguistic possibilities but their ordering or sorting beforehand. *Accordingly, englishing is the result of the sorting practice I call relanguaging, not the sorting practice itself.*

An example is when a teacher picks up a linguistically heterogeneous statement a learner has made and relanguages it into classroom englishing by *sorting out* all Khayelitshan resources. This example can be illustrated with a relanguaging circle, a model that I will invoke at various points throughout the analyses presented in this work:

Circle I: 'Sorting out'

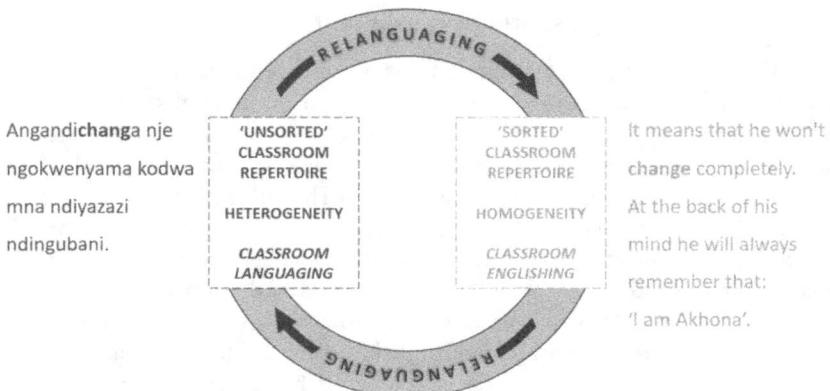

The learner's statement (in black) 'Angandi**chang**a nje ngokwenyama kodwa mna ndiyazazi ndingubani' *(He can change me only superficially but me, I know who I am)* instantiates the heterogeneous unsorted classroom repertoire via classroom languaging (see the black box in the circle). The teacher then relanguages (top arrow) this statement by *sorting out* the Khayelitshan resources but keeping the verb 'change' that the learner assembled in 'angandi**chang**a'. She says (here in grey): 'It means that he won't **change** completely. At the back of his mind he will always remember that: "I am Akhona"' (Grade 5 English Lesson 16.05.2016). Here, the contrast between the teacher's englishing and the learner's heterogeneous classroom languaging makes relanguaging visible. The teacher sorted out the Khayelitshan resources, repositioned 'change' as a Standard English resource, overall balanced[12] the classroom repertoire towards homogeneity and then demonstrated how to english (see the grey box in the circle).

This is how relanguaging itself – here in its homogenising direction as *sorting out* (top arrow) – can be made visible at the threshold of linguistic heterogeneity and homogeneity. Relanguaging is a process of larger linguistic ordering in space but becomes most tangible in its manifestation as a watchful rephrasing of something that was actualised from the classroom repertoire a moment ago, as in the above example. Relanguaging is the sorting practice that under translanguaging, with its focus on individual repertoires, is said to take place hidden in the minds of speakers. I posit here that a conceptualisation of repertoires as *spatial* instead of *individual* and of linguistic resources as *material* allows for making this sorting practice visible. Considering that the classroom repertoire is heterogeneous to begin with, we can posit that every act of englishing that we observe is the result of relanguaging. This is what it means for me in this book to base my analysis on the premise of heterogeneity as the norm. Throughout Chapters 4–6, a more nuanced and complexified picture of this relanguaging will emerge.

2.4.2 Relanguaging as 'bringing together'

Above, I described relanguaging as a homogenising move performed on the classroom repertoire, reinventing it to make englishing possible. In the relanguaging circle, we were therefore concerned with the top arrow. However, *re-* can also stand for 'back' to some original place, which, in this case, is the heterogeneity of the full classroom repertoire with Standard English and the Khayelitshan repertoire in their unsorted[13] foldedness. At points where homogeneity had been foregrounded in the classroom repertoire – say when the teacher had been reading from a Standard English story or was englishing for other reasons – relanguaging means to reconnect the Standard English resources with the Khayelitshan resources, *bringing together* the statist and the Khayelitshan repertoire again so that the full, heterogeneous classroom repertoire can be drawn on. Relanguaging is then a heterogenising move on the classroom repertoire and again it manifests itself most visibly at the threshold of homogeneity and heterogeneity as 'watchful rephrasing'. The relanguaging circle illustrates this once more:

Circle II: 'Bringing together'

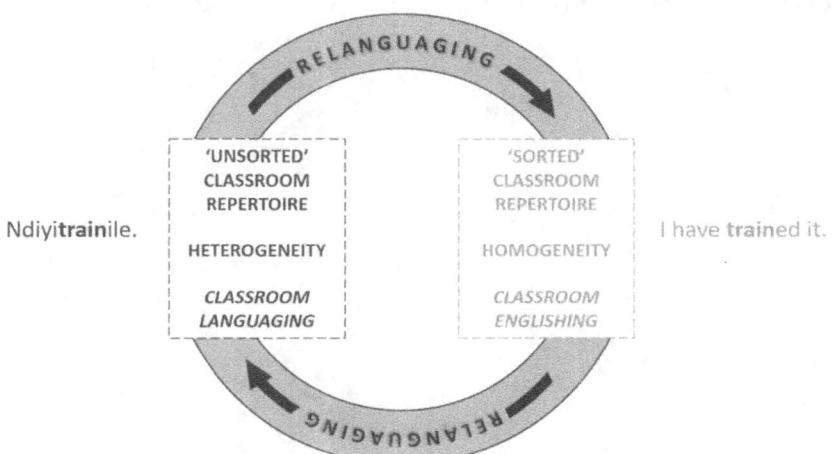

The teacher here reads the sentence 'I have **train**ed it' (in grey) from a story and then relanguages it into 'Ndiyi**train**ile' *(I have trained it)* (in black). We see relanguaging as *bringing together* (bottom arrow), systematically preparing classroom languaging. Here, the primary ordering principle is then not the rules and resources of one statist repertoire and also not the rules of a different set of regularly co-occurring linguistic resources (i.e. a 'code') but the interactional aim of making learners understand something – in this case the vocabulary item 'train'. In pursuit of that aim, the teacher brings 'train' together with Khayelitshan morphology (*ndi-*, *-yi-* and *-ile*), assembling *in situ* resources from the full, folded classroom repertoire.

2.4.3 The relanguaging circle

The practice of relanguaging underlines the teacher's pivotal role regarding the order of the classroom repertoire. With relanguaging, teachers manage two competing pressures: they draw on the full classroom repertoire (classroom languaging) to give learners linguistic clues to make sense of Standard English stories, task instructions and exam questions, and they demonstrate how to english – how to homogenise the classroom repertoire by *sorting out* those resources that don't count as Standard English and then actualising those that do. Therefore, they constantly relanguage back and forth, not between a first and a second language, but between heterogeneity and homogeneity, between languaging and a nomolanguage. The two relanguaging directions of homogenisation and heterogenisation can at this stage be summarised like this:

Circle III: Two directions of relanguaging

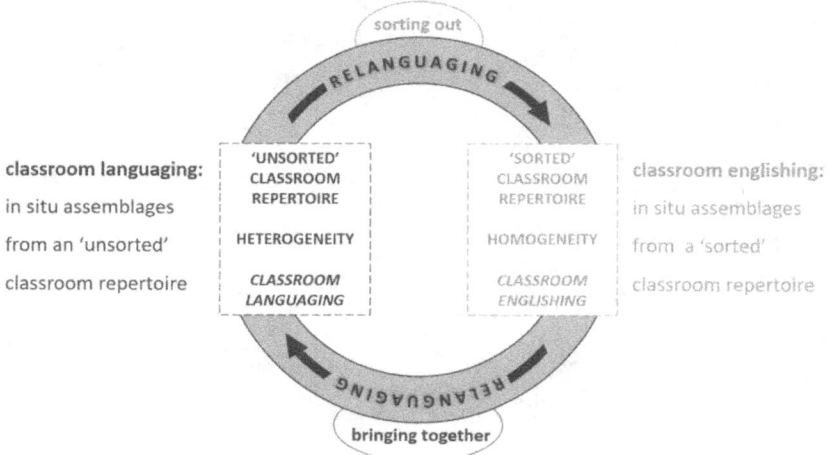

Depending on whether the classroom repertoire is balanced towards heterogeneity or homogeneity at certain points during an activity, we will see relanguaging as a *sorting out* or a *bringing together* of the resources in the classroom repertoire. *Sorting out* results in an ensemble of linguistic possibilities that is limited mostly to the confines of Standard English and actualised in classroom englishing. *Bringing together* results in the full classroom repertoire being available for classroom languaging. We have now seen relanguaging as larger processes of linguistic ordering in space. What will also count in my analyses, however, are the fine-grained details of the results of these processes, of classroom englishing and classroom languaging. Deep-dives into such detail will reveal relanguaging to be a more complex phenomenon than what we have seen so far.

This chapter introduced and explained the analytical viewpoint and concepts that help me in my experiment of walking the other way. I have explained the concepts that will help me to locate myself as an analyst on the languaging side with regard to the heterogeneous practices (languaging) and the homogenised nomolanguages that are relevant in the Khayelitshan English classroom. The conceptual considerations I presented are therefore aimed at developing an alternative to linguistically seeing like a state – i.e. to looking from nomolanguages to languaging. It is central for this new vision to dissolve the default conflation of linguistic features and nomolanguages in linguistic analyses that I discussed at various points throughout this chapter. Just how difficult this task is and how it requires many more detours becomes clear in what follows.

3 A Linguistic Ethnography for Seeing More

3.1 From Taxis to Classrooms[1]

3.1.1 Becoming slightly less 'you'

The school is located in Khayelitsha, about 28 km from Cape Town's city centre. It sits at the intersection of an area dominated by government housing[2] and one of Khayelitsha's huge informal settlements, densely packed with corrugated iron shacks. The primary school covers Grades R–7,[3] employs 30 teachers and accommodates around 1,000 learners. As a low-fee public school it belongs to Quintile 2 (according to the poverty ranking of schools in South Africa), which marks the 'second poorest' category.[4] Schools in Quintile 1 are the poorest in the country and those in Quintile 5 the best resourced ones. Under apartheid, Khayelitsha Primary was administered by the Department of Education and Training (DET) and only Black staff and learners were allowed there (Christie, 1995). While this situation is no longer stipulated by law, the fact that the learner and teacher body at the school is exclusively Black has not changed – as is the case for many former DET schools in South Africa, due to continuous residential segregation and unequal access to financial resources (Banda, 2003; Fataar, 2009).

Accordingly, the learners come from working-class families, mostly at the lower end of the socioeconomic spectrum. Slightly better-off parents likely send their children to schools outside of Black townships like Khayelitsha (see Section 1.5). Some of the children come to school with dirty uniforms and often the clothes they wear are too small. These are clues to a lack of financial security, and often also of parental care, at home. Teachers told me that for many learners the only warm meal they receive is the one provided by the school. Staff often spoke about how many parents suffer from alcohol addiction, struggle to look after their children and show no interest in their schooling careers. During my time at the school, I have encountered plenty of drunk parents coming to pick up their children or to complain about something to the teachers.

For a German, middle-class, White woman, Khayelitsha Primary was not an easy space to fit in. How to get to the school and then how to adapt to and become accepted at the research site were my biggest concerns when I started my first research project (for my master's degree) in 2013 (Krause, 2014).[5] The PhD project that this book is based on was to follow in 2016 at the same school, but the heavy lifting of gaining access and establishing myself at the research site took place back then. I was in Cape Town for five months and at the school for three months. I didn't have a car, neither did I have any contacts in Khayelitsha, except for the staff member of the literacy non-governmental organisation (NGO) that is active at Khayelitsha Primary and that established the contact between me and the school management. I had volunteered for this same NGO in an inner-city Cape Town school during my first stay in South Africa as a high-school graduate in 2009. We kept in touch and as the NGO extended its reach into townships, it became the link between me and my future research site. It was Andiswa[6] who worked – and still works – at the school for this NGO, who instructed me how to get to the school via public transport, i.e. via minibus taxis:

> Go to the Cape Town taxi rank, find the lane towards Khayelitsha, ask whether the taxi is going to 'Site B', if so, get on. When you get to Khayelitsha, tell the driver you need to go to Highschool A[7] and then I will pick you up there. (Andiswa, Field Notes 2013)

I had previously taken taxis. Even daily. But mostly through Cape Town's more immediate surroundings, not out to the townships via the N2 highway. In his walking ethnography of the N2, Twidle (2017: 66) describes this highway as 'a corridor of motorist anxiety and middle-class paranoia'. While it is easy for middle-class South Africans to avoid going into the townships, they cannot avoid the highway. It links the residential and more industrial suburbs to the city, takes you to the airport or straight to your coastal holiday domicile. Or to Khayelitsha. The N2 is 'a space where we are all in it together – though not, of course, all in the same way' (Twidle, 2017: 63). Whites are normally in their private cars. This explains the startled reactions I got from taxi drivers and passengers on my now almost daily trips to the township. Why would a White girl go to Khayelitsha? And why by taxi? Minibus taxis constitute a largely unregulated, highly flexible and efficient transport industry, used mostly by the working class that often lives in townships and works in the city (Clark & Crous, 2002). This part of the population, as a remnant of apartheid racial segregation, is, in turn, Black or Coloured, not White like me.

While taking taxis was a practical matter for me, for people at the school it mattered in a way that I didn't anticipate. 'How did you get here?', I was often asked by staff and teachers at the school entrance when they saw me walking instead of driving through the school gate:

Me: By taxi. I got off at the police station (an established 'stop') and walked.
Lihle:[8] Why do you not come by car?
Me: I don't have a car.
Lihle: Why do you not have car?
Me: I'm a student, I can't afford a car.
Lihle: Ah ok. Aren't you scared here in Khayelitsha?
Me: No, I'm fine.[9]

Exchanges similar to this one often ensued during my first days at the school. It mattered how I got there, because in South Africa forms of transport index social class. Social class, in turn, has historically been closely tied to race (Bowker & Star, 1999; Posel, 2001). While the entanglement of race and class is loosening, racial residential segregation persists. In Cape Town, working-class areas equal Black or Coloured areas, while middle-class areas are more mixed but have a high proportion of Whites. Public transport remains almost exclusively a non-White affair (Seekings, 2008). In South Africa, you buy yourself free from the perceived (and actual) dangers of using public transport as soon as you can. The middle class, and with it the majority of Whites, *can* sooner than others.

Moving around like everybody else also meant that I had relatable stories to tell. From particularly complex routes the taxi took (having me feel lost and sometimes anxious), via interesting conversations with passengers, to flat tires, smoking engines and the umlungu (*white person*) figuring out how to collect passenger fares – a job you get whenever you sit in the passenger seat. Out of necessity rather than strategically, taxis helped me mitigate my foreignness at the school. Me taking public transport surprised people, because it contrasted with the behaviour of other Whites who would occasionally visit. NGO workers or departmental officials come in their private cars and with particular agendas. Taxis made categorising me as 'another White visitor' more difficult. They cut across associations of class, race and expected behaviour, blurring on my behalf the lines of segregation so firmly implemented under apartheid: *We* live here, *You* live there. *We* can't afford, *You* can afford. *We* take taxis, *You* drive cars. *We* are Black, *You* are White. It is not that taxis made me *We*, but they made me slightly less *You*.

3.1.2 Languaging, trust and classroom access

Another essential step in becoming less *You* at the school was learning not only to move around like everybody else, but also to speak like everybody else. While I wouldn't claim that I ever became a fluent Khayelitshan languager, my friends, also outside Khayelitsha, would often tell me that when I xhosa, I tend to speak 'isiXhosa saselokishini', the 'Xhosa' of the location (i.e. township). I therefore have sufficient skills in actualising the repertoire of the area to, for example, hypothesise about which languaging resources learners and teachers in the classroom might be familiar with from their day-to-day language practices. When I first arrived at the school, however, I had almost no Khayelitshan languaging skills.

Coming from a background of African Studies and having learned Swahili for five years at university, I came prepared to learn rather quickly the workings of Khayelitshan morphology, because they are similar in many ways. I had taught myself basic greeting procedures and some verbal structures so that I could immediately begin to ask people how to say this or that. I wrote everything down in my field journal, creating random vocabulary lists like this one:

```
thengisa - sell                    yimalini - how much?
Tshintsha - to change              kwakhona - again
Weather - imozulu                  ↳ Ubage kwakhona
Themba - to trust                  -buza - to ask
-ongeza - add more                 ↳ ubuzile - he asked
Imozulu yasekapa iyatshintsha. - The weather in CT is changing.
```

Picture 1 Field notes 2013

The different handwritings show that sometimes teachers or staff would write words down for me if I struggled with spelling. Turning the research participants into my informal language teachers was a great way to break the ice and to start conversations during coffee and lunch breaks. I didn't make any attempts at getting access to classrooms for the first three weeks but invested that time to get a sense of what was going on at the school more broadly (Heath & Street, 2008), while working towards gaining the teachers' trust. I aimed at making sure that they saw me at the school consistently and at creating as many opportunities as possible for casual chats. Learning to language their way was a great way of doing this.

I have not only acquired Khayelitshan languaging when at the school, but have intensively pursued xhosing skills academically from 2015 onwards to prepare for the next research for the PhD. I completed a major in Xhosa Communication at the University of Cape Town (UCT), which put emphasis on mastering the grammar of Standard Xhosa with its noun class system and complex morphology. Towards the end of the course, I became a tutor and also started to give private classes. In March 2017, I started lecturing parts of the same Xhosa Communication course that I had previously completed. From March 2017 until June 2018, I lectured students in first year (beginner), second year (intermediate) and towards the end those in the third year (advanced) of the course.

In my teaching I have – with the support of the course convener – focused less on Standard Xhosa and as much as possible on mostly urban, but also rural spatial repertoires, which share many characteristics with Khayelitshan languaging. For teaching preparation this meant transcribing languaging from different samples of these repertoires that came, for example, from radio show broadcasts in Cape Town and from conversations recorded in different research projects in rural and urban settings. I also analysed the morphology in song texts and in social media posts. The development of these resources has made me very familiar with the actualisations of different spatial repertoires that are similar to Khayelitshan languaging, helping me a great deal in transcribing and analysing my own classroom data.

This groundwork of taxiing and languaging was the basis for getting a sense of the research site, for learning to fit in and for eventually gaining access to the classrooms and being able to observe and record classroom practices. Gaining the trust necessary for the last step was a particularly bumpy ride. Given the fact that heterogeneous language practices – known widely as 'code-switching' – are officially unwanted in the classroom, the prospect of a researcher being particularly interested in them and observing and documenting them, didn't sit well with teachers and school management. They feared that I would uncover and leak to officialdom teachers' language practices in the classrooms. This fear was very present when I started the first research in 2013. I had to repeatedly explain my exact research interest and why I wasn't going to leak any of the information I obtained to the departmental authorities.[10]

About a week into hanging out at the school, I used a staff meeting to address these issues. One of the main points I made at the time – one that I am still convinced of – is that understanding how teachers in such linguistically complex situations make teaching and learning work is of great interest for education systems around the world. I gave the example of Germany, where linguistic heterogeneity in classrooms is increasing, meeting teachers who aren't prepared for the task of languaging flexibly. What could we, therefore, learn from Khayelitshan teachers globally? This staff meeting made a start in convincing teachers that I was no danger to them. Not being in a rush, being there every day, helping out in the library, and always being open to chat about why I was constantly writing into this fieldnote book of mine, did the rest. I was allowed into the classrooms and teachers were happy to do interviews with me. So I completed my inquiry into the language attitudes and practices of teachers in early 2014.[11]

In 2015, when I was already thinking about returning to the school for further research, the same NGO that established the contact in the first place offered me a position as centre manager in a bigger literacy programme they had just started at that school. From March 2015 until March 2016, I worked at Khayelitsha Primary, mainly coordinating volunteers who were working with children from Grade 3 (the grade just before the change to English medium instruction). The children in the programme were identified as 'at risk' of not reaching the levels of literacy in English aimed at in these grades. One volunteer would work with two children at a time for an hour, following a specific programme of literacy support exercises. I also worked with the children myself, which equipped me with valuable background knowledge about the languaging skills and struggles with which 'at risk' learners enter into Grade 4, one of the grades in focus in my PhD research.

The job also meant more time at the school, more conversations, more trust, more Khayelitshan languaging. When I approached the principal after a while about the possibility of doing further research – now focused on English teaching – he was open to the idea and so were the English teachers. The second project reported on here was off to a good start.

3.1.3 Observation, stimulated recall and a writing task

The first part of data collection was the recording of language practices in the classroom while taking supplementary field notes. I recorded with a small device that has sufficient strength to adequately record voices in a confined space. No other observers were with me. The presence of an umlungu – normally this only happens when departmental subject advisors come to observe lessons – can distract learners and influence teachers to deviate from their usual language and teaching practices. The Grade 5 English teacher described the situation like this:

T: [...] they didn't perform the same as when we are alone in class, without them in the classroom. They seem to change. Just to accommodate this person or they're shy, let me just put it that way.
R: Do you feel like that was always the case when I was there or did they also get used to me a bit?
T: Yes they were getting used to you because I always told them that Achwayitile[12] works in our school. She's been here for a long time. She understands Xhosa. She's also an English teacher.[13] Don't mind her when she is here. She is here just to see how we do things in our school. She's not here to judge you. So just be yourself when she is here. I tried to tell them, yes. But I could see the first time she came, all the time before they say anything they will have one look at Achwayitile before they answered. (Interview Grade 5 Teacher)

My presence in the beginning certainly deroutinised classroom practices (McIntyre, 1980; Setati, 2005). The teachers spoke to the learners on my behalf and gradually I became less of a disturbance and mundane teaching routines set in. I sat at the back of the classrooms in order to distract learners and teachers as little as possible. The complete lessons were sound recorded. The teacher's voice is clearly audible throughout, some learners' voices can also be heard and supplement the overall teacher-focused data. I accompanied the recording with field notes (Jewitt *et al.*, 2016) and teachers often – but not always – provided me with the material (e.g. worksheets, textbooks, etc.) they deployed in the lesson. Sometimes, especially if teachers had forgotten that I was supposed to join the class for that lesson and I had to remind them again shortly before, I just sat down, as it didn't seem appropriate to ask them for any material.

I conducted the bulk of my classroom observations from February to May 2016. The major part of the transcriptions had to be completed before I conducted the interviews. I was interested in teachers' implicit knowledge about their own classroom languaging and wanted to elicit this knowledge using stimulated recall interviews (Calderhead, 1981; Dempsey, 2010), playing instances of their own classroom language practices for the teachers. I therefore had to make an initial selection from the gathered material, resulting in a recursive research process of jumping back and forth between classrooms and analysis. Stimulated recall has the advantage that it

> brings informants a step closer to the moments in which they actually produce action. It gives them the chance to listen or view themselves in action, jog memories, and give answers of 'I did', instead of 'I might have'. (Dempsey, 2010: 349–350)

The stimulated recall interviews were conducted by me and my first PhD supervisor Tessa Dowling – a fluent Khayelitshan languager and Xhosa lecturer. Her long-standing linguistic expertise allowed her to ask questions about morphology that I couldn't have come up with at the time. There were three English teachers in the Intermediate Phase. We spoke with the Grade 4 teacher for one hour and with the Grade 5 teacher for almost two hours. With the Grades 6 and 7 teacher, I spoke alone and without stimulated recall, as he tends to get very nervous and insecure when confronted with his own teaching practices. Nevertheless, the interview was about an hour long and yielded some interesting results.

Towards the end of my research, I spontaneously supplemented the teacher-centred research with a learner-centred element. When observing classroom languaging, the question 'What would language education look like if we no longer posited the existence of separate languages?' (Makoni & Pennycook, 2007a: 36) began ringing ever louder in my ears. I wanted to know what languaging techniques learners would display in their writing when let completely off the 'nomolanguage hook'. I therefore administered a writing task with a picture story that learners were supposed to describe using the language resources of their choice. I will explain the exact nature of the task in Section 6.1. For now, we turn to the analytical strategies I applied to make sense of the data.

3.2 An Experimental Linguistic Ethnography

3.2.1 Digging in an open field

Central to my experiment is developing a counter-perspective to the statist lens. The latter normalises categorisation and simplification and therefore, the alternative lens has to normalise heterogeneity (Section 1.7). Analytically this means avoiding surface-level identification and categorisation of linguistic phenomena and taking individual features of languaging seriously. This endeavour had me dig in an open field, careful not to get caught up in established categories of sensemaking from linguistics, while trying to understand what I still consider to be linguistic phenomena. Discarding linguistics was not an option, but neither was relying on it. I needed the orientation to detail the pattern-finding tools of the discipline, but I simultaneously needed to unsettle its traditional objects of knowledge: nomolanguages. I needed a systematically limited linguistics.

It helped that I am not a trained linguist. Instead, I have a multidisciplinary background, shaped by my studies, and now my work, at the Institute of African Studies in Leipzig. There, the aim has been to provide students with broad access to various fields and themes: history, political science and linguistic anthropology, to name but a few. When acquiring tools to access different research fields and to analyse various types of data, ethnography was as present as praxeology and conversation analysis (CA) – approaches that also inspire the methodology at hand. What lies at the foundation of this book is the constant critical questioning and the de- and reconstruction of analytical categories that are so prominent in Leipzig's African Studies. Here, the struggle with the deeply imperial and colonial history of area studies is often and thoroughly addressed. 'Africa' as some alleged unit of analysis is constantly unsettled – to the great despair, but also to the inspiration of students and lecturers alike. With hindsight I recognise this critical stance also at the heart of this book.

Linguistics as a discipline gradually became more relevant for me when I was already working on my PhD and lecturing Xhosa Communication at the School of Languages and Literatures (African Languages Section) at the University of Cape Town (Section 3.1.2). I came to appreciate the systematic deep-dives into the (morphological) fine grain that linguistics allows for. In this study, insights from Bantu language scholars proved particularly valuable (Morrison, 2018; Nurse & Philippson, 2003; Pahl *et al.*, 1971). Simultaneously, my lack of formal training had me retain a certain naivety and suspicion towards linguistics, making it easier to keep my distance from many common-sense categories and descriptors. I was thereby sheltered from an overwhelmingly linguistic ideology of linguistics. What linguistics is and could be, and what constitutes its object of knowledge, remained malleable for me throughout this work. I combine linguistic tools with other methods, inviting 'reflexive sensitivity to the processes involved in the production of linguistic claims and to the potential importance of what gets left out' (Rampton et al., 2004: 4). A framework that accommodates much of what I have in mind here is linguistic ethnography (LE) (Creese, 2010; Madsen, 2018; Rampton et al., 2004). It

> combines ethnographic methodology (observations, interviews etc.) with micro-analysis of recorded interactions (employing tools from conversation analysis and linguistics), and it sees social and linguistic categories and structures as being produced and reproduced through practices in everyday life. (Madsen, 2018: 392)

I somewhat stretch and adapt the approach of LE to fit the task at hand, which is to make visible new things about languaging in Khayelitshan English classrooms. The methodological bricolage I put together allowed me to conduct the experimental enquiry I aimed at here and to discover and analyse the ordering of classroom language practices captured in the term *relanguaging*.

3.2.2 Noticing relanguaging and my own statist vision

When engaging with the transcribed data in order to select sequences for stimulated recall, I was aided by CA and to some degree by grounded theory, approaches that have the analyst look into the data with an open mind, not too strongly influenced by preconceived ideas or existing theories. Instead, the particularity of one's material takes centre stage and it is the analyst's creative task to find patterns within the data (Böhm, 2003; Creswell, 2007; Deppermann, 2001; Schegloff, 1996; Ten Have, 1999). The parts of the data that I subjected to close investigation were identified not based on a predefined analytical aim 'but by "noticings" of initially unremarkable features of talk or of other conduct' (Schegloff, 1996: 172) that seemed to accomplish something in the English classroom.

An initially unremarkable feature I noticed because it was so prominent across classrooms, was that teachers spent a lot of time on what I coded initially as 'saying things differently'. Teachers would take Standard English resources from the teaching material and say them anew and differently. In the process, they often entangled – as I saw it – Standard English resources with different resources from the classroom repertoire, for example with Khayelitshan morphology. I later came to describe this as the 'heterogenising' direction of relanguaging that produces classroom languaging by *bringing together* various resources (see Section 2.4.2). Other times, teachers would rephrase heterogeneous classroom languaging via Standard English resources – now the 'homogenising' direction of relanguaging that produces englishing by *sorting out* Khayelitshan resources (see Section 2.4.1). 'Saying things differently' or 'rephrasing' occurred in a variety of classroom activities, accomplishing different things like trying to make learners understand the content of stories or poems, helping them make sense of task instructions or even nudging them into passing tests. It became the core phenomenon that I wanted to focus on in the teacher interviews. I picked examples that I thought of at the time as exemplifying this practice to play for stimulated recall.

After the interviews, I matched the transcripts of the stimulated recall snippets with what teachers said about them, ending up with a combination of transcribed classroom languaging excerpts ready for detailed linguistic analysis, combined with data from the interviews and my experiences at the research site, which added an ethnographic dimension. However, I didn't exclusively focus on the classroom data for which I had teacher comments, but also reviewed the material in its entirety several times throughout the process of analysis. This recursive analytical process of cross-checking the material with emerging interpretations is common in grounded theory (Böhm, 2003; Creswell, 2007), but also CA is a hermeneutic process. It revealed relanguaging as a phenomenon that is 'more complex than first noted' (Psathas, 1994: 52), but most importantly it showed that during the initial noticing, pattern-finding and data selection process, I as an analyst still saw in accordance to how the state sees. I noticed more often the instances of relanguaging that went from homogeneity to heterogeneity – the former apparently anchored as the norm and the latter as the interesting exception in my analytical vision. I therefore have more teacher comments on heterogenisation than on homogenisation and later I found several instances of classroom languaging and englishing that I could have played for teachers as well.

Finding this statist bias in my initial data selection and analysis made me *feel* how difficult it is to develop and apply a lens that normalises linguistic heterogeneity. The very things I noticed when looking at the material speak to my own entrenchment in the nomolanguage ideology, to my own 'seeing like a state'. I tried to mitigate the pull of the statist, homogenising vision by including various pieces of data that I only 'saw' later on, after better understanding my own bias. The thought experiment outlined in the introduction helped me to notice whenever I strayed off into conventional directions and reminded me to turn around again and to keep walking the other way. This was specifically important during fine-grained linguistic analyses that I introduce below.

3.2.3 Tying ethnography down with Bantu linguistics

Classical linguistic approaches have been developed and used based on the assumption that the linguistic features analysed are parts of bigger structures (nomolanguages) (Section 2.1). Yet, this doesn't render their achievements in illuminating linguistic patterns and their meanings invalid. Instead of discarding linguistics, it seems promising to disentangle it from statist categorisation projects and put it there 'where "language" and everything dependent on it, actually live' (Silverstein, 1998: 403) – in this case into the Khayelitshan English classroom. In this particular space, scholars of Bantu linguistics (Demuth, 2000; Katamba, 2003; Nurse & Philippson, 2003), and more specifically of Nguni nomolanguages (Koopman, 1999; Ngcobo, 2013; Pahl et al., 1978), can help us in understanding classroom language practices.

Morphological analysis, for example, makes it possible to identify the affordances of tense and aspect morphology studied under the Bantu paradigm (Nurse, 2003), as well as the significance of morphological noun class agreement (Nurse & Philippson, 2003) in getting things done in the classroom. Most important here are Nurse and Philippson (2003) who assembled a variety of distinguished Bantu linguists in a book that has something to say about almost every feature studied under the Bantu paradigm. With specific reference to Standard Xhosa and its morphology I draw a lot on Pahl et al. (1971), who write themselves in Standard Xhosa.

Fine-grained linguistic analysis is a good starting point for an LE that partly aims at

> *'tying ethnography down'*: pushing ethnography towards the analysis of clearly delimitable processes, increasing the amount of reported data that is open to falsification, looking to impregnate local description with analytical frameworks drawn from outside. (Rampton et al., 2004: 4)

Linguistics is this external analytical framework and I use it to ground my analyses in the details of the linguistic features used by learners and teachers in the classroom. But when accounting for linguistic features as elements of a spatial practice, it is not enough to consider what such features have *generally* been found to afford speakers, i.e. their meanings and grammatical functions as codified in grammars and dictionaries. Instead, we need to know what they afford speakers in particular spaces. Therefore, we need to know how a specific spatial repertoire in question is constituted (see Section 2.3.2 for the Khayelitshan English classroom repertoire). Then, we need to ask what exactly speakers accomplish – or want to accomplish – with the choice of particular linguistic features in that space. I ask these questions from a praxeological perspective aided by CA. We will see below how these two approaches work together in this experiment.

3.2.4 Spatial practices and conversation analysis

Epistemologically, LE leans towards social constructivism and post-structuralism, with their emphasis on social and linguistic order being established and changed through practices (Creese, 2010; Madsen, 2018). If we emphasise the systematicity of the practices that are assumed to produce and structure the social world, we find ourselves close to praxeological (Reckwitz, 2002; Schatzki, 2005) and conversation analytical approaches (Deppermann, 2001; Goodwin & Heritage, 1990; Psathas, 1994; Schegloff *et al*,. 2002). They both take the orderliness of social interaction seriously, conceptualising it as being 'produced by the parties in situ' (Psathas, 1994: 2) through (linguistic) practices and actions that are systematic to the point where even their smallest details are used to accomplish something, i.e. to produce sociability (Deppermann, 2001; Schatzki, 2005). I assume of (here linguistic) detail that it accomplishes something in an orderly way and that to discover this orderly way is my analytical task (Psathas, 1994; Ten Have, 1999).

I see linguistic features not primarily as mental elements but rather as *things* that are *used* (Section 2.3.2). Looking at which things are used by whom, how and at what point of a given activity, is my analytical entry point to shed light on the other elements, like the 'understanding, know-how, states of emotion and motivational knowledge' (Reckwitz, 2002: 249–250) of teachers and learners that structure their languaging. Accordingly, I take very seriously the definition of languaging as a *practice* and what it implies.

Pennycook (2010: 8) notes that scholars often add the term practice or the suffix '–ing' to language without defining what practice as a theoretical concept adds to the idea of languagING. I here profit from making the implications of the practice ING explicit. One of the premises I build on is summarised by Pennycook. He writes that

> it is not that we use language as a pre-given entity in context, but rather that we produce language in our repeated local activities. Furthermore, these activities are parts of bundled practices, and as such they are always social, always historical and always local. (Pennycook, 2010: 46)

Translanguaging scholarship often speaks about language as a social practice, but has nevertheless been marked by a certain methodological individualism, focusing on linguistic features belonging to individual repertoires (discussed in Sections 2.2.3 and 2.3.1). The social practice part has therefore often remained underemphasised (Canagarajah, 2011: 4–5). Thinking with Pennycook, if languaging is seen as a spatial practice – which includes the social, local and historical dimensions he mentions – then producing language in repeated local activities describes well how certain linguistic features become more or less sedimented parts of spatial repertoires that are in turn 'handled and shaped by practices' (de Certeau, 1985: 137). A practice, in turn,

> is a routinized type of behaviour which consists of several elements, interconnected to one another: forms of bodily activities, forms of mental activities, 'things' and their use, a background knowledge in the form of understanding, know-how, states of emotion and motivational knowledge. (Reckwitz, 2002: 249–250)

If languaging is a practice, then we can posit that participants' linguistic choices aren't random. Practices are carried out 'above all, in order to do something' (Reckwitz, 2002: 254–255). Feature selection is goal directed, as speakers choose those that make sense to them in a given situation (García & Wei, 2014; Jørgensen, 2008). Schatzki summarises this view when writing about practices that people mostly

> do what makes sense to them to do; more elaborately, they are almost always performing bodily doings that, in the current circumstances, constitute the actions that make sense to them to perform. (Schatzki, 2005: 55)

Exploring their linguistic choices, we therefore have to ask: 'Why that now (Schegloff & Sacks, 1973)? What is getting done by virtue of that bit of conduct, done that way, in just that place?' (Schegloff *et al.*, 2002: 5). With that we are in the domain of CA, which offers itself for analysing languaging as a spatial practice, because one of its axioms is that

> every action is simultaneously context shaped (in that the framework of action from which it emerges provides primary organisation for its production and interpretation) and context renewing (in that it now helps constitute the frame of relevance that will shape subsequent action). (Goodwin & Heritage, 1990: 289)

The notion of *context* as actively shaping talk in interaction and in turn being renewed by it, is reminiscent of current interactional sociolinguistics' notion of *space* as transforming and being transformed by practices (Section 2.3.2). Conversation analysts see speakers not only as drawing on, but also as oriented towards, shaping the interactional space. Talk is therefore 'treated as both displaying an understanding of prior and projecting subsequent conversational actions' and this treatment enables 'simultaneous analysis (a) of the organisation of action and (b) of understanding in interaction' (Goodwin & Heritage, 1990: 288). The tools from (Bantu) linguistics described above, allow me to analyse *which* features teachers and learners use *how* and *when*. With the additional CA approach, I can also ask *why* they use them, because grammatical and lexical choices are treated 'as sets of resources which participants deploy, monitor and manipulate' (Schegloff *et al.*, 2002: 15) to get things done. One of CA's principles with regard to getting things done with talk that is central for the classroom space is 'recipient design'. It intimates that when choosing linguistic features, speakers consider the knowledge of their addressees (Goodwin & Heritage, 1990: 293). This situation is amplified in a language classroom, where teachers have to consider in their linguistic choices the resources that the majority of learners in class can realistically already access. I am interested in the knowledge that teachers have in this regard and how it structures their languaging.

Deppermann (2001: 18) defines CA not as strictly applying a set of methods but as a 'kreative Tätigkeit' (*a creative activity*), allowing analysts to explore new paths and 'play' with their data, as long as such analytical paths are made rigorously transparent. This freedom, therefore, is not an invitation to casual analysis and convenient categorisation. Summarising phenomena under general headings like 'code-switching' or 'translanguaging' is not the interest of conversation analysts. Instead, they 'investigate individual practices for what they are being used to accomplish in a particular sequence and setting, rather than relying on categories imported from other, even similar settings' (Schegloff *et al.*, 2002: 18).

While these axioms of CA underlie big parts of my analyses, I also go beyond the 'particular sequence and setting' and beyond the traditional domain of linguistics and CA.

3.2.5 Opening linguistics up by following features and asking teachers

CA and linguistics are normally confined to what is displayed by speakers in the immediate interaction in question. However, I often don't only consider what linguists have to say about certain features and what the CA lens allows me to see about what they accomplish in one situation. Instead, I am inspired by the Actor Network Theory (ANT) mantra 'follow the actors' (Latour, 2005: 29). In ANT, objects or things (in my case linguistic features like lexemes, prefixes or suffixes) are seen as having agency in the production of sociability (Latour, 2005; Law, 2004). Therefore, as I follow the teachers step by step, going along with their linguistic choices as they read stories or explain instructions in class, I sometimes go on analytical tangents to follow particular linguistic features through different spaces at the school and beyond.

This method of following features helps to get a fuller picture of which particular affordances they might offer in the English classroom. In Section 5.2, I trace the noun class prefix 'u-' through Bantu linguistic scholarship, through different classrooms and through the teacher interviews, where it pops up as well. I then consider what teachers themselves have to say about their use of this prefix, before I draw conclusions regarding *what 'u-' can do*.

Asking teachers in stimulated recall interviews about their use of language resources in class relies on the praxeological idea that even though practices – like languaging – are routinised behaviours, people can often explain them in quite some detail in retrospect (Garfinkel, 1967: vii). When asked specific questions, they can often give their view on why they 'x-ed instead of y-ed' (Schatzki, 2005: 59) – e.g. why they used a certain linguistic feature and not another. Via the stimulated recall interviews, I exploit exactly this ability of teachers to reflect on and explain concrete elements of their languaging.[14]

Following features through different spaces, enrolling teachers' expertise and drawing on my own local (linguistic) knowledge are methods that help me to discover new perspectives that would remain hidden in a purely linguistic and/or conversation analytical enquiry (Blommaert, 2007). The ethnographic and ANT-inspired approach of 'following features and asking teachers' described in this last section is then a tool for

> '*opening linguistics up*': inviting reflexive sensitivity to the processes involved in the production of linguistic claims and to the potential importance of what gets left out. (Rampton *et al.*, 2004: 4, emphasis in original)

And, on the other hand, linguistics and CA are instruments for

> '*tying ethnography down*': pushing ethnography towards the analysis of clearly delimitable processes, increasing the amount of reported data that is open to falsification, looking to impregnate local description with analytical frameworks drawn from outside. (Rampton *et al.*, 2004: 4, emphasis in original)

Taken together, these approaches constitute the methodological backbone of this study – *an LE for seeing more* in Khayelitshan English classrooms.

4 An Eagle Learning to Fly and an Analyst Learning to See

4.1 Before the Story Begins

4.1.1 Introducing the teacher and 'going along' with the story

On 16 May 2016, I arrived at Khayelitsha Primary during morning assembly when learners and teachers gather in the schoolyard for about 15 minutes as the principal addresses some issues relevant to everyone, but mostly gives enthusiastic speeches about the importance of getting a good education. I joined the crowd and as we were all dispersing again I went up to the Grade 5 teacher to remind her that I was going to join one of her lessons that day. As usual, she was friendly and welcoming and confirmed that I could come in for the English period after the lunch break.

The Grade 5 teacher is 41 years old and when I began my PhD research she had been at the school for about two-and-a-half years. She is originally from KwaZulu-Natal and self-identifies as a Zulu speaker but is a fluent Khayelitshan languager. Of the three teachers, she was the one most understanding and supportive of my research. I was able to record 14 of her English lessons. What stands out about her teaching is that she speaks very slowly in class and she commented on that herself in an interview: 'If you notice when I'm in class I speak slowly so that they can hear each and every word that I speak or that I say' (Interview Grade 5 Teacher). This matches my impression of her as being rather serene and calm in the classroom, mostly seeming confident in herself and her teaching strategies. She is also the only teacher who is not apologetic about her heterogeneous languaging in class. She doesn't seem to feel like she has anything to hide, which might also explain why she let me observe lessons where learners were being assessed (Chapter 5).

In the course of this chapter, we will see that for this teacher stimulated recall and the focus on linguistic features were a great entry point to tell us about her linguistic strategies in teaching. She often provided very specific accounts of why she did what at a certain point.

When I entered her classroom on 16 May 2016, the learners were just cleaning up their desks and settling down and the teacher was sorting some papers. There were 35 learners in class on that day, seated in rows facing the blackboard. As it was the middle of May and my classroom observations had started in February, the learners were used to me by now and barely noticed when I walked in and sat down at the back with my recorder. The bell rang and the teacher got up and greeted everyone with: 'Good afternoon Grade 5!' and the class responded in a chorus: 'Good afternoon educator!' – a routine repeated in all of this teacher's classes, varying depending on the time of day from good morning to good afternoon. The teacher then turned to a story in the textbook that was going to be the focus of this lesson.

The textbook is provided by the Department of Basic Education (DBE) for Grade 5 English as a first additional language (EFAL) learners (Baker *et al.*, 2012a) and the story in question talks about a man who catches a young eagle in the forest, brings it home and keeps it together with his fowls, ducks and turkeys. Here, I am not giving any more information about what happens in the story, because I 'go along' with it in my analyses and the events will unfold in the pieces of transcribed classroom data that I look into. At various points of the analyses, certain languaging resources or the teacher's interview comments send me on tangents away from the story into teaching scenarios in other classrooms or onto unexpected analytical paths. These tangents mostly serve to unsettle nomolanguages, to illuminate details of teachers' knowledge that informs their classroom languaging, to highlight practices that are shared by teachers at Khayelitsha Primary or to situate their classroom language practices in the wider institutional dynamics of South African education. However, I always return to the story so it can guide us into the next analysis.

I invite you to follow the teacher's (re)languaging throughout one lesson, and to put yourself in her shoes while she nudges the learners into understanding the story's content and into englishing. The focus is on providing in-depth insights into the particular ensemble of linguistic possibilities – the spatial repertoire – of the Khayelitshan English classroom during a specific activity, and into how the teacher strategically orders such possibilities via relanguaging.

4.1.2 How to relanguage a story and what to expect in this chapter

I start this analytical experiment from the conceptualisation of the classroom repertoire as heterogeneous, with the Khayelitshan repertoire and the statist repertoire of Standard English folded into each other (Section 2.3.2). Beginning from this heterogeneous ensemble of linguistic possibilities, the relanguaging moves with which the teacher orders it have to be explained. To illustrate what relanguaging means in this part of the lesson, let's look at an example (analysed in detail in Section 4.5.1):

1	T:	**But soon it became more graceful and confident.**
2	C:	**But soon it became more graceful and confident.**
3	T:	But as an eagle flew, yaqalisa ke ngoku yaqhela, yomelela. Yayeka
4		ukuthini? Ukoyika. It stopped being scared. It got used to it as it was flying.
5		Iqhubekeka ukubhabha. Yaphela isithini? Iqhela and it became confident.
6		**It flew higher and higher into the sky until it was just a tiny dot in the**
7		**distance.**

The **bold print** in Line 1 shows the Standard Written English (SWE) from the story as read by the teacher. Her reading I see as a form of englishing that is immediately determined by the teaching material – a reshaping of SWE into oral englishing. In Line 2, learners repeat in a class chorus what the teacher has read. This chorus englishing is a direct imitation of the teacher – the learners don't need to read and turn SWE into oral englishing, they need to listen and repeat. The normal print from Lines 3 to 5 then shows the relanguaged version of this part of the story that in itself contains classroom languaging – where there is no watchfulness towards the boundaries of Standard English – and englishing, which instantiates a homogenised repertoire (Line 4). The **bold print** (Lines 5–7) then shows the teacher reading the next sentence from the story. The class chorus will repeat it and this particular reading activity will continue in the same sequential order.

The by now familiar circle (Section 2.4) illustrates what goes on in this sequence in terms of relanguaging:

Circle IV¹

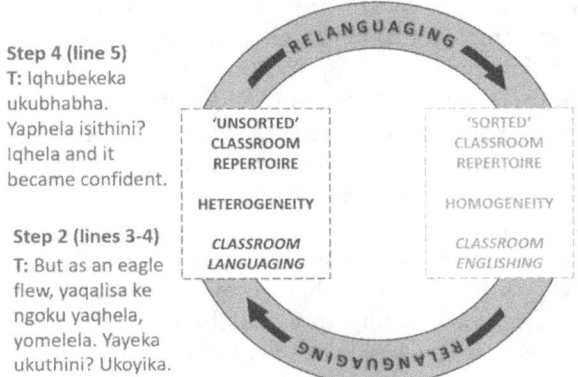

Step 4 (line 5)
T: Iqhubekeka ukubhabha. Yaphela isithini? Iqhela and it became confident.

Step 2 (lines 3-4)
T: But as an eagle flew, yaqalisa ke ngoku yaqhela, yomelela. Yayeka ukuthini? Ukoyika.

Step 1 (lines 1-2, reading)
T: But soon it became more graceful and confident.
C: But soon it became more graceful and confident.

Step 3 (line 4)
T: It stopped being scared. It got used to it as it was flying.

Step 5 (line 6-7, reading)
T: It flew higher and higher into the sky until it was just a tiny dot in the distance.

Step 1: We see **relanguaging** as *sorting out* (Lines 1–2). As the teacher reads from the Standard English story and the learners repeat, the classroom repertoire gets relanguaged – *sorted out* – and thereby balanced towards Standard English. The resources from the textbook play a big role in this homogenising move, because all the teacher has to do in order to tilt the balance of the classroom repertoire towards Standard English is to read from the story.

Step 2: We see **relanguaging as *bringing together*** (Lines 3–4) that begins from the homogenised language of the story that had taken centre stage for a moment. The teacher then entangles the resources from the story with others from the classroom repertoire, not adhering to the boundaries of Standard English, thereby balancing the classroom repertoire towards its heterogeneous starting point.

Step 3: We see **relanguaging again as *sorting out*** (Line 4), but this time the teacher doesn't revert to the language from the story. Rather, she assembles more easily accessible Standard English resources to demonstrate englishing while clarifying content.

Step 4: We see **relanguaging again as *bringing together*** (Line 5) as the teacher re-entangles resources from the story (like 'became' and 'confident') with others from the classroom repertoire, not restricting herself to the boundaries of Standard English.

Step 5: The circle repeats with **relanguaging again as *sorting out*** (**Lines 6–7**) via the chorus reading activity, as described under Step 1.

This is a necessarily schematic representation that exemplifies what we will see throughout this chapter in terms of relanguaging as a spatial, linguistic ordering process. The details that constitute it will now become the focus of this chapter, as well as the situated institutional and social dynamics in which they are entangled and by which they are co-constituted. The upcoming analytical deep-dives into small linguistic elements will reveal the Khayelitshan English classroom to be a space of specific linguistic possibilities that remain invisible through the statist lens that looks from nomolanguages to languaging. By paying attention to such detail and by 'following features and asking teachers', we will see that, in Khayelitsha, the ability not only to teach – but also to learn – how to english rests on the ability to relanguage. This skill of teachers and learners, however, remains hidden from educational administrators (and linguists) who see like a state and it can therefore not be tested or be otherwise accounted for as it stands.

The very notion of relanguaging also becomes more complex throughout this chapter, as it turns out that linguistic heterogeneity and homogeneity don't necessarily constitute the threshold at which this sorting practice emerges. It can also occur within the confines of a homogenised, statist repertoire at the threshold of what are likely inaccessible and likely accessible Standard English resources for learners (e.g. Section 4.5.6). The insight that linguistic heterogeneity and homogeneity aren't always an analytically relevant dichotomy, here gained through detailed empirical investigations, marks the point where analysts stop linguistically seeing like a state. This chapter is my own journey as analyst towards that point.

The Grade 5 teacher has the first word, to give us some background about the reading activity that dominates this lesson and – in the process – about the linguistic resources she thinks her learners (don't) have access to.

4.1.3 Learners who seldom go to the malls

With regard to the structure of the reading activity, I was impressed with how the learners always knew when exactly to start their group chorusing. Chick (1996: 29–30) has also noted the often 'remarkably rhythmic manner' with which teachers and learners synchronise such 'chorusing sequences', based on 'their shared, implicit knowledge of the discourse conventions associated with conventional interactional styles'. While this style of verbal interaction is certainly conventionalised for reading activities across classrooms at the school, I was still interested in how the teacher herself explained the rationale behind this practice. We therefore played a sequence from this lesson to her during the interview and asked her about it.

Interview Excerpt a[2]	
T = Teacher	R1 = Researcher 1 (Lara Krause, author) R2 = Researcher 2 (Tessa Dowling, supervisor)

1	R1:	How do they [the learners] manage to read in a choir really on point? They have
2		a rhythm...
3	T:	I train them. As I have said before. I speak in a rhythm in class. Because if I can
4		just walk inside the class: 'Hello Grade 5 how are you today bla bla bla [speaking
5		very fast]', they won't understand, because they don't speak English at home. And
6		they aren't exposed to English speaking people. They stay in Khayelitsha full
7		time. I think they seldom go to the malls [in Cape Town]. They use this mall [in
8		Khayelitsha]. So I try by all means to speak in a rhythm and I train them that when
9		they speak, even when they speak their language they must speak slowly,
10		especially in class.

She confirms here what many studies of classroom interaction in South Africa and other post-colonial settings have found: chorusing activities and other 'safe-talk' are common strategies to cope with the discrepancy between the language of learning and teaching (LoLT) and the language practices that teachers and learners control with some fluency (Chick, 1996; Kapp, 2004; McKinney *et al.*, 2015). But my main reason for quoting this excerpt is that her response shows how she sees languaging as a spatial practice, since she connects the resources that her learners can or cannot access to the spaces they (don't) language in regularly:

- the 'home' in Khayelitsha where learners don't English (a5–a7);
- the 'malls' in Cape Town's more immediate surroundings where people do English (a7);
- and 'this mall' in Khayelitsha where nobody Englishes (a7–a8).

For her, space has an important impact on how her learners language, influencing the linguistic resources they can understand and to which they have access. In terms of spatial repertoires, the learners are therefore able to actualise the linguistic possibilities of their home and lifeworld in Khayelitsha. However, they rarely move in spaces – like the malls in Cape Town – with different ensembles of linguistic possibilities that might intersect some more with the statist repertoire of Standard English and feature less of the language resources characteristic for Khayelitsha. These shopping centres outside Khayelitsha are examples of the spaces where learners would become 'exposed to English-speaking people' but they 'seldom' go there. This makes Khayelitshan English classrooms different from Cape Town's inner-city or suburban classrooms that are embedded in a network of englishing spaces, bringing learners into regular contact with this practice. There, in contrast to Khayelitsha, exposure to englishing is not limited to the school environment but also occurs in surrounding spaces.

Against this background, when actualising the classroom repertoire, the teacher chooses strategies that, in her view, give learners a real chance to understand and follow the lesson. This leads here to a slow, repetitive and rhythmic reading activity with chorusing sequences and extensive mediation. I now turn to the details of this activity and the classroom repertoire that emerges in this lesson.

4.2 Looking for Interesting Birds and Interesting Linguistic Features

4.2.1 Animals unsettling nomolanguages

The lesson begins with the teacher drawing the learners' attention to the pictures allocated around the text of the story in the book (Baker *et al.*, 2012a: 51). She asks what the learners see in the pictures, making them focus on these visual resources that form part of the classroom repertoire during this activity. Some learners raise their hands and verbalise – or 'language' – these pictures along the lines of 'I see the chicken', 'I see the egg' and 'I see the eagle' (Grade 5 English Lesson 16.05.2016). The format of these short subject-verb-object sentences is quite representative of learner contributions in English classrooms in situations where the teacher's language policy is English-only – this is not always the case, as we will see. There is rarely an occasion when learners experiment with more complex constructions. What we can take from these responses is that at least some learners in the classroom are familiar with the animal names that feature in the story – such as 'chicken' and 'eagle' – and that these resources are available in the classroom repertoire.

After this warm-up, the teacher begins the reading activity described above, while the learners have their books in front of them. I now zoom into selected parts of this activity.

Picture 2   You can fly

Lesson Transcript A			
T = Teacher C = Class L = Learner (individual)	**bold print** normal print *(italics)* [underlined]	= = = =	language as read from the story classroom languaging/englishing *(englishing added by the author)* [body languaging][3]

1	T:	A certain man went through a forest, looking for any interesting bird that he could
2		find. Please read after me.
3	C:	A certain man went through a forest, looking for any interesting bird that he could
4		find.
5	T:	He caught a young eagle, brought it home and put it among his fowls and ducks
6		and turkey and gave it chicken food to eat, even though it was an eagle, the king
7		of birds.
8	C:	[reading after teacher]
9	T:	What is an eagle in Xhosa? What is an eagle? Yes?
10	L:	Ukhozi (Eagle).
11	T:	Ukhozi! The king of birds. The bird that can fly up high. It is the only bird that
12		can fly up high, that's why they call it 'the king of birds'. The story is talking
13		about a man who was looking for any interesting bird. The word 'interesting'
14		means, 'into enikisa umdla' *(something that gives interest)*. Kubhalwa efuna ke
15		le ntaka, azokuyifuya any [expansive arm gesture] ntaka that is interesting *(It's*
16		*written that he wants this bird, he will breed any bird that is interesting)*. Noba
17		yeyiphi intlobo yentaka eyayizomnika ntoni? Umdla *(No matter which type of*
18		*bird that will be what? Interesting)*. **He caught a young eagle, brought it home**
19		**and put it among his fowls.** When we talk about the fowls, sithetha ngeenkuku
20		ezithiwani? Ezifuywayo apha ekhaya *(When we talk about the fowls, we talk*
21		*about chicken that are what? That are bred here at home)*.

I see the teacher's reading as the first step in her relanguaging strategy. Teachers often remark that learners 'can't read' (Interview Grade 4 Teacher) or at least struggle when it comes to reading by themselves. In their written form, the Standard English resources in the classroom repertoire might therefore be inaccessible to many. By transforming SWE into englishing, the teacher tilts the classroom repertoire not only towards Standard English but also towards the oral. Learners can now imitate her, rather than relying on the visual clues of SWE alone.

After reading the first two sentences, the teacher's question in A9 ('What is "eagle" in Xhosa?') aims explicitly at *bringing together* Standard English with other elements of the classroom repertoire and a learner responds with 'ukhozi' (A9–A10). In cooperation with the learners, the teacher now starts assembling and validating a more heterogeneous classroom repertoire, signalling a space that is inclusive of linguistic flexibility in this activity, instead of restricting it to Standard English. In this space, 'ukhozi' is now an available and also *legitimised* resource for meaning-making.

Yet, I promised to ask some unsettling questions regarding nomolanguages. So, is 'ukhozi' actually a Khayelitshan resource and, for that matter, a likely familiar one for most learners? This question wouldn't usually arise. Nomolanguages, in the administrative logic of the state, are attached to territories and population groups: These children live in Khayelitsha, Khayelitsha is categorised as an Xhosa-speaking area; therefore, the children speak Xhosa. 'Ukhozi', then, is an Xhosa word –part of the linguistically and administratively defined set of resources that counts as Standard Xhosa – and therefore the learners know it. It is part of their 'first language' (L1), 'home language' or 'mother tongue'. But learners' languaging in some of the questions they ask towards the end of this lesson – seemingly very interested in what an eagle eats – shows more accurately how they normally talk about animals in Khayelitsha. For example, a learner asks:

Ieagle iyayitya iandaconda? *(Does the eagle eat an anaconda?)*

Another asks:

Miss, ieagle abantwana becrocodile ibatya xa besandoqgiba ukuphuma phantsi komhlaba? *(Miss, does the eagle eat the children of a crocodile as they are coming out of the earth?)*

The learners here prefer to use not only 'ieagle' – which the teacher also sometimes uses in the lesson as we will see – but also other animal names like 'anaconda' and 'crocodile' that had not been mentioned before; they don't use Standard Xhosa resources. Animal names are a word field that illustrates how analytically attaching words to nomolanguages can misguide our assumptions regarding the linguistic resources to which learners have access. An encounter during a different research project conducted by Tessa Dowling, this time in a rural area in the Eastern Cape, further illustrates this point. She was interested in which noun class prefixes young speakers would use for certain nouns, one of which was the Standard Xhosa word for tortoise *(ufudo)*. The following exchange ensues when she shows a young girl, who would self-identify as Xhosa speaking, a picture of a tortoise and asks:

Researcher: Usibiza njani esi silwanyana? *(How do you call this animal?)*
Girl: Uskolpati *(Tortoise)*.
Researcher: Awulazi igama elithi 'ufudo'? *(Don't you know the word 'ufudo'?)*
Girl: Inoba ligama lenu lesiNgesi? *(Could it be that it is your English word?)*[4]

The girl's response 'uskolpati' is the word for tortoise that is conventionally associated with Afrikaans: 'skilpad'. The Standard Xhosa word for tortoise found in traditional Xhosa folk tales and in dictionaries is 'ufudo'; however, as the exchange shows, the girl is not familiar with this word and even wonders whether it might be English. This little anecdote shows that, when conceptualising language in terms of spatial repertoires, we can see that 'uskolpati' is, and 'ufudo' is not, an element of this girl's routinised language practices, since the latter is not part of the ensembles of linguistic possibilities that she regularly actualises.

This additional information complexifies the question of how to interpret the collaborative relanguaging of 'eagle' into 'ukhozi' at the beginning of this lesson. Instead of connecting the Standard English resource 'eagle' to a more familiar one ('ukhozi'), for some learners the opposite might be true and 'eagle' might be the more and 'ukhozi' the less familiar resource at play. To them, in fact, the teacher might rather be teaching a Standard Xhosa vocabulary item instead of clarifying a Standard English one.[5] This example illustrates the inadequacy of constructs such as L1 and second language (L2) to capture language use in language teaching in Khayelitsha. It also supports the findings of other scholars who show that the nomolanguages structuring South African schooling – also the African nomolanguages often used in early primary school and proclaimed to be children's 'mother tongues' – don't reflect the actual routinised language practices of learners (Banda, 2018; Ditsele, 2014; Dowling, 2011; Sibanda, 2019). Animals then – like more examples to come – illustrate the advantages of talking about Khayelitshan languaging instead of trying to make such languaging fit into a statist 'Xhosa' box that implies a boundedness that we are here to unsettle further.

4.2.2 Finding -fuya in Khayelitsha

In Section 3.2.5, I argued that in order to gain further insight into the complexity of a local linguistic situation and to make explicit the knowledge and motivation that might underlie situated classroom language practices, it can be useful for the analyst to follow an object (Latour, 2005) – in this case a specific linguistic feature – across different spaces and activities. This method is useful to make sense of the last part of Lesson Transcript A and the teacher helps us with the tracing.

Repetition of Lesson Transcript A (A14–A21)	
T = Teacher C = Class L = Learner (individual)	**bold print** = language as read from the story normal print = classroom languaging/englishing *(italics)* = *(englishing added by the author)* [underlined] = [body languaging]

14 T: [...] interesting means, into enikisa umdla. Kubhalwa efuna ke le ntaka,
15   azokuyifuya any [expansive arm gesture] ntaka that is interesting *(It's written that*
16   *he wants this bird, he will breed any bird that is interesting).* Noba yeyiphi intlobo
17   yentaka eyayizomnika ntoni? Umdla *(No matter which type of bird that will be*
18   *what? Interesting).* **He caught a young eagle, brought it home and put it**
19   **among his fowls.** When we talk about the fowls, sithetha ngeenkuku ezithiwani?
20   Ezifuywayo apha ekhaya *(When we talk about the fowls, we talk about chicken*
21   *that are what? That are bred here at home).*

When we played this sequence for stimulated recall, we first asked the teacher about her use of the verb '-fuya' *(breed)* in azokuyi*fuy*a (A15) and ezi*fuy*wayo (A20).

Interview Excerpt b	
T = Teacher	R1 = Researcher 1 (Lara Krause, author) R2 = Researcher 2 (Tessa Dowling, supervisor)

1	R1:	I'm learning Xhosa for example and I've for example never heard the word
2		ukufuya, right? So do you think all the learners understand that word?
3	T:	In English or in Xhosa?
4	R1:	In Xhosa when you say 'ezifuywayo apha ekhaya'.
5	T:	Yes they do understand it.
6	R1:	Do you think they know it from where they come from or is it used also here, like
7		in the urban?
8	T:	It is used yah in their everyday life. Because some of the parents have the goats,
9		the chicken. They know that 'umama ufuy' iinkuku' (*mother breeds chicken*) and
10		so on.
11	R2:	So ligama eliqhelekileyo (*So it is a common word*).
12	T:	Ligama *(it is a word)* that they hear almost every day. Even if they don't have
13		iinkuku (*chicken*) here in Cape Town but in the Eastern Cape they know.

The first thing to note is that if we were guided by an analytical lens that attaches words to nomolanguages, we wouldn't have asked this question about '-fuya' in the first place. We would have taken for granted that learners know it, because 'it is Xhosa' and 'Xhosa is their L1'. For us, however, this verb seemed unlikely to be part of the Khayelitshan repertoire, because we connected it to rural farming activities rather than to township life. However, we learn from the teacher that the presence of animals like goats and chickens (b8–b10), urban farming activities and the fact that many learners come from, or have family ties to, the rural Eastern Cape explain that '-fuya' features in the linguistic inventory of Khayelitsha and is available as a resource in the English classroom.

What the teacher tells us about '-fuya' and its usage history in Khayelitsha and the Eastern Cape also helps in understanding exactly what this verb affords the teacher here. Nowhere in the original text of the story is there any talk of 'breeding'. Rather, the man is said to have 'caught' the eagle and 'put' it among his fowls. I argue that '-fuya' here is a key word in the teacher's classroom languaging that accomplishes two things in this short sequence:

1. In A15, '-fuya' helps to frame a somewhat odd and distant activity of catching birds in a forest within the context of a familiar activity of breeding animals that learners often observe in their immediate

surroundings. A Standard English resource like 'breed' wouldn't have had the same agency in her languaging, because even if some learners might know it, it has not accompanied them through the relevant activities and spaces and therefore couldn't have gained the same meaning for them.

2. In A20, the teacher then enrols '-fuya' to teach the new vocabulary item 'fowls'. She says: 'When we talk about the fowls, sithetha ngeenkuku ezithiwani? Ezifuywayo apha ekhaya' *(When we talk about the fowls, we talk about chicken that are what? That are bred here at home)*.

Here, '-fuya' helps the teacher to point out that 'fowls' in fact denote particular types of chicken – those that are bred at home, or domesticated. The verb allows the teacher to shed light on quite a nuanced distinction between two Standard English resources: chicken and fowls.

The case of '-fuya' shows how analytically attaching linguistic features to spatial repertoires makes us ask new questions, which can in turn make visible the agency of particular words in their own right. Throughout this chapter, I will illustrate with more examples why nomolanguages are often analytical distractions, while a spatial orientation can further our understanding of situated classroom languaging. For now, I want to draw attention to another strategy of teaching vocabulary that we can read from Lesson Transcript A.

4.2.3 Accessing Standard English 'any' way

In A14–A15, the teacher says: 'Kubhalwa efuna ke le ntaka, azokuyifuya any [expansive arm gesture] ntaka that is interesting' *(It's written that he wants this bird, he will breed any bird that is interesting)*. We now wanted to know how she views her use of the word 'any' – a Standard English resource from the story – that she assembles with a variety of other resources from the classroom repertoire. We asked the teacher during the interview why she thinks she used it at this point in front of 'intaka' *(bird)*. She replies:

> Sometimes I use the words just so that they can understand how to use it or they, they understand the meaning of that word. Because as I teach, I also use my body language: 'any' [making expansive arm gesture similar to what she did in class]. (Interview Grade 5 English Teacher)

Body languaging is indeed often part of her teaching with which she tries to keep the learners interested and focused during the lesson. In this case, the expansive gesture is a specific clue to help learners understand the word 'any'. It could be argued (as I will do more extensively in Section 5.3.5) that her gesture is just another languaging resource from the classroom repertoire, which she enrols to relanguage 'any'. Her comment further reveals that she deems it possible for learners to disassemble 'any' from the Khayelitshan resources it is surrounded by in her classroom languaging, grasp its meaning and 'understand how to use it' as a Standard English resource. In her view, it seems perfectly possible to infer the meaning of 'any' from 'Kubhalwa efuna ke le ntaka, azokuyifuya any [expansive arm gesture] ntaka that is interesting', as she relies on her learners to dis- and reassemble languaging resources, make sense of them in new combinations and learn Standard English vocabulary in the process.

We begin to see that this teacher's classroom might be a space where 'English language teaching can escape its narrow vision of itself as a monolingual enterprise, as a place where English is taught only in its own presence' (Pennycook, 2010: 141). Rather, by *bringing together* the Standard English resources from the story with various others into a heterogeneous classroom repertoire through her relanguaging, the teacher exploits linguistic (and semiotic) fluidity and heterogeneity to provide learners with points of access into the statist repertoire of Standard English. Linguistic homogeneity and heterogeneity aren't mutually exclusive in this space but engaged in a productive push-and-pull relationship and heterogeneous classroom languaging might well be assembled with an eye on Standard English. I find it therefore misleading to describe such language practices as translanguaging, suggesting that linguistic heterogeneity means always a transcendence or an unwatchfulness towards, rather than a negotiation of, linguistic fixity. More complex accounts are necessary that aren't stuck on either side of an alleged binary between linguistic heterogeneity and homogeneity (see also Jaspers & Madsen, 2019; Otsuji & Pennycook, 2010). To find more such negotiation processes at the threshold of heterogeneity and homogeneity, we have to see what happens next in the story of the eagle.

4.3 Seeing Morphemes Guide the Change into a Chicken

4.3.1 It was going to sound like a poem

After having caught the bird, the man keeps it with his chickens and feeds it chicken food. The eagle never attempts to fly, because none of its chicken friends ever do. One day, after five years, a biologist walks through the man's garden and spots the eagle among the chickens. He is shocked and says to the man that this bird is not a chicken but an eagle. It then says in the story: 'Yes, said its owner, but I have trained it to be a chicken'. At this point, the following transcribed teaching sequence (Lesson Transcript B) starts, with the class repeating this sentence that the teacher read out before. This is a sequence we have also played in full for the teacher in the interview, in order for her to comment on it.

76 Relanguaging Language from a South African Township School

Lesson Transcript B		
T = Teacher	bold print =	language as read from the story
C = Class	normal print =	classroom languaging/englishing
L = Learner (individual)	*(italics)* =	*(englishing added by the author)*
	[underlined] =	[body languaging]

1   C: Yes, said its owner, but I have trained it to be a chicken.
2   T: It is no longer an eagle, it is a chicken, even though it measures four and a half
3   meters from wingtip to wingtip.
4   C: [reading after teacher]
5   T: The man agreed, yes, it is an eagle, **but I have trained it to be a chicken**.
6   Sendiyiqeqeshile ngoba mayitshintshe ibe yintoni? Inkuku *(I have already trained*
7   *it because it should change into what? A chicken)*. Mayibe yinkuku, ingabi saba
8   ieagle *(It shall be a chicken, it shall no longer be an eagle)*. He says it is no longer
9   ukhozi *(an eagle)*. Ayiselulo ukhozi, ngoku seyintoni? Seyichicken *(It is no*
10   *longer an eagle, now it is already what? It's already a chicken)*. Why? Because I
11   have trained it. Ndiyitrainile kuba mayiyeke ukuba lukhozi, ibe yichicken *(I have*
12   *trained it because it shall stop being an eagle and be a chicken)*. For five years, a
13   man has kept this eagle with the chicken, so that it will change its ways of being
14   the eagle to a, to become a chicken.

Before diving into the morphological details to see what exactly they accomplish here, we can look at this sequence again in terms of the teacher's main relanguaging moves from B5 to B14:

Circle V

Step 1 (B5)
The man agreed, yes, it is an eagle, but I have trained it to be a chicken.

Step 4 (B11)
Ndiyitrainile kuba mayiyeke ukuba lukhozi, ibe yichicken.

Step 3 (B10-B11)
Why? Because I have trained it.

Step 2 (B6-B9)
Sendiyiqeqeshile ngoba mayitshintshe ibe yintoni? Inkuku. Mayibe yinkuku, ingabi saba ieagle. He says it is no longer ukhozi. Ayiselulo ukhozi, ngoku seyintoni? Seyichicken.

Step 5 (B12-B14)
For five years, a man has kept this eagle with the chicken, so that it will change its ways of being the eagle to a, to become a chicken.

(Circle diagram labels: RELANGUAGING, HETEROGENEITY, HOMOGENEITY)

Step 1 instantiates a sorted, homogenised classroom repertoire as the teacher Englishes and in part repeats a sentence from the story: '...but I have trained it to be a chicken' (B1 and B5). This sentence, together with 'It is no longer an eagle, it is a chicken...' (B2) is also what then gets relanguaged into heterogeneous classroom languaging in Step 2. Then, the teacher homogenises the classroom repertoire again, returning to the language resources from the story in Step 3, to then bring these resources together again with others from the classroom repertoire in Step 4. Then, she Englishes a summary of the important points from this sequence, tilting the balance of the classroom repertoire towards linguistic homogeneity again in Step 5.

These relanguaging processes from B5 to B14 therefore mainly revolve around two statements made by the eagle's owner in the story:

(i) I have trained it to be a chicken.
(ii) It is no longer an eagle, it is a chicken.

In the remainder of this section, I discuss what exactly the linguistic (mostly morphological) features that the teacher enrols here afford her, as she tries to make her class understand these two statements that are important for the story.

Learners who are at the proficiency level that the curriculum presupposes for Grade 5 EFAL might be able to pick up that the owner's training is the reason why the eagle is no longer an eagle and that the animal had been subtly forced into becoming a chicken by being kept and treated like one. The sequence of events would be clear through the use of the perfect tense in 'I have trained it', and the present tense in 'It is a chicken', indicating that the training is over and the eagle is now a chicken. For the learners in her classroom, however, as the teacher tells us in the interview, these lines were

> just not going to make any sense. 'It's no longer an eagle, it is now a chicken'. Ok. It was going to sound like a poem maybe. (Interview Grade 5 Teacher)

Her statement vividly illustrates how opaque she deems this language for the learners and how unlikely they are to arrive at a meaningful interpretation of what is happening. To make this Standard English 'poem' accessible without spending time on long explanations, the teacher relanguages it into heterogeneous classroom languaging (Steps 2 and 4). The inaccessible resources here get entangled with a variety of morphological affordances from the classroom repertoire. Below, I look into some of these affordances in detail.

4.3.2 'se-', '-ile', sequences and causes

Graphic A illustrates the timeline of the story, showing the essential causal connection over time between the act of training the eagle and its change into a chicken. As the teacher indicated above, most learners wouldn't have been able to access this content without her help.

Graphic A

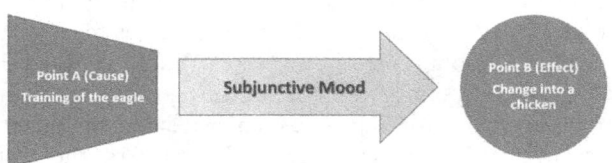

The following analysis first looks into how the employed tense and aspect morphology clarify the order in which the events unfold in the story. I start by describing the morphology the teacher uses to talk about the main event at Point A. Then, I look at the subjunctive mood, which is represented by the arrow in the graphic, illustrating the sequence of events and the causal connection between Points A and B in the story. Lastly, I analyse the morphology used to describe the effects of the training at Point B.

Repetition of Lesson Transcript B (B5–B12)		
T = Teacher	**bold print**	= language as read from the story
C = Class	normal print	= classroom languaging/englishing
L = Learner (individual)	*(italics)*	= *(englishing added by the author)*

5	T:	The man agreed, yes, it is an eagle, but **I have trained it to be a chicken.**
6		Sendiyiqeqeshile ngoba mayitshintshe ibe yintoni? Inkuku *(I have already trained*
7		*it because it should change into what? A chicken).* Mayibe yinkuku, ingabi saba
8		ieagle. *(It shall be a chicken, it shall no longer be an eagle).* He says it is no longer
9		ukhozi *(an eagle).* Ayiselulo ukhozi, ngoku seyintoni? Seyichicken *(It is no*
10		*longer an eagle, now it is already what? It's already a chicken).* Why? Because I
11		have trained it. Ndiyitrainile kuba mayiyeke ukuba lukhozi, ibe yichicken *(I have*
12		*trained it because it shall stop being an eagle and be a chicken)*

In her relanguaged version of this part of the story, the teacher adopts the voice of the eagle's owner when expanding on (i) 'I have trained it to be a chicken'. She starts by saying 'sendiyiqeqeshile' (B6), which features the following morphological components (see Appendix A for glossing conventions):

se-	-ndi-	-yi-	-qeqesh-	-ile	
COMP	SM1P	OM9	train	ANT	*(I have already trained it.)*

The completive 'se-' in combination with the anterior (perfect) '-ile' indicates an action that has already been completed. Bantu linguists have described this combination as a common morphological constellation 'where prefixes and finals combine to show tense-aspect' (Nurse & Philippson, 2003: 121). The final '-ile' adds more meaning relevant to this context, since it tends to be used for completed actions 'whose consequences or relevance live on' (Nurse & Philippson, 2003: 125), which here applies to the training of the eagle (Point A). The consequence that the eagle is now a chicken (Point B) continues to be relevant throughout the story. 'Ndiyitrainile' in B11 also features the suffix '-ile' and thereby marks the training as completed, while, however, putting less emphasis on this by not adding the completive 'se-'. The linguistic form of 'ndiyitrainile' and its connection to 'sendiyiqeqeshile' will receive more attention in a different context (Section 4.4.3). For now, we see that the rich morphology with regard to tense and aspect prevalent in Khayelitshan languaging affords the teacher resources to create a clearer timeline for the learners, which in turn gives them a better chance to understand the relations of cause and effect in the story. At this point, they are now sure to know that the eagle had been trained in the past and that the effects of this training continue to be important in the present.

4.3.3 'ma-', connection and authority

The complexity of the language in the story makes it necessary for the teacher to break the narrative up into pieces. This can disrupt the flow and the connections between events in the story and the teacher is now reconnecting those events into a flowing sequence. For this purpose, after 'sendiyiqeqeshile' has established that the training of the eagle is completed and has an effect that will continue to be relevant in the story, the teacher now relies heavily on the hortative 'ma-' and the subjunctive mood – both grammar affordances from the Khayelitshan repertoire that are available to the teacher and the learners in the English classroom. We will see that especially 'ma-', which she uses repeatedly in different constellations, helps her to redesign this sequence in some ways like a dramatic dialogue, creating a vivid picture for her learners of how, and with what authority, the owner has trained the eagle.

Below is the morphological make-up of the forms she uses after 'sendiyiqeqeshile' in B6 where she says: 'Sendiyiqeqeshile ngoba mayitshintshe ibe yintoni? Inkuku' *(I have already trained it because it should change and become what? A chicken).*

ngoba	-ma-	-yi-	-tshintsh-	-e		
because	HORT	SM9	change	SUBJ	(...because it should change...)	
i-	-b-	-e	y-	-in-	-to-	-ni?
SM9	become	SUBJ	COP10	NPx9	thing	what? (...and become what?)
In-	-kuku.					
NPx9	chicken	(A chicken.)				

Firstly, the conjunction 'ngoba' *(because)* clarifies that the man trained the eagle with a particular intention. The teacher now expresses this intention using the hortative 'ma-' and the subjunctive mood. Pahl *et al.* call 'ma-' a 'deficient verb'. They posit that it regularly forms part of commands and 'udla ngokubonakalisa ukugunyazisa' *(is often used to show the exercise of authority)* (Pahl *et al.*, 1971: 134). It is not used by itself but always attached to a verb in the subjunctive mood. 'Sendiyiqeqeshile ngoba mayitshintshe...' could be Englished as 'I have trained it, because it should better change...'.

This construction here initiates a sequence of commands that is continued with 'ibe' *(and it should become)*, which is a subjunctive form without 'ma-', followed by the rhetorical question: 'yintoni?' *(what?)* and the answer: 'Inkuku' *(A chicken)*. The subjunctive in Khayelitshan languaging is marked in the positive by the final vowel '-e' and is described as 'Uhlobo lolandelelwano' *(the mood of a sequence/series)*, being a mood 'ezichaza izenzeko ezilandelelanayo' *(which explains events that follow each other)* (Pahl *et al.*, 1971: 131). The subjunctive occurs frequently in commands (Nurse & Philippson, 2003: 595) and, as Gough (1993: 39) puts it, when it is used 'there will be an assumption of conceptual connexity or continuity unless otherwise indicated'. 'Sendiyiqeqeshile ngoba mayitshintshe ibe yintoni? Inkuku', can thus be Englished like this: 'I have trained it, because it should better change and become what? A chicken', with 'and' expressing lexically what the teacher here expresses via the subjunctive mood: the conceptual continuity between the command to change and the subsequent command to become a chicken.

When languaging in Khayelitsha, the learners connect sequential events through morphological changes in verbs (as in the subjunctive mood). They now have to learn that in Standard English such connections are made lexically through 'and', 'and then' or other conjunctions. From my own experience, I can say that going the reverse route, from the lexical to morphological expression of a sequence, was one of the most difficult parts of learning to language in Khayelitsha. In turn, for these learners, conjunctions aren't elements they routinely use to express a sequence and I argue that enrolling Khayelitshan affordances like 'ma-' and the subjunctive into the classroom repertoire during this activity ensures that they follow the plot events.

We are still at the same point in the story, where the man tells the biologist that he has trained the eagle to be a chicken. This training and the change into a chicken have already been relanguaged once, as shown above. However, the teacher continues to clarify the same scenario in B7–B8 and B11–B12, using the same combination of the hortative 'ma-' expressing a command followed by a simple subjunctive.[6] All these versions of that combination express the same situation: the change from an eagle to a chicken. First, it is framed as a command – or at least a wish – for the eagle to become a chicken and to no longer be an eagle (B7–B8: 'mayibe yichicken, ingabi saba ieagle') and other times as a command to stop being an eagle (B11–B12: 'mayiyeke ukuba lukhozi, ibe yichicken').

However, through these repetitions, every framing of the eagle's change is marked at least once by 'ma-'.

I argue that 'ma-' is a grammatical affordance that formalises the 'voice of authority' of the eagle's owner. Without 'ma-', learners would have had to understand this voice of authority from context and for the teacher to make it explicit via exclusively Standard English resources would have been rather laborious (e.g. 'It should better change...'). 'ma-' is a sedimented feature of the Khayelitshan repertoire and is often used in commands in direct speech. In fact, the learners often addressed it to me when they wanted me to come with them, saying: '*Ma*sihambe!' *(Let's go!)*. Teachers also use 'ma-' in commands in class, for example, when instructing learners to open their books: '*Ma*sivule iincwadi!' *(Let's open the books!)*. The Grade 4 teacher also used 'ma-' when teaching the pronunciation of '-th-' [ð] in 'throwing', saying: '*Ma*silume ulwimi!' *(Let's bite our tongue!)* (Grade 4 English Lesson 01.02.2016).

By using 'ma-' so frequently in her version of this sequence, the teacher reshapes it into something resembling a dramatic dialogue. In the original story, the owner merely recounts to the biologist that he has trained the eagle to be a chicken, but the teacher here lets the owner speak to the biologist, describing emphatically and repeatedly how and with what intention, and also with what authority, he has trained the eagle. In contrast to how reading activities in township schools are normally described (Section 1.6) in terms of rote-learning and chorus chanting (Chick, 1996; Kapp, 2004), I find that looking into their linguistic fine grain might uncover them to be quite dense and meaningful (further discussed with a different reading activity in Section 5.3.5).

4.3.4 Making visible morphological affordances and a didactics of explicitness

As the teacher put it so vividly, for her learners this part of the story 'just wouldn't make any sense. It would sound like a poem maybe' (Interview Grade 5 Teacher as quoted in Section 4.3.1). Up to now, I have shown how the tense and aspect morphology in 'sendiyiqeqeshile' as well as 'ma-' and the subjunctive are the teacher's morphological tools from the classroom repertoire to make part of this 'poem' accessible for the learners by showing how the training of the eagle (Point A) has led to the change into a chicken (Point B). Her use of the subjunctive drives the story forward, connecting the unfolding events (Gough, 1993: 39) and allowing a clear timeline to emerge.

The sequence and causal connection of the events in the story are, however, not the only things the teacher has clarified. If we compare the meaning conveyed with 'Sendiyiqeqeshile ngoba mayitshintshe ibe yintoni? Inkuku', with the original sentence from the story: **'I have trained it to be a chicken'** (Lesson Transcript B), we see that neither the process of the actual change of the eagle, nor the authority with which the man commands it to change, are explicitly formalised in the sentence in the story. This information is, however, essential for the learners to understand what kind of moral concerns might be hidden in this story, for example: Is it possible – and if so, is it morally sound – to force a living creature to change so drastically?

Without the teacher's help, such nuances of meaning would have to be induced by the learners from the overall context of the story, to be read between the lines, so to speak. However, the language of the story is dense and complex. The teacher's interventions show that she knows well that the learners at this stage don't have sufficient access to the necessary Standard English resources and can therefore neither decipher the concrete meaning of parts, nor the rough content of the whole story without her help. Especially the affordances of 'ma-' in this context help the teacher to build what I call a *didactics of explicitness* that brings out the nuances of the story that are otherwise likely to remain hidden from her learners. Such explicit-making strategies will become visible at various points throughout this book, as teachers implement them in several different ways.

Through her relanguaging, the teacher brings together Khayelitshan affordances such as the tense and aspect morphology ('se-' and '-ile'), 'ma-' and the subjunctive mood with the Standard English of the story (e.g. 'eagle' and 'chicken'). This *bringing together* of heterogeneous resources in the classroom repertoire offers the learners additional resources to make meaning of this 'poem' in a less restricted linguistic space that allows for flexibility and fluidity in making sense of linguistic fixity. Canagarajah (2018: 47) has argued that 'since space is expansive, it provides resources for participants to construct alternate spaces within bounded and hegemonic places, to suit their interests'. It seems that we are observing the teacher doing exactly that – creating possibilities that suit the interest of English teaching in a space that is also structured by strong prescriptions of monolingualism voiced by educational officials, school management and parents (Section 2.2.1). Spatial repertoires offer the opportunity to resist such prescriptions, and resulting practices can also be subversive, as we will see in Chapter 5.

The fine-grained linguistic details with which the teacher resists prescriptions of monolingualism, affordances such as 'ma-', '-se-' or '-ile' in this case, are normally not 'seen' in studies on classroom translanguaging, because there it is not the minute linguistic detail that is of interest, but the fact that constructed language boundaries aren't being adhered to in the first place. Jaspers and Madsen (2019: 11) note that translanguaging – in similar ways to other new descriptors like metrolingualism (Pennycook & Otsuji, 2015) and polylanguaging (Jørgensen *et al.*, 2011) – makes us notice particular types of language practices (heterogeneous ones mostly), but often doesn't 'help us to dive into the fray of their detailed interactional analysis'. I argue that the nuances of teachers' linguistic strategies in the classroom can only be understood if we also make visible the nuances of the linguistic features that constitute them. The value of looking closely without being distracted by nomolanguages or other rather abstract categories will be shown throughout this work.

4.3.5 What 'ayiselulo' can do that 'no longer' cannot do

With 'ma-' and the subjunctive having clarified the conditions of getting from A to B on the timeline, the teacher now takes advantage of a different piece of familiar aspect morphology with which she situates 'It is no longer an eagle', at Point B of the timeline as an effect of the completed training. Talking about this sentence in the interview, the teacher says: 'Something would go wrong there if I didn't explain it to them' (Interview Grade 5 Teacher), because, as will be discussed in more detail below, the language in this sentence is confusing for the learners for several reasons.

The teacher relanguages 'It is no longer an eagle' into 'ayiselulo ukhozi', which is morphologically made up like this:

ayi-	-se-	-lu-	-lo
NEGSM9	PERS	COP11	ABS11
u-	-khozi		
NPx11	eagle		*(It is no longer an eagle.)*

The morpheme '-se-' in this example is found behind the subject marker (SM), not in front of it like the completive aspect explained in Section 4.3.2. It is referred to as the 'persistive' aspect, because it describes an action as still being performed or a state as still persisting at the time of the utterance. Again, in Standard English this aspect would be expressed lexically with 'still' and not morphologically (Nurse & Philippson, 2003: 128).

In this example, the persistive '-se-' is used in a negative construction, indicating that a state that had persisted before (the bird being an eagle) doesn't persist anymore at the time of the utterance – as expressed lexically in the story with 'no longer'. The combination of '-se-' with the identificative copulative of noun class 11 '-lu-' – a prefix form used only with reference to nouns and pronouns (Oosthuysen, 2015: 86) – clarifies that the persistive aspect refers to the state of a noun in class 11 rather than to the performance of an action. The Standard English resource 'no longer' retains the same form, regardless of whether it is used to describe the state of a noun (like here in 'It is no longer an eagle') or of an activity (e.g. 'It is no longer helping me'). The Khayelitshan repertoire, on the other hand, offers '-sa-' to express the (non)persistence of an activity (e.g. 'Ayi*sa*ncedi' – 'It is *no longer* helping') and '-se-'when describing the state of nouns (e.g. 'Ayi*se*lothando'/'Ayi*se*lulo uthando' – It is *no longer* love). Accordingly, even if learners at times get lost regarding the overall context of the story, the teacher nudges them – via familiar morphology – into understanding the rather unusual but here crucial event of *something* no longer existing in its previous essential form, i.e. no longer being an eagle.

Another affordance of this morphological representation of the persistive aspect is that it takes away the risk of 'no longer' being mistaken for a length measure. This is a likely scenario, especially because the part of the sentence that follows suit in the story*:* **'...even though it measures four and a half meters from wingtip to wingtip'** (B2–B3), actually features the measurement unit 'meters'. When we asked our teacher in the interview if she thinks learners would have been likely to confuse 'no longer' with 'longer' referring to length, the following exchange ensues:

Interview Excerpt c	
T = Teacher	R1 = Researcher 1 (Lara Krause, author) R2 = Researcher 2 (Tessa Dowling, supervisor)

1 R2:   Would it be the word 'longer' that they would struggle with? What would be the
2   difficulty there? Is it that they would think 'long' is 'not short'?
3 T: Yes as in the length.
4 R1:   So that's why then the translation into...
5 T: Yes.
6 R2:   You knew they would, that would be a new...
7 T: Something would go wrong there if I didn't explain it to them.

She agrees that 'longer' could have easily been mistaken for a length measure instead of being understood as marking a duration of time. We don't know whether she would have identified this potential source of confusion without our cue, but nevertheless her remark in c7 shows her experience with learners' interpretations of Standard English resources that aren't part of their routinised language practices: 'something will go wrong'. She indicates that such experience helps her to identify these potential pitfalls, which could complicate meaning-making for her learners. Her use of familiar aspect morphology disambiguates here, clearly distinguishing 'no longer' from any connection to the length of the bird's wings and thereby removing potential stumbling blocks, preventing confusion. We will see further on (e.g. Section 4.5.6) that the anticipation of stumbling blocks and sorting them out before they can cause confusion among learners is part of the many relanguaging moves by this teacher.

4.3.6 Affordances of noun class agreement in tracking the eagle

We are still at the point of the story where the owner tells the biologist that the eagle is now no longer an eagle but a chicken.

Repetition of Lesson Transcript B		
T = Teacher C = Class	**bold print** = normal print = *(italics)* =	language as read from the story classroom languaging/englishing *(englishing added by the author)*

1 C: Yes said its owner, but I have trained it to be a chicken.
2 T: It is no longer an eagle, it is a chicken, even though it measures four and a half
3   meters from wingtip to wingtip.
4 C: [reading after teacher]
5 T: The man agreed, yes, it is an eagle, **but I have trained it to be a chicken.**
6   Sendiyiqeqeshile ngoba mayitshintshe ibe yintoni? Inkuku *(I have already trained*
7   *it because it should change into what? A chicken).* Mayibe yinkuku, ingabi saba
8   ieagle *(It shall be a chicken, it shall no longer be an eagle).* He says it is no longer
9   ukhozi *(an eagle).* Ayiselulo ukhozi, ngoku seyintoni? Seyichicken *(It is no*
10   *longer an eagle, now it is already what? It's already a chicken).* Why? Because I
11   have trained it. Ndiyitrainile kuba mayiyeke ukuba lukhozi, ibe yichicken *(I have*
12   *trained it because it shall stop being an eagle and be a chicken).* For five years, a
13   man has kept this eagle with the chicken, so that it will change its ways of being
14   the eagle to a, to become a chicken.

'It is no longer an eagle' (B2) features the pronoun 'it', which Haspelmath *et al.* (2001: 1130) call a 'referential device'. 'It' here indexes that which used to be an eagle. Those familiar with the working-outs of gender in Standard English don't run the risk of understanding 'it' as referencing, for example, the owner of the eagle, who would be referred to as 'he'. However, for our learners, 'it' may not be an unambiguous referential device, especially in such an unlikely context of something changing its essential way of being. Instead, there is potential for 'referential conflict', where the learners can perceive 'more than one possible candidate for the referent of a referential expression' (Haspelmath *et al.*, 2001: 1130). If relying on Standard English, the teacher would be left with only one possibility to disambiguate this for the learners, namely by using the full noun phrase again, as in: 'The eagle is no longer an eagle'. This would still confront them with a rather odd piece of language. The teacher solves this difficulty by relanguaging 'It is no longer an eagle' into 'Ayiselulo ukhozi', which is morphologically made up like this:

ayi-	-se-	-lu-	-lo
NEGSM9	PERS	COP11	ABS11
u-	-khozi		
NPx11	eagle		*(It is no longer an eagle.)*

The NEGSM 'ayi-' refers to a noun in class 9 and is here used as an anaphora which can either be taken to index 'intaka' *(the bird)* or a 'generic it' (Pahl *et al.*, 1971: 72). The combination of the COP for noun class 11 ('lu-') and the ABS for the same class ('-lo') results in '-lulo', which follows the aspect marker '-se-' and is, in turn, employed as an anaphoric expression unambiguously referencing 'ukhozi' *(eagle)* as the only word in this immediate context that is in class 11. What 'Ayiselulo ukhozi' illustrates well is the extensive noun class system (see Appendix B for tables with the agreement morphology) that is a sedimented feature of the Khayelitshan repertoire. Here, 'agreement, both anaphoric and grammatical, radiates out from the head noun across the noun phrase and into the verb' (Nurse & Philippson, 2003: 31). Morrison (2018: 54) shows how speakers 'easily manipulate the system for both stancetaking and reference tracking purposes'. Other (Bantu) linguists have also emphasised the role of noun class agreement in reference tracking (Comrie, 1999; Contini-Morava, 2002). Contini-Morava (2002: 36), for example, summarises that noun classes help speakers 'to identify the intended referent of so-called agreeing elements in discourse by restricting their range of possible reference to a noun of a particular class'.

Compared to the spatial repertoire of Khayelitsha and the statist repertoire of Standard Xhosa, Standard English offers only three genders that are reflected in pronouns that can be used as referential devices: 'it', 'she' and 'he'. The latter two are mostly used for humans, with some exceptions, for example, individual pets, leaving 'it' for all other nouns. The only plural option is 'they'. The specificity of referential relationships therefore has to be inferred from context or via syntactic signals much more frequently than in Khayelitshan languaging, where a wide variety of referential devices can be used to express such relationships in morphologically explicit ways.

'Ayiselulo ukhozi' (It [=something in noun class 9] is no longer it [=something in noun class 11], an eagle [noun class 11]) clearly shows the learners that it is the state of the eagle (and not of anybody or anything else) that no longer persists. I argue that the teacher's 'referential choice' (Haspelmath *et al.*, 2001: 1124) is helping the learners to track the different actors and what is happening to them throughout the story, so that they can make sense of what might otherwise strike them as an opaque 'poem'. Again, noun class agreement can be an instrument in a didactics of explicitness, because it conveys information and connections that would have to be inferred from context in Standard English.

This morphologically explicit and clear reference tracking is only possible, because explicit noun class agreement is part of learners' and teachers' routinised day-to-to language practices. Therefore, the Khayelitshan English classroom offers this specific ensemble of linguistic possibilities from which the teacher can actualise these noun class–specific reference tracking devices and enrol them in her classroom languaging. An English classroom in an ex-Model C school in Cape Town's suburbs wouldn't offer the same possibilities, because teachers and learners there often don't share the same routinised language practices and teachers wouldn't be able to recruit noun class agreement morphology for clarification. Zooming into linguistic particularities, therefore, can position township classrooms as spaces of specific linguistic affordances and possibilities rather than as linguistic dead-ends marked solely by the alleged lack of Standard English (Section 1.5). So, it is worth looking closely for a while longer.

4.3.7 Becoming a chicken with 'se-' and '-yi-'

Since it has been established now that the eagle 'is no longer an eagle', the teacher moves on to explain what it is now, by relanguaging 'It is a chicken'.

Repetition of Lesson Transcript B	
T = Teacher C = Class	**bold print** = language as read from the story normal print = classroom languaging/englishing *(italics)* = *(englishing added by the author)*

1 C: Yes said its owner, but I have trained it to be a chicken.
2 T: **It is no longer an eagle, it is a chicken, even though it measures four and a half**
3   **meters from wingtip to wingtip.**
4 C: [reading after teacher]
5 T: The man agreed, yes, it is an eagle, **but I have trained it to be a chicken.**
6   Sendiyiqeqeshile ngoba mayitshintshe ibe yintoni? Inkuku *(I have already trained*
7   *it because it should change into what? A chicken).* Mayibe yinkuku, ingabi saba
8   ieagle *(It shall be a chicken, it shall no longer be an eagle).* He says it is no longer
9   ukhozi *(an eagle).* Ayiselulo ukhozi, ngoku seyintoni? Seyichicken *(It is no*
10   *longer an eagle, now it is already what? It's already a chicken).* Why? Because I
11   have trained it. Ndiyitrainile kuba mayiyeke ukuba lukhozi, ibe yichicken *(I have*
12   *trained it because it shall stop being an eagle and be a chicken).* For five years, a
13   man has kept this eagle with the chicken, so that it will change its ways of being
14   the eagle to a, to become a chicken.

In B9, she enrols the completive 'se-' again ('*se*yintoni' and '*se*yichicken'), to express that the change of the eagle into a chicken has now been completed and we are at Point B of the timeline.

Repetition Graphic A

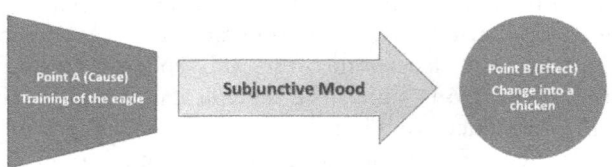

While the first completive 'se-' encountered was used in the verbal construction '*se*ndiyiqeqeshile' (Section 4.3.2), it now occurs in the nominal constructions '*Se*yintoni?' and '*Se*yichicken'. Their morphological make-up looks as follows:

se-	-yi-	-nto-	-ni	
COMPL	COP9	thing	INTER	*(It is already what?)*

This rhetorical question directs the learners' attention to which state has already been reached:

se-	-yi-	-chicken	
COMPL	COP9	chicken	*(It is already a chicken.)*

As explained in Section 4.2.1, in Khayelitshan languaging different versions of animal names circulate and the teacher therefore freely draws on 'inkuku' *(chicken)* and 'chicken' interchangeably in her classroom languaging. The latter here has the advantage of keeping language use close to that of the original story.

To clarify that the animal's transformation has now been completed, the teacher again draws on noun class agreement and tense and aspect morphology. As a direct follow up of 'ayiselulo ukhozi' discussed above, she relanguages what is narrated in the story in the simple present tense ('it is a chicken', B2) into 'seyintoni' and 'seyichicken'. These constructions include the COP of noun class 9 ("-yi-"), an anaphora which here has the same referent as the 'ayi-' (NEGSM of noun class 9) in 'ayiselulo', namely 'intaka' (noun class 9: *bird*). The 'se-' in the initial position (completive) in 'seyintoni' and 'seyichicken' then contrasts with the foregoing '-se-' in the T(A) position (persistive) in 'ayiselulo'. The whole construction shows that the same 'it' (the bird) that is no longer an eagle is now already a chicken:

'Ayiselulo ukhozi, ngoku seyintoni? Seyichicken'.

It (class 9) is no longer it (class 11), an eagle, now it (class 9) is already what? It (class 9) is already a chicken.[7]

Aspect morphology in combination with noun class agreement has – so I argue – clarified a central turning point in the story. A turning point that the teacher further elaborates on, as we will see in the next section.

4.3.8 'Because' and 'why' we have to disentangle words from nomolanguages

From B11 comes the point where the teacher clarifies why the change from an eagle into a chicken has occurred.

Repetition of Lesson Transcript B (B9–B14)

9   T: [...] no longer ukhozi. Ayiselulo ukhozi, ngoku seyintoni? Seyichicken *(It is no*
10   *longer an eagle, now it is already what? It's already a chicken).* Why? Because I
11   have trained it. Ndiyitrainile kuba mayiyeke ukuba lukhozi, ibe yichicken *(I have*
12   *trained it because it shall stop being an eagle and be a chicken).* For five years, a
13   man has kept this eagle with the chicken, so that it will change its ways of being
14   the eagle to a, to become a chicken.

In B10–B11, the teacher explains again the reason for the transformation by asking: 'Why [is it a chicken]? Because I have trained it. Ndiyitrainile uba mayiyeke ukuba lukhozi, ibe yichicken'. The question word 'why' followed by 'because' is used to emphasise the causal connection between the training (Point A) and the subsequent change (Point B). 'Why' and 'because' are familiar Standard English resources to the learners, as they are frequently used in classroom languaging to draw attention to causal connections and I have quite often observed lessons throughout Grades 4–7 that revised the joining of sentences via conjunctions such as 'because' and 'but'.

But 'why' and 'because' are also Khayelitshan resources, which I have heard used many times outside the classroom. Especially conjunctions such as 'because' occur regularly. Deumert (2013: 64) points out that 16 out of 19 urban Xhosa interviewees (interviewed 'in Xhosa') used 'because' and 'but' frequently. These little words therefore illustrate well how the statist repertoire of Standard English and the Khayelitshan repertoire are indeed *folded into each other* in the English classroom. For the analyst who looks for borrowing, code-switching or translanguaging – thus seeing to a degree 'in conformity to how the state sees' (Silverstein, 2014: 18) – nothing stands out about 'Why? Because I have trained it' (B10–B11). Had the teacher said: 'Why? Kuba I have trained it', 'kuba' *(because)* would be a clear indication of heterogeneous classroom languaging, because, since it is clearly excluded from Standard English, 'kuba' would be recognisable as a Khayelitshan resource. However, in Khayelitsha 'kuba' and 'because' are synonyms – two options for the same conjunction, one as Khayelitshan as the other.

'Why' and 'because' can be just as much Khayelitshan resources as '-fuya' and 'ma-' discussed above. The difference is that they are also

Standard English resources, codified in the corpus of that statist repertoire. And because linguistic features in linguistic analyses are per default conflated with nomolanguages (see Section 2.1.2), 'why' and 'because' are invisible as Khayelitshan linguistic possibilities. It is only spatial association and a disentangling from nomolanguages that allow us to perceive them as such.

Then, it also becomes clear that, via relanguaging, the teacher is in fact *making* 'why' and 'because' Standard English words, as we can see by reinvoking the familiar relanguaging circle:

Repetition of Circle V

Step 4 (B11)
Ndiyitrainile kuba mayiyeke ukuba lukhozi, ibe yichicken.

Step 2 (B6-B9)
Sendiyiqeqeshile ngoba mayitshintshe ibe yintoni? Inkuku. Mayibe yinkuku, ingabi saba ieagle. He says it is no longer ukhozi. Ayiselulo ukhozi, ngoku seyintoni? Seyichicken.

HETERO- | HOMO-
GENEITY | GENEITY

Step 1 (B5)
The man agreed, yes, it is an eagle, but I have trained it to be a chicken.

Step 3 (B10-B11)
Why? Because I have trained it.

Step 5 (B12-B14)
For five years, a man has kept this eagle with the chicken, so that it will change its ways of being the eagle to a, to become a chicken.

Contrasting it with the heterogeneous classroom languaging in Step 2, 'Why? Because I have trained it' in Step 3 is clearly a homogenisation and a close entanglement of 'why' and 'because' with the Standard English resources from the story ('I have trained it'). It is only in the space of the English classroom and through the teacher's sorting of linguistic features in watchfulness towards the boundaries of Standard English, that these two resources, that otherwise could also be Khayelitshan, are positioned as part of the homogenised, statist repertoire. Teaching to english in Khayelitsha often means to demonstrate that already familiar resources can *count as English* in other spaces. Learning to english in Khayelitsha accordingly also means to understand this. Relanguaging is a mechanism through which teachers can make this point.

By looking more closely at 'why' and 'because' I also realised that, in terms of the didactic strategies, there is a parallel between the teacher's use of morphemes such as 'ma-' (see Section 4.3.3 and Steps 2 and 4 in Circle V) and her use of 'why' and 'because'. All these resources allow her to make information that is implicit in the Standard English story linguistically explicit. 'Why' and 'because' formalise the causal connection between the training of the eagle and its change into a chicken, like 'ma-' had formalised the voice of authority that makes the eagle change into a chicken. I argue that what we observe in both cases is a 'didactics of explicitness' with which the teacher foregoes potential confusion among learners. This communality would remain hidden when analysts look for translanguaging, because 'Why? Because I have trained it', wouldn't be analysed conjunctively with instances of heterogeneous languaging such as 'Ndiyitrainile ukuba mayiyeke ukuba lukhozi ibe yichicken'. Only the latter would count as translanguaging and the former would be ignored. It becomes possible to analyse them together and to discover that they both instantiate a didactics of explicitness, when we link linguistic features to spatial repertoires instead of nomolanguages and when we conceptualise the ordering of these features in interaction in terms of relanguaging. If we stop seeing like a state, therefore, linguistic homogeneity or heterogeneity don't necessarily signify different languaging or teaching strategies or a binary that legitimises separate analyses of one or the other. In this light, the distinction between monolingual language use and fluid languaging begins to crumble.

The importance of analytically linking linguistic features to spatial repertoires instead of nomolanguages becomes even more clear when looking at two other key resources in this relanguaging activity: 'sendiyiqeqeshile' *(I have already trained it)* and 'ndiyitrainile' *(I have trained it)*. We played B5–B14 as stimulated recall in the interview and asked the teacher about these resources in particular. Her elaborate answer warrants pursuing a few analytical tangents below.

4.4 Relanguaging 'Train' while Training the Eagle

4.4.1 It's like when you preach in church

Repetition of Lesson Transcript B (B5–B14) as played in interview	
T = Teacher	**bold print** = language as read from the story normal print = classroom languaging/englishing *(italics)* = *(englishing added by the author)*

5	T:	The man agreed, yes, it is an eagle, **but I have trained it to be a chicken.**
6		Sendiyiqeqeshile ngoba mayitshintshe ibe yintoni? Inkuku *(I have already trained*
7		*it because it should change into what? A chicken).* Mayibe yinkuku, ingabi saba
8		ieagle *(It shall be a chicken, it shall no longer be an eagle).* He says it is no longer
9		ukhozi *(an eagle).* Ayiselulo ukhozi, ngoku seyintoni? Seyichicken *(It is no*
10		*longer an eagle, now it is already what? It's already a chicken).* Why? Because I
11		have trained it. Ndiyitrainile kuba mayiyeke ukuba lukhozi, ibe yichicken *(I have*
12		*trained it because it shall stop being an eagle and be a chicken).* For five years, a
13		man has kept this eagle with the chicken, so that it will change its ways of being
14		the eagle to a, to become a chicken.

We started the conversation about this sequence like this:

R1: Yah that is, maybe I'm not gonna ask anything. Maybe you can just tell us what you, what you did there, because the language that you are using is just so interesting.
T: I'm using Xhosa. More especially for the more-time learners. The slow learners. Because there are some learners who don't understand a bit. (Interview Grade 5 teacher)

After this, the teacher continues to elaborate on how the 'slow learners' struggle to understand any English. We then directed her attention back to this concrete instance of classroom languaging that we had played for her. We were particularly interested in her use of the forms 'sendiyiqeqeshile' and 'ndiyitrainile', which, apart from the additional completive aspect 'se-' in '*se*ndiyiqeqeshile' (see Section 4.3.2) convey close to synonymous meanings. In 'ndiyitrainile', however, the verb root is not '-qeqesh-' *(train)* but '-train-'. To prompt the teacher to comment further, we picked up on the fact that she said 'I'm using Xhosa', and the following exchange ensues:

Interview Excerpt d	
T = Teacher	R1 = Researcher 1 (Lara Krause, author) R2 = Researcher 2 (Tessa Dowling, supervisor)

1	R1:	Ok and then you say you speak Xhosa, but at the same time also sometimes you
2		say something like 'seyichicken' or 'ndiyitrainile'. How would you describe that
3		kind of language? Because…
4	R2:	You use '-qeqeshile' and then you also use '-trainile'.
5	T:	Ndiyiqeqeshile, ndiyitrainile. So that when I say that word in English: 'I have
6		trained', they already, some of them they pick up the minute you say
7		'ndiyiqeqeshile', 'ndiyitrainile'. Then they just put them together. The meaning
8		of 'qeqeshile' is 'to train'.[8]
9	R1:	And then you say 'ndiyitrainile' and then you say 'train'.
10	T:	Yes. Sometimes I don't even go there. They, they pick it up and say it themselves.
11	R2:	Oh wow.
12	T:	Yah it helps. You, you try to change an English word into a Xhosa word. Because
13		the word 'train' is an English word. It's not a Xhosa word but I can say
14		'ndiyitrainile' instead of saying 'ndiyiqeqeshile'.
15	R1:	And so do you use that as a tool?
16	T:	Yes, I do.
17	R1:	Have you learned that? Has somebody in your training taught you?
18	T:	No, no.
19	R1:	How did you come up with it?

20	T:	Sometimes it just come. Just like when you preach in church. The words just come
21		on their own. It just, it just comes, I don't know how it happens but I was not
22		trained at school. At school they said that when you teach English you mustn't do
23		code-switching. But to me it came that here this is not a Model C School. Some
24		children speak English full time, at home, the more that they used [sic]. The
25		people that work there are Xhosa. When they go to buy they speak Xhosa when
26		they pay at the till. So I just change it myself.

The first point I want to make relates to the last part of the transcript (d20–d26). Asked how she came up with the linguistic mediation using '-qeqeshile' and '-trainile', the teacher gives us some insight into relanguaging as a spatial practice. She compares her classroom languaging to preaching in church – she, like the majority of teachers at the school, regularly attends church on weekends – where 'the words just come on their own' (d20–d21) and she 'doesn't know how it happens' (d21). The fact that the teacher doesn't consciously strategise about which languaging resources to use is typical of practices as highly routinised forms of behaviour (Reckwitz, 2002; Schatzki, 2005). In the above excerpt, she is nevertheless able to retrospectively give us a deep insight into how and why she used '-trainile' instead of '-qeqeshile' (Garfinkel, 1967: vii; Schatzki, 2005). Her account shows how she chooses the linguistic features according to what makes sense to her in her quest to make her learners understand the meaning of the word 'train' in the context of the story.

Her preaching in church analogy also reminds us how (re)languaging is always a spatial practice as it is influenced by the institutional as well as the physical space in which it is done. In church, preaching is influenced by institutionalised ideas of what happens during a church service as well as by written language from the Bible, etc. Township worshipping is characterised by spontaneous prayer, where people often pray at length in eloquent but unrehearsed utterances that integrate aspects of the written word from the Bible in ways that are accessible for the local congregation. In fact, it could be investigated whether, in the space of a church, relanguaging is also a relevant mechanism in that it prepares for praying and preaching. It is therefore not far-fetched for the teacher to make connections between her church and her classroom languaging, which is also influenced by the spatial particularities of the Khayelitshan English classroom. These particularities are, for example, a learner population with very limited englishing experiences, centralised curricula that transport teaching materials with quite complex Standard English into the space and the institutionalised rule that the aim of activities in this classroom is not to spread the word of God but to teach how to english.

For this teacher, such spatial particularities are important as we can read from her comparison of the township school with a 'Model C

School' (d23). In the former, so she has decided herself, 'code-switching' is a necessary part of teaching English, while in ex-Model C schools things might be different. In fact, a little bit later in the interview, asked about what she thinks the differences would be between teaching in a township versus teaching in an inner-city or suburban school, the teacher says:

> Code-switching. Because if I can teach English in the English speaking area then there will be no need for me to code-switch. And teaching English in the Xhosa area, it's, it's a bit hard. It's challenging. Because as I've said you have to cater for the slow learners as well. (Interview Grade 5 Teacher)

According to this teacher, classroom languaging is thus strongly influenced by the linguistic space in which a school is located. In her estimation, there would be 'no need to code-switch' in classrooms in 'English speaking areas'. Adding a different perspective to her elaboration here, we could also say that the spatial repertoires of classrooms in an 'English speaking area' – compared to township classrooms – in fact offer only restricted possibilities for such heterogeneous language practices. As pointed out in Section 4.3.6, in an ex-Model C school English classroom, teachers and learners often don't share the same routinised language practices, which limits the variety of linguistic resources available for classroom languaging.

In this view, then, township classrooms become linguistically more demanding spaces, necessitating substantial relanguaging efforts to order the variety of resources available. At the same time, they also become spaces of substantial linguistic possibilities, letting the repertoire of ex-Model C classrooms appear restricted. This change of perspective towards a resource-oriented view of township classrooms is supported by research from Guzula *et al.* (2016) looking at practices in an after-school literacy club. They show how far what they call 'languaging-for-learning' in exploratory discourse can in fact be more productive 'when the teacher and learners share linguistic repertoires' (Guzula *et al.*, 2016: 223) than in spaces where this is not the case.

The resource richness of township classrooms that looks like a comparative advantage from a perspective that takes heterogeneity as the norm, is turned into a disadvantage through the statist lens, which is concerned with assessing successful language teaching and learning via standardised tests. These tests assume that (emergent) mastery of a homogenised repertoire such as Standard English can only be assessed monolingually. Especially in Chapter 6, where I discuss learners' heterogeneous writing practices, I will ponder – with those learners' and their teachers' help – on options of systematically teaching and assessing englishing *from within* linguistic heterogeneity. For now, however, let's return to Interview Excerpt d, from which more insights into the linguistic complexity of Khayelitshan English classrooms can be gained.

4.4.2 Tracing 'train' through townships

Repetition of Interview Excerpt d (d12–d14)

12 T: Yah it helps. You, you try to change an English word into a Xhosa word. Because
13   the word 'train' is an English word. It's not a Xhosa word but I can say
14   'ndiyitrainile' instead of saying 'ndiyiqeqeshile'.

The teacher's remark that 'the word "train" is an English word. It's not a Xhosa word...' is in line with the conventionalised, statist view of nomolanguages. Accordingly, the teacher described what she is doing here as 'changing an English word into a Xhosa word'. Before looking at what exactly it is that she accomplishes here with 'ndiyitrainile', I invite you to once again unsettle the nomolanguage ideology by tracing some whereabouts of 'train' outside the statist repertoire of Standard English:

'Train' in Khayelitsha: From personal experience, I can say that the noun 'trainer' features a lot in Khayelitshan languaging because it is a resource used in the comments on soccer matches on TV and radio. The verb root '-train-' in turn can often be heard in conversations around soccer training, e.g. 'Sitraine kakhulu izolo' *(We trained a lot yesterday)*. It is also used for activities aimed at improving one's physical shape, e.g. becoming fit through exercising.

'Train' in Gugulethu: While I don't have written or sound recorded documentation of the use of this particular verb in Khayelitsha except in this classroom scenario, it was recorded in the neighbouring Cape Town township Gugulethu[9] by Seabe (2014), who conducted interviews with former members of criminal gangs, who had joined voluntary organisations. The township is a space very similar to Khayelitsha in terms of migratory dynamics and the resulting language practices discussed in Section 1.2. In an interview, a volunteer says:

> Ndiqale ndatraina, and ukutraina ndayithand' into, ukuyithanda kwam yabasegazini ukuba no akhonto ndiyenzayo elokishini.... Bendikade ndikwizinto zee gangsters, ndisenza yonke into elapha phandle but now ndina two years ingqondo yam ayisekho kweza zinto. *(I started with training and I loved it. When I loved it, it was in my blood that I am not doing anything in the township... I used to be in these things of gangsters, doing everything that is out there but now it's been two years and my mind is no longer there).* (Seabe, 2014: 71, englishing by Seabe, my emphasis)

Apart from the fact that this entire quote is an illustration of the type of heterogeneous languaging that is also prevalent in Khayelitsha, I here merely want to point out that the verb root '-train-' features twice in the first sentence in 'ndatraina' and 'ukutraina'. This illustrates how this verb root has been travelling far beyond Standard English and is indeed a sedimented part of the spatial repertoire of townships like Gugulethu and Khayelitsha. So, when the teacher says: 'Train is not a Xhosa word', she is right in the sense that 'train' doesn't belong to the administratively defined set of linguistic features called Standard Xhosa that – through the statist lens – is spoken by people in Khayelitsha. However, if we look at language in terms of spatial repertoires, then '-train-' – similarly to 'because' and 'why' discussed in Section 4.3.8 – becomes visible as a Khayelitshan resource. This perspective influences the interpretation of what exactly 'ndiyitrainile' accomplishes in this sequence, as we will see below.

4.4.3 'They just put them together'

Repetition of Lesson Transcript B (B5–B14)	
T = Teacher	normal print = classroom languaging/englishing *(italics)* = *(englishing added by the author)*

5   T: The man agreed, yes, it is an eagle, **but I have trained it to be a chicken**.
6   Sendiyiqeqeshile ngoba mayitshintshe ibe yintoni? Inkuku *(I have already trained*
7   *it because it should change into what? A chicken).* Mayibe yinkuku, ingabi saba
8   ieagle *(It shall be a chicken, it shall no longer be an eagle).* He says it is no longer
9   ukhozi *(an eagle).* Ayiselulo ukhozi, ngoku seyintoni? Seyichicken *(It is no*
10   *longer an eagle, now it is already what? It's already a chicken).* Why? Because I
11   have trained it. Ndiyitrainile kuba mayiyeke ukuba lukhozi, ibe yichicken *(I have*
12   *trained it because it shall stop being an eagle and be a chicken).* For five years, a
13   man has kept this eagle with the chicken, so that it will change its ways of being
14   the eagle to a, to become a chicken.

As noted earlier, the forms 'sendiyiqeqeshile' (B6) and 'ndiyitrainile' (B11) convey nearly synonymous meanings. I now jump to the beginning of Interview Excerpt d, where the teacher explains why she uses both forms:

Repetition of Interview Excerpt d (d5–d10)	
T = Teacher	R1 = Researcher 1 (Lara Krause, author) R2 = Researcher 2 (Tessa Dowling, supervisor)

5   T: Ndiyiqeqeshile, ndiyitrainile. So that when I say that word in English: 'I have
6   trained', they already, some of them they pick up the minute you say
7   'ndiyiqeqeshile', 'ndiyitrainile'. Then they just put them together. The meaning
8   of 'qeqeshile' is 'to train'.
9   R1:   And then you say 'ndiyitrainile' and then you say 'train'.
10 T: Yes. Sometimes I don't even go there. They, they pick it up and say it themselves.

The teacher's explanation is strongly reminiscent of what Celic and Seltzer (2011: 3) promote as an essential part of translingual pedagogy: 'Putting language practices alongside each other makes possible for learners to explicitly notice language features, an awareness needed to develop linguistic abilities'. I argue – based on the tracing of 'train' above – that '-qeqeshile' and '-trainile' are both equally Khayelitshan and are therefore accessible for learners. Of both resources then, '-trainile' is more similar to 'trained' from the story and the teacher uses it directly following 'trained' (B11), with a pronunciation that clearly emphasises the similarity of the verbs: 'Because I have *train*ed it. Ndiyi*train*ile…'. By putting them 'alongside each other' (Celic & Seltzer, 2011: 3), she emphasises the similarities between the language resources familiar to the learners and those used in the story, blurring the perceived boundaries between the familiar Khayelitshan repertoire and the complex Standard English of the teaching material. With '-trainile' she 'bridges' words and emphasises connections and meaning overlaps – a strategy recognised as productive in translingual pedagogy (García & Wei, 2014: 131) as well as in more traditional approaches to 'second language teaching', where it would fall under the use of 'cognates' (Graves *et al.*, 2013: 29). This then is an example of how what is promoted as new approaches to pedagogy under translanguaging is actually often already firmly grounded in South African teachers' practices (see also Banda, 2018; Probyn, 2015).

The teacher also thinks that her learners are already able 'to explicitly notice language features', as she is convinced that with '-qeqeshile', 'trained' and '-trainile' available in the spatial repertoire during this activity, the learners will be able to 'put them together' and arrive at the meaning of the targeted resource 'train'. She presupposes that her learners aren't prevented from picking up this particular resource by the Khayelitshan morphology she assembled around it ('ndi-'; '-yi-'; '-ile'). The teacher assumes that the learners can recognise such morphology as being separable and mobile and are able to dis- and reassemble it on their own. This would mean that they also know which features belong where in the statist view. Therefore, to teach vocabulary in the way the teacher does here with 'train', she doesn't see the need to continue her relanguaging to the point where she sorts out all of the Khayelitshan resources and says the word 'train'. Instead, the learners can do part of the relanguaging as they 'pick it up and say it themselves' (d10). In this particular case, if we assume that learners are already familiar with the verb root '-train-', then what they can learn from this sequence is that 'train', when disassembled from Khayelitshan morphology, in fact counts as a Standard English word.

The Grade 5 teacher is not alone in ascribing such skills of dis- and reassembling morphemes to her learners. The Grade 4 English teacher uses the morpheme '-ish-a' (Koopman, 1999) with the verb root '-mean' in 'meanisha' in a lesson recorded on 8 February 2016 and when asked about it she says that she wants to teach the learners the vocabulary item 'mean' and adds: '"u-sha" [in meani*sha*] they know is Xhosa' (Interview Grade 4 Teacher). Thus, she points – even more explicitly than the Grade 5 teacher above – to the learners' ability to recognise '-ish-a'[10] 'as a separable suffix' without confusing it to be 'part of the target language set' (Dowling & Krause, 2018: 13). Rather, she assumes that they are able to sort the resources out, to dis- and reassemble '-ish-a' as needs be, and also that they know where it belongs in the statist view – namely to Standard Xhosa. Teachers see their learners as relanguagers with substantial metalinguistic awareness, who are able to sort out and put together morphological affordances as the space demands it. In Chapter 6, we will see that it is not only the teachers who assume their learners have these sorting skills but also some learners indeed display them in their writing when given the opportunity.

To summarise the findings of this section, I want to emphasise what the teacher also said in this long interview sequence:

Repetition Interview Excerpt d (d22–d26)

22 T: At school [teacher training college] they said that when you teach English you
23   mustn't do code-switching. But to me it came that here this is not a Model C
24   School. Some children speak English full time, at home, the more that they used
25   [sic]. The people that work there are Xhosa. When they go to buy they speak
26   Xhosa when they pay at the till. So I just change it myself.

The message that 'when you teach English you mustn't do code-switching' (d22–d23) is powerful as it is also communicated by educational authorities that urge schools 'to reduce the amount of code-switching and code mixing in order to ensure maximum exposure to the LoLT' (Western Cape Government, 2017). Township parents (see Section 1.5) also criticise teachers in this regard (Lombard, 2007; Ndimande, 2012) and the principal of Khayelitsha Primary stands behind this message as well. In the interview I conducted with him for my MA thesis, he said that the teachers:

> tend to teach English in Xhosa. That's why we have problem with our children, because they mustn't code-switch, we call it a code-switching. They must teach English even Grade 4. They must be taught the language of the lesson, of the learning area. All the learning area, the language of the learning area is English. (Interview Principal Khayelitsha Primary 2014)[11]

But what both teachers' classroom languaging and their own interpretations of it imply, is that they deem all language resources to be equally valuable in teaching English. This attitude and the resulting heterogeneous language practices appear in this light as a courageous act of resistance against such deficit orientations produced by a statist perspective on linguistic heterogeneity. Regardless of what they are being told and what they are being chastised for, in light of their experience with the affordances and constraints of Khayelitshan schooling, the teachers 'just change it themselves' (d26) – 'it' here being dominant ideas of monolingualism as the only valid approach to English teaching.

In their classroom languaging, teachers often overcome the idea of having to teach a new target language that is separate from learners' usual languaging. Instead, in line with what is promoted in translingual approaches to pedagogy, they help their learners in gaining access to a 'unique repertoire of meaning-making resources' (García & Wei, 2014: 80). 'Ndiyitrainile' and 'meanisha' are such 'unique meaning-making resources' that teachers assemble from the particular inventory of linguistic possibilities afforded by the Khayelitshan English classroom. Those resources escape the eyes of educational authorities and state administrators – and in their detail often also the eyes of analysts who are entangled in the statist vision – or only become visible as disturbances, because they unsettle the boundaries between nomolanguages that are necessary for statist homogenisation and categorisation. However, I argue that it is precisely the teachers' use of these placed resources that adds immense value to their teaching by pointing out paths into Standard English via accessible resources. But this in itself doesn't help township teachers' reputation in the eyes of educational stakeholders who 'see like a state' and can only overlook the effective strategies behind such practices that lie in their nuances. The conflict between the statist vision and the potential of township teachers' heterogeneous language teaching strategies will be further illuminated throughout this work.

I argue that the teacher's heterogeneous classroom languaging that I analysed here is not an instance of translanguaging but a product of relanguaging in this reading activity, as she never loses sight of Standard English resources and the fact that it is her job to teach them. Fluidity and fixity therefore co-constitute each other and nomolanguages aren't transcended in the English classroom, as can be made visible by taking one final look at the relanguaging circle that contains Lesson Transcript B in the next section.

4.4.4 Summarising the story and sorting out Khayelitshan resources

I spent much time discussing the linguistic fine grain of the language resources the teacher uses to make the story more accessible for her learners. The relanguaging circle helps to resurface from these morphological deep-dives in order to visualise again how these linguistic details are part of a toing and froing between heterogeneity and homogeneity that orders the English classroom as a linguistic space in this activity:

Repetition of Circle V

Step 4 (B11)
Ndiyitrainile kuba mayiyeke ukuba lukhozi, ibe yichicken.

Step 2 (B6-B9)
Sendiyiqeqeshile ngoba mayitshintshe ibe yintoni? Inkuku. Mayibe yinkuku, ingabi saba ieagle. He says it is no longer ukhozi. Ayiselulo ukhozi, ngoku seyintoni? Seyichicken.

Step 1 (B5)
The man agreed, yes, it is an eagle, but I have trained it to be a chicken.

Step 3 (B10-B11)
Why? Because I have trained it.

Step 5 (B12-B14)
For five years, a man has kept this eagle with the chicken, so that it will change its ways of being the eagle to a, to become a chicken.

My analyses up to now comprised what happens from Steps 1 to 4, where we are currently. Step 4 marks a point where the classroom repertoire is unsorted and balanced towards heterogeneity. The move towards Step 5 is now the final *sorting out* that wraps up the teacher's mediation of this section of the story by summarising the essential points: An eagle was kept with chickens so that it changed into a chicken itself.

Having disentangled the ensemble of linguistic possibilities by *sorting out* Khayelitshan resources that were still prevalent in Step 4, the teacher now englishes this summary in Step 5. Such relanguaging as *sorting out* had up to now mainly been accomplished by reading from the Standard English story or by assembling resources that remained very close to the language of the story (Step 3), with the teaching material central to this process. Now, the teacher does the *sorting out* more independently from the textbook, becoming the main agent in homogenising the classroom repertoire. She closes down on the possibilities of an otherwise heterogeneous linguistic space, by restricting herself to englishing. She is being watchful towards the boundaries of Standard English. This move demonstrates the skill that English learners in Khayelitsha have to master: abandoning those elements from an ensemble of linguistic possibilities that don't fit the required statist repertoire and choosing those that fall within its confines. In other words, learners themselves have to become relanguagers when learning how to english in Khayelitsha. They need to learn to sort out heterogeneous spatial repertoires so that they can produce a homogenised one that counts as Standard English – and it is exactly this skill that the teacher demonstrates here.

Throughout this chapter, I have so far illustrated the details of the linguistic features that constitute the teacher's classroom languaging and englishing in this reading activity and that are, in turn, products of heterogenising or homogenising relanguaging moves performed by handling and shaping the classroom repertoire. Along the way, I have gone on plenty of other analytical excursions to make visible teachers' local expertise that underlies their language practices. But where do we stand with regard to what happens in the story? As my next analytical point of interest requires us to jump forward significantly in the plot, I here insert a brief summary to bridge the gap.

4.5 What the Story and the Spatial Lens Teaches Us

4.5.1 Of clumsiness and verbiness

So far, the analysis has taken us to the point where the owner of the eagle explains to the biologist that he has trained the eagle to be a chicken. The story further unfolds with the biologist responding: **'No, it is an eagle still. It has the heart of an eagle and I will make it fly high up in the sky'**. The owner then claims that it is impossible for the eagle to fly, because it is now a chicken. However, he lets the biologist test it. In the owner's garden, the eagle really doesn't fly. It just jumps down from whichever pedestal the biologist puts it on, in the hope that it would start flapping its wings. The biologist then decides that the conditions in the garden aren't favourable and takes the eagle to a high mountain and sets it free. Eventually, the eagle starts flapping its wings and flies. This is where the teaching sequence transcribed below sets in. In C1, the learners repeat after the teacher a sentence in the story that describes what the eagle's first flying attempts look like.

Lesson Transcript C		
T = Teacher C = Class	bold print = normal print = *(italics)* =	language as read from the story classroom languaging/englishing *(englishing added by the author)*

1 C: At first it was clumsy and it wobbled, as it flew.
2 T: Iyaqala ke ngoku, iyabhabhazela kabi *(It starts now, it flaps about badly)*: clumsy.
3   Ibingekho... kubonakala uba loo mntu oyenzayo lo, laa nto, wenza into
4   angayiqhelanga *(It wasn't... it is visible that the someone who is doing that thing
5   is doing something s/he is not used to)*. **But soon it became more graceful and**
6   **confident.**
7 C: **But soon it became more graceful and confident.**
8 T: **But as an eagle flew,** yaqalisa ke ngoku yaqhela, yomelela *(..., it started getting*

9	used to it and became strong). Yayeka ukuthini? Ukoyika (*It stopped being*
10	*what? Being scared*). It stopped being scared. It got used to it as it was flying.
11	Iqhubekeka ukubhabha (*It continues to fly*). Yaphela isithini? (*It ended up doing*
12	*what?*) Iqhela (*It gets used to it*) and it became confident. **It flew higher and**
13	**higher into the sky until it was just a tiny dot in the distance. It never**
14	**returned. It was an eagle, though it had been kept as a chicken.**

I begin by focusing on C1–C6 and before we go into the morphological deep-dive, we can take a look at what happens there in terms of relanguaging:

Circle VI

Step 2 (C2–C4)
T: Iyaqala ke ngoku iyabhabhazela kabi: clumsy. Ibingekho... Kubonakala uba loo mntu oyenzayo lo, laa nto, wenza into angayiqhelanga.

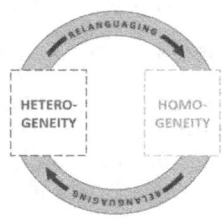

Step 1 (C1)
C: At first it was clumsy and it wobbled as it flew.

Step 3 (C5–C6)
T: But soon it became more graceful and confident.

Starting, as usual, from the unsorted classroom repertoire, the chorus reading of a sentence from the story (Step 1) balances the repertoire towards homogeneity. Step 2 then instantiates the result of relanguaging as *bringing together* resources from the classroom repertoire into a heterogeneous ensemble, shedding light on the vocabulary item 'clumsy'. Step 3, the reading of the next sentence from the story, then balances the classroom repertoire towards homogeneity again.

The language of the actual story in C1 is now grammatically very dense and complex. Alongside the adjective 'clumsy' – which is not only a Standard English but also a likely familiar Khayelitshan resource as I will explain – it features the regular past tense of the highly idiosyncratic verb 'wobble', followed by the irregular past tense form 'flew'.[12] These two verb forms are likely to be unfamiliar to most learners and so is the lexical expression of simultaneity via 'as' in the subordinate clause 'as it flew'. The picture so nicely painted by 'wobbled as it flew' – a huge bird struggling to balance its body while flying – therefore does little for most learners. Let's look at the resources the teacher uses to make this scene more understandable and easier to visualise:

In contrast to the verb forms 'wobbled' and 'flew', the adjective 'clumsy' is likely to be familiar to learners, since it can often be heard in Khayelitshan utterances such as 'Ndiclumsy!' *(I am clumsy!)*. 'Clumsy' is definitely part of the Khayelitshan repertoire; however, while learners are likely to use it in their day-to-day languaging, they might not be aware of its particular usage and shade of meaning as a Standard English resource.

In the story, 'clumsy' is used as an adjective referring to 'it' (the eagle). In her relanguaged version, however, the teacher uses 'clumsy' to refer to the act of flying. This doesn't change the meaning, because the description of the eagle as clumsy in the story results from how it is flying. In C2, she uses the verb '-bhabhazela', which is explained very vividly in Kropf's (1915: 17) dictionary as: 'flap about, as a duck attempting to fly'. This verb conveys the semantics of 'being clumsy' and 'wobbling' while 'attempting to fly' in one package and the following adverb 'kabi' *(badly)* reinforces the helplessness and clumsiness already included in this verb form. The teacher then ends with 'clumsy', as if summarising for the learners that if a bird bhabhazelas badly it can be described as 'clumsy'. The verb '-bhabhazela' illustrates why Bantu nomolanguages are described as being 'verby', since 'the verb is pivotal in the sentence, it incorporates much information, and may stand alone as a sentence' (Nurse & Philippson, 2003: 30). The verb '-bhabhazela' carries so much graphic content that it gives learners access to everything described in the highly complex sentence in C1. This verbiness appears as a useful, efficient affordance here, allowing the teacher to quickly cut to the core of the issue, while still providing cues for the visualisation of the eagle's flying attempt in all its detail.

After her use of '-bhabhazela' has clarified the meaning of 'clumsy' in the particular context of learning to fly, the teacher gives a more general definition of what it means to be 'clumsy' in C3–C4, saying: 'Ibingekho… kubonakala uba loo mntu oyenzayo lo, laa nto, wenza into angayiqhelanga' *(It wasn't… it is visible that the someone who is doing that thing is doing something s/he is not used to)*.

The impression of the general applicability of this definition is induced firstly by her use of SM15 (-ku-) as a 'generic it' (Pahl *et al.*, 1971: 72) in

ku-	-bon-	-akala	
SM15	see	NEUT	*(it is visible)*

The neuter extension, which has the allomorph '-akal-', is also described as a 'potential extension', indexing 'the ability to undergo an action […] as may be indicated by the Standard English suffix *-able* or *-ible*' (Pahl *et al.*, 1989: 706). This extension therefore turns the common verb '-bona' *(see)* into '-bonakala' *(be visible)*, while retaining a connection to the frequently used root verb '-bon-'. 'Kubonakala' allows the teacher to bring in the concept of 'visibility' – a useful affordance in an activity that isn't directed at introducing additional vocabulary that learners potentially don't know (e.g. 'visible'), but at helping her learners access the meaning of 'clumsy'. I argue that the Khayelitshan resources available in the classroom help her to take 'clumsy' out of the immediate context of the story and point to its more generic meaning. Other Khayelitshan resources that help the teacher in this quest are the verb '-enza' (*do*) and the nouns 'umntu' (*a person*, here: *someone*) and 'into' (*a thing*, here: *something*). A general definition emerges: Someone is 'clumsy' when it is visible that s/he is doing 'into angayiqhelanga' (*something that s/he is not used to*).

The teacher's use of '-qhela' in 'angayiqhelanga' instead of the phrasal verb 'used to' in this sentence is also an interesting case. Research on L2 learning shows that phrasal verbs sometimes pose problems for learners, especially if, in their familiar languaging, such verbs don't feature (Matlock & Heredia, 2002: 252), as is the case for Khayelitshan languaging. This can then cause 'confusion as to whether a word such as *on*, as in *turn on*, is functioning as a particle in a phrasal verb or a preposition in a verb + preposition combination' (Matlock & Heredia, 2002: 252, emphasis in the original). In the example relevant here, in sentences like 'They are doing something that they aren't used to', the 'to' then is a particle in a phrasal verb, whereas learners with limited access to Standard English know these little words as locative prepositions. Such complexities around phrasal verbs often lead to their avoidance – even by quite advanced learners (Matlock & Heredia, 2002: 257).

I argue that in this case '-qhela' is a convenient resource firstly for the teacher herself to avoid a phrasal verb. We might recall that in Interview Excerpt d, she produces this sentence: 'Some children speak English full time, at home, the more that they used' (d24), not complying with Standard English rules regarding the phrasal verb herself. Secondly, by using '-qhela' instead she also avoids potential confusion on the part of the learners. A writing piece (discussed in Section 6.2.5) also shows a learner employing a strategy that seems to avoid phrasal verbs. So, these Standard English resources might pose a particular challenge in the Khayelitshan English classroom.

In summary, this relanguaged sequence shows how heterogeneous resources offered by the classroom repertoire allow the teacher to not only make the content of the story more accessible but also teach vocabulary, providing a general understanding of 'clumsy', so that learners may use it for their own purposes, not only when languaging in Khayelitsha but also when englishing. Further, the resources may also allow her to cover up her own insecurities regarding Standard English resources at certain points. Rather than demonstrating unconventional englishing, the teacher circumvents that scenario by exploiting the full classroom repertoire.

This example shows once more the manifold and complex functions of classroom languaging. Existing conceptualisations of language that group together heterogeneous language practices under terms like code-switching or translanguaging in classroom research make rather general functions associable with such practices (see Sections 2.2.2 and 2.2.3). These categories then tend to reify heterogeneous language practices as fundamentally different from homogenised ones. If we want to understand the nuanced strategies behind teachers' classroom languaging in Khayelitsha, focusing exclusively on linguistic heterogeneity makes us underestimate the situated linguistic complexity that lies exactly in the relationality of heterogeneity and homogeneity.

The spatial lens that I suggest doesn't discriminate: heterogeneity and homogeneity are co-constituting the same space and relanguaging forces us to keep an eye on the constitution of the classroom repertoire and how it changes. Relanguaging appears to be a useful descriptor so far, because looking for it means looking for the push-and-pull between linguistic heterogeneity and homogeneity, between fluidity and fixity – that is while looking for translanguaging means looking only for those practices that overstep nomolanguage boundaries. To show relanguaging, analysts are forced to look at exact wordings beyond the level of the sentence and at the details of feature combinations down to the level of morphology. Therefore, we can no longer single out one of the two dimensions of language. Functions of relanguaged language in the classroom – whether they materialise in englishing or classroom languaging – must in each instance be determined under the consideration of the momentary constitution of the classroom repertoire, the goal of the given activity and as much other ethnographic information as possible.

4.5.2 Of grace and confidence

Repetition of Lesson Transcript C (C7–C14)		
T = Teacher C = Class	**bold print** = normal print = *(italics)* =	**language as read from the story** classroom languaging/englishing *(englishing added by the author)*

7   C: But soon it became more graceful and confident.

8   T: But as an eagle flew, yaqalisa ke ngoku yaqhela, yomelela *(..., it started getting*

9   *used to it and became strong).* Yayeka ukuthini? Ukoyika *(It stopped being what?*

10   *Being scared).* It stopped being scared. It got used to it as it was flying.

11   Iqhubekeka ukubhabha *(It continues to fly).* Yaphela isithini? *(It ended up doing*

12   *what?)* Iqhela *(It becomes used to it)* and it became confident. **It flew higher and**

13   **higher into the sky until it was just a tiny dot in the distance. It never**

14   **returned. It was an eagle, though it had been kept as a chicken.**

The last relanguaging circle (Circle VI) ended where this one begins, with the sentence read from the story in C7:

Circle VII

Step 4 (C11-C12)
T: Iqhubekeka ukubhabha. Yaphela isithini? Iqhela and it became confident.

Step 2 (C8-C9)
T: But as an eagle flew, yaqalisa ke ngoku yaqhela, yomelela. Yayeka ukuthini? Ukoyika.

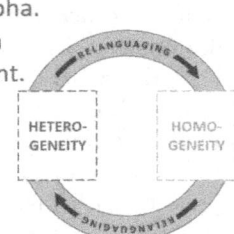

Step 1 (C7)
C: But soon it became more graceful and confident.

Step 3 (C10)
T: It stopped being scared. It got used to it as it was flying.

Step 5 (C12-C14)
It flew higher and higher into the sky until it was just a tiny dot in the distance.

In Step 1, the learners are confronted with the abstract adjectives 'graceful' and 'confident', used in the story to describe how the eagle's flying improves. Step 2 then shows how the teacher exploits the full classroom repertoire, having relanguaged these adjectives via less abstract Khayelitshan resources, while conveying the same message. Instead of 'more graceful and confident', in her relanguaged version the eagle 'yaqhela, yomelela' (*became used to [flying] and became strong*) and stopped 'ukoyika' (*being scared*). From this point, the teacher then sorts out the Khayelitshan resources and Englishes the next two sentences (Step 3). When englishing, she also moves away from the abstract adjectives 'graceful' and 'confident' and models instead the use of more accessible Standard English resources which are nevertheless challenging. For example, in 'It got used to it as it was flying' (C10), the teacher demonstrates how to use the phrasal verb 'to get used to', a verbal construction she seemed to avoid in the earlier sequence.

The negotiation of the push-and-pull between heterogeneity and homogeneity in the teacher's quest to get all learners on board is shown once again when she brings together Standard English and Khayelitshan resources in Step 4. 'Iqhubekeka ukubhabha' (*It continues to fly*) (C11) stands out, because the teacher at this stage no longer uses the verb for 'flying clumsily' ('-bhabhazela') as she did in C2 (p. 101), where the eagle's clumsiness was the focus of her explanations. Instead, she now uses '-bhabha', which simply means 'fly', no longer integrating the element of clumsiness. Without having to explain the adjective 'graceful', which would be of little use to the learners at this level, the teacher exploits the multilayered and nuanced semantics of familiar verbs to illustrate the progression from 'clumsy flying' ('-bhabhazela') to 'flying' ('-bhabha'). Then, the teacher returns to the original vocabulary from the story when she says: 'Iqhela and it became confident'. Through this heterogeneous assemblage, she positions 'becoming confident' as the result of 'getting used to doing something' ('-qhela') – an example of how classroom languaging in its heterogeneity can be assembled with an eye on Standard English. She then tilts the classroom repertoire towards homogeneity again, as the last two sentences of the story are read (Step 5).

Overall, even though the complexity of this passage requires the teacher to mostly bring together Standard English with a lot of Khayelitshan resources to keep the learners afloat, she also sorts out those resources in between and demonstrates how to english. In this sequence, for example, she circulates various Standard English resources in the classroom repertoire that don't feature in the story itself ('get used to', 'stopping to be scared' etc.) but that seem more useful for learners at this stage than words such as 'graceful' and 'confident'. It has been argued that the discourse practices in township English classrooms 'are incompatible with the need to use the language at cognitively demanding levels in other subjects' (Kapp, 2004: 260). I argue that here we actually see a teacher demonstrating for her learners a useful skill of rephrasing complex terms via more accessible language and thereby also giving them the opportunity to pick up Standard English vocabulary and phrases that they can realistically employ and that are useful beyond the English classroom. A high-resolution lens is needed to see such detail, one that takes individual linguistic features seriously but still sees them as connected to the rest of the spatial repertoire. So far, spatially looking for relanguaging seems to allow for this.

This teacher's relanguaging competencies with which she orders the classroom repertoire for the purposes of English teaching in this complex linguistic space speak of her experience and routine as the pivotal figure between statist curriculum expectations that don't see local linguistic heterogeneity, and the linguistic skills and struggles of her learners – she can see both sides of the equation and mediates between them. While this helps her in her teaching, it doesn't count in her score when departmental officials measure her ability to teach or speak English via standardised tests (Section 1.5). How the vision of state administrators could be broadened in this regard is a question that accompanies me through this work, but for now we remain caught up in the eagle story for a bit longer.

The story now comes to an end. The eagle flies away and never returns. At this point, 24 minutes of the 45-minute lesson have passed and the teacher has time left to discuss the story with the class. We will see that, as the textbook language retreats into the background, the teacher still uses a good deal of relanguaging to sort out the classroom repertoire, demonstrating ways of englishing that she deems accessible for her learners, less constrained by the complex Standard English of the story.

4.5.3 Of eagles, human beings and Tarzan

This part of the lesson begins with the teacher briefly summarising the story. Then, she contextualises it by referring to human development, saying:

> When you are small, you know nothing. You only learn the ways of human beings from the other human beings as you grow up. This eagle knows nothing about the life of an eagle, because it was taken away while it was very small. It was raised as a chicken, it was kept with the chicken, it learned the behaviour of the chicken. (Grade 5 English lesson 16.05.2016)

This piece forms part of her explanation and summary that stretch over about five minutes in total. What stands out in this snippet is that it is Englished all the way through. We are therefore on the *sorting out* train of relanguaging here that produces englishing. In fact, the last part of the lesson, where the teacher is no longer directly engaging with the textbook language, features several larger chunks of englishing that the teacher then doesn't relanguage (heterogenise) again. She therefore often foregrounds the statist repertoire of Standard English, a point to which I will return. For now, content is important.

The teacher spends some time comparing the experiences of the eagle in the story with those of human beings. For this purpose, she brings in the story of Tarzan (which some learners probably know in its Disney version), who grew up among apes and didn't know how humans behaved until they actually arrived in the jungle. Tarzan's human heart, however, resulted in him getting married to another human being – just like the eagle eventually flies, because 'it has the heart of an eagle'. After having drawn this parallel, the teacher returns her focus to the eagle story and this is where Lesson Transcript D begins.

Lesson Transcript D		
T = Teacher L = Learner (individual)	normal print *(italics)*	= classroom languaging/englishing = *(englishing added by the author)*

1	T:	Now today we are talking about an eagle that was raised as a chicken. But when
2		it was placed on the highest mountain, it began to fly, even though he was never
3		taught to fly before. Nobody taught him how to fly but it just happened
4		automatically. Why? Because he is not a chicken, he is an eagle. What do you
5		learn from this story? Is this story too difficult for you? Is it difficult? What does
6		this story teach you? Likufundisa ntoni eli bali? *(What does this story teach you?)*
7		Yes! [to learner who raised his hand]
8	L:	Ndithethe isiXhosa? *(Can I speak Xhosa?)*
9	T:	Ewe *(Yes).*

10	L:	Mna, eli bali lindifundisa ukuba ungabo yithatha enye into uyenze enye into (*As*
11		*for me, the story teaches me that you mustn't go and take one thing and change it*
12		*into something else*).
13	T:	He says it teaches him that you mustn't take one thing and try to change it to
14		become something else. What do you say? 'Ungabo yithatha enye into uyijike,
15		uyenze enye into', utsho uLisakhanya[13] (*'You mustn't take one thing and then*
16		*turn it into something else', says Lisakhanya*). What do you think? Or what can
17		you say on that? When he says 'ungabo yithatha', which means you mustn't take
18		a horse, you mustn't tame it you must leave it in the wild [...]

As usual, taking the heterogeneous classroom repertoire as the starting point, we can visualise this sequence in a relanguaging circle as well:

Circle VIII

Step 6 (D17-D18)
T: When he says 'ungabo yithatha', which means you mustn't take a horse...

Step 4 (D14-D15)
T: "Ungabo yithatha enye into uyijike, uyenze enye into", utsho uLisakhanya.

Step 2 (D6-D10)
T: Likufundisa ntoni eli bali? Yes!
L: Ndithethe isiXhosa?
T: Ewe.
L: Mna, eli bali lindifundisa ukuba ungabo yithatha enye into uyenze enye into.

Step 1 (D1-D6)
T: Now today we are talking about an eagle that was raised as a chicken.[...] What does this story teach you?

Step 3 (D13-D14)
T: He says it teaches him that you mustn't take one thing and try to change it to become something else. What do you say?

Step 5 (D16-D17)
T: What do you think? Or what can you say on that?

In Step 1, the teacher only Englishes in her summary of the story, having 'sorted out' all Khayelitshan resources. Step 2, beginning with her relanguaging of 'What does this story teach you?' into 'Likufundisa ntoni eli bali?' is an important act of reordering the classroom repertoire to allow for heterogeneity. It signals for the learners that her language policy for this exploratory activity of discussing the story is not English-only. Instead, the door to other linguistic possibilities is opened. As we will see in Section 6.1.1, there are also times when this teacher doesn't open this door. The fact that her classroom language policy is not always the same explains why the learner here first ratifies whether it is ok to respond 'in Xhosa' (D8).

Looking at his response (D10), an important conceptual point arises that needs clarification here. In the statist view, what the learner produces here looks like Standard Xhosa, because it doesn't feature any resources that would fall outside of its codified corpus. However, throughout this work I have argued that codification in such a corpus is not a sufficient condition to speak about resources as 'Xhosa' or 'English' (e.g. Sections 4.2.1 and 4.4.2). Instead, we need to consider the linguistic space in which they are used and whether the relevant statist repertoire is folded into it as an ordering principle to orient and be watchful towards. I argue that Standard Xhosa is not a relevant ordering principle during the oral classroom activities I have been investigating here. Adherence to this code is not policed or consistently approximated by teachers – quite the opposite: As we will see in Section 6.1.1, learners are sometimes even encouraged to 'code-switch' so that they can practice englishing without having to completely homogenise the classroom repertoire. I have also shown in Section 4.2.1 (with regard to animal names), and will show with other examples (Section 4.5.5 and 4.5.6), that learners language freely in their responses, assembling a heterogeneous rather than a statist, homogenised repertoire. The point is that when this learner asks whether he can 'speak Xhosa', it is likely that he means whether he is confined to Standard English or if he is allowed to draw on familiar languaging resources. From this perspective, his response then merely *coincides* with what would elsewhere count as Standard Xhosa and is not a product of his watchful adherence to this code. In the space of the English classroom during this oral activity, I therefore count his response as assembled from a heterogeneous repertoire without watchful adherence to Standard Xhosa. Accordingly, it appears in Step 2 on the classroom languaging side of the relanguaging circle.

Turning now to this response, it is insightful to look into the morphological details of its core part 'ungabo yithatha enye into uyenze enye into':

u-	-nga-	[ham]b-[i]	u]-	[y]o	yi-	thatha
SM2S	SUBJNEG	go	you	go and	OM9	take
enye	into	u-	-y-	-enz-	-e	enye	into
one	thing	SM2S	OM9	make	SUBJ	another	thing

(You mustn't go and take one thing and then change it into another thing.)

Throughout the whole lesson, the process of changing one thing into another had been discussed only with reference to concrete examples like the story of the eagle or of Tarzan. This learner now answers on a more abstract level, formulating a general 'lesson learned' from the story that can be applied beyond this immediate context. Instead of talking about the eagle or Tarzan, he speaks of 'enye into' (*one thing*) being made into 'enye into' (*another thing*). The learner's use of 'ungabo'[14] (*you mustn't go and*) shows that he judged the man's actions as morally problematic. Even though the learner is not englishing in his response, it still shows that through the teacher's mediation he has gained access to this quite complicated story and is able to abstract and learn from it. The teacher, through her flexible language policy in the classroom, offers him the chance to express this understanding, while he might have been silenced had she insisted on a policy of monolingualism. In Section 6.1.1, I will show how learners are indeed silenced in a lesson where this same teacher insists on 'English-only'.

The teacher now picks up the learner's response and sorts out the Khayelitshan resources, replacing them with Standard English ones, demonstrating for the class again the practice of englishing (Step 3 [D13–D14]). In Step 4, she orients towards heterogeneity and accessible resources again by repeating the learner's response in indirect speech (D14–D15). The *sorting out* of the classroom repertoire resulting in the Englished questions in Step 5 exemplifies what is typical for this teacher, namely that she almost always Englishes the rather sedimented elements of classroom discourse that occur regularly and independently of the particular topic of the lesson – like these general questions addressed at her learners. Asked about a similar instance in an interview, she explains that she knows which words and expressions her learners can already access, because she uses them so regularly in class. She goes on to say: 'I no longer code-switch when I get there' (Interview Grade 5 Teacher). This shows how she keeps an eye on her learners and their linguistic skills and struggles and uses the opportunities she gets to expose them to familiar englishing so that they can 'bank' the words – an expression she used for when learners really remember words and how to use them.

In Step 6, as the last heterogenising move I discuss here, she uses part of the learner's response to teach some vocabulary. She explicitly quotes the expression 'ungabo yithatha' and brings it together with Standard English resources, demonstrating how it could be Englished as 'it means you mustn't take...'. Here, the teacher turns the linguistic features used by the learner into an opportunity to introduce those resources needed to english the expression. This also sends the message to learners that their contributions are valued resources in the classroom – again a message that is emphasised by advocates of translingual pedagogy (Celic & Seltzer, 2011; García & Wei, 2014). Another example in the next section will illustrate this further.

4.5.4 To some it will appear as a question

In reaction to the learner's contribution discussed above, the teacher gives a few examples of how humans have changed (i.e. domesticated) certain animals such as horses and dogs. She then tells a personal story about how her own dog bit her at the weekend, even though it is domesticated and she feeds it every day. The teacher points out that somewhere in the back of their minds, dogs will always be wild. She then refers back to the story and goes on to say:

Lesson Transcript E	
T = Teacher	normal print = classroom languaging/englishing (italics) = (englishing added by the author)

1 T: Somewhere somehow into oyiyo *(the thing that you are)* can be activated
2   automatically. [reprimands learner for disturbing the class] Into oyiyo *(the thing*
3   *that you are)*, what you are can always come back to you. You can be changed but
4   what you are can always come back to you. This is not a chicken, it is an eagle. But
5   it was raised as a chicken. But it automatically started flying. No one taught it how
6   to fly but it flew, because it has the heart of an eagle. Ilukhozi ekugqibeleni *(It is*
7   *an eagle after all)*.

This sequence is mostly Englished. I argue that tilting the classroom repertoire towards Standard English is easier for the teacher in this part of the lesson, because her englishing is no longer directly dependent on – and entangled with – the textbook language. Because those resources are often far out of reach for learners in Khayelitsha at the level of Grade 5, the teacher has to spend a lot of time relanguaging them, bringing them together with familiar resources in order to make them accessible. Now that the written material no longer asserts its presence so strongly, the teacher can choose more appropriate Standard English resources. For example, in E4 she doesn't have to integrate formulations like 'it was an eagle, though it had been kept as a chicken' (C14, p. 102) with complex past tenses but can use simpler main clauses like 'This is not a chicken, it is an eagle' (E4).

There are indications here that, whenever the teacher engages less directly with the standardised written material, it becomes easier for her to foreground the linguistic homogeneity actually targeted in the classroom. Such findings add some nuance to research on classroom code-switching which has found that heterogeneous languaging often occurs when teachers directly engage with and mediate written text with learners (Ferguson, 2003). I want to emphasise at this point that written teaching material developed by educational authorities thus seems to actively prompt, or even force teachers into classroom languaging, leaving them with less possibilities for englishing in ways that would be accessible for their learners. An understanding of languaging as a spatial practice and of speakers actualising *spatial* rather than *individual* repertoires means that the material actively shapes language use in the classroom – a point that needs to be considered in discussions about how English teaching in township classrooms could be optimised and that I will return to later.

The overall watchfulness towards Standard English displayed in Lesson Transcript E, here makes 'into oyiyo' (E1–E2) and 'ilukhozi ekugqibeleni' (E6) appear as poignant interjections. While 'ilukhozi ekugqibeleni' summarises what the teacher said before, namely that the eagle is an eagle after all, we were interested in the role of 'into oyiyo' at the beginning of the sequence. We asked her if she thinks the learners would have understood the construction 'what you are', if she didn't precede it with this Khayelitshan resource. She says:

Interview Excerpt e		
T = Teacher	R1 = Researcher 1 (Lara Krause, author) R2 = Researcher 2 (Tessa Dowling, supervisor)	

1	T:	If I just said: 'what you are'?
2	R2:	Yes.
3	T:	Some of them, not the whole class. Yes, some of them would have got it, but to
4		some it will appear as a question, because it starts with 'what'.
5	R1:	Ah interesting! I remember also that one lesson where you did: 'Put this into a
6		question form', and some of them would keep the structure like a statement and
7		just put the 'what' and the question mark.
8	T:	Yes.
9	R1:	So 'What you are?' [and then] question mark, instead of: 'What are you?'
10	T:	To them it will sound as if I am saying: 'What are you?', yes.
11	R1:	Interesting, I didn't...
12	R2:	Not: 'What you are...'
13	T:	'What you are...' it's because of that word 'what', to them it will sound as a
14		question.

This example shows how, based on her experience, the teacher routinely anticipates which words will be problematic for the learners. Here, she makes the potential pitfall she sees around 'what you are' very explicit. Words like 'who', 'when', 'where', 'why' and 'what' are mainly taught and used as question words at this level, but advanced Englishers would be able to distinguish this function from their function as relative pronouns. They would also be unlikely to take 'what you are' to be a question, because the word order indicates otherwise.

From e5 to e7 of the interview excerpt, I reference another lesson of this teacher recorded on 20 April 2016, where learners had to change statements into questions. Many of them in fact responded by inserting a question word and a question mark, without changing the word order. This may be prompted by Khayelitshan languaging, where the word order in statements and questions is often identical. The teacher's assumption that many learners would interpret 'what you are' as a question is therefore very likely. They then wouldn't be able to make sense of the abstract statement the teacher is trying to make here.

With 'into oyiyo' this potential confusion is foregone – another example of how detailed knowledge about the Standard English resources her learners likely can or cannot access guides her classroom languaging. By asking specific questions about particular languaging resources rather than focusing on when a 'switch between nomolanguages' is said to occur, we here get nuanced insights into the teacher's substantial background and motivational knowledge that shapes her classroom languaging. Contrary to public and partly academic discourse, township teachers often know a whole lot about Standard English and the specific challenges their learners face when trying to access it. Teachers' expertise remains hugely underestimated if we don't look closely at their languaging, ask new questions and take time to listen (see also Bua-Lit Collective, 2018). The importance of teachers' local expertise will remain a focus throughout this book, but for now it is time to listen to another learner's comment on the story.

4.5.5 'Change' between a language and languaging

Shortly after Lesson Transcript E, the teacher briefly returns to the Tarzan example again and remarks how he also 'was human after all', emphasising the connection between Tarzan's and the eagle's story. She encourages learners again to share their own thoughts on the story and this is where the next transcript starts.

Lesson Transcript F		
T = Teacher L = Learner (individual)	normal print = *(italics)* =	classroom languaging/englishing *(englishing added by the author)*

1   L: Ndicinga ukuba mna Miss mhlawumbi ukuba ndizalwe ndilahlekele endaweni
2   efihlakeleyo umntu azame ukundichanga akanokwazi ukundichanga.
3   Angandichanga nje ngokwenyama kodwa mna ndiyazazi ndingubani *(I think that*
4   *for my part Miss, if maybe I was born and then got lost in a hidden place and*
5   *someone tried to change me, s/he wouldn't be able to change me. S/he can change*
6   *me only physically but me, I know who I am).*
7   T: He says if someone can take him away and try to change him, he can always
8   remember who he is. It means that he won't change completely. At the back of his
9   mind he will always remember that: 'I am Akhona, even if I am trained to be that
10   whatever, to be that thing'. But at the back of his mind he will always know that:
11   'I am Akhona and it will never be easy to change me'.

Here, I want to first draw attention to a verb in this case that retains a connection between the learner's contribution and the teacher's Englished version: 'change'. In the learner's response, the verb appears three times in 'ukundi*change*a' and 'angandi*change*a' (F2–F3). In the teacher's version, 'change' then appears stripped of Khayelitshan morphology in F7, F8 and F11. The relanguaging circle illustrates this:

Circle IX

Step 1 (F1-F3)
Miss mhlawumbi ukuba ndizalwe ndilahlekele endaweni efihlakeleyo umntu azame ukundi**change**a akanokwazi ukundi**change**a. Angandi**change**a nje ngokwenyama kodwa mna ndiyazazi ndingubani.

Step 2 (F7-F11)
He says if someone can take him away and try to **change** him, he can always remember who he is. It means that he won't **change** completely. At the back of his mind he will always remember that: 'I am Akhona, even if I am trained to be that whatever, to be that thing.' But at the back of his mind he will always know that: 'I am Akhona and it will never be easy to **change** me.'

In contrast to 'train' (Section 4.4.2), I have not heard 'change' used with Khayelitshan morphology anywhere apart from this occasion. Rather than enrolling a comparably sedimented part of the Khayelitshan repertoire, it seems that here the learner assembles 'change' – a resource that was often used in this lesson – *in situ* with Khayelitshan morphology into a new meaning-making resource functional in this activity. If we remember how the Grade 4 and Grade 5 teachers spoke about their learners' ability to recognise morphological features as separable and mobile and to 'just put them together' (d7, p. 96), it would seem that this is exactly what this learner demonstrates here with 'ukundi*change*a' and 'angandi*change*a' (F2).

When the teacher then relanguages this learner's contribution into accessible classroom englishing, 'change' remains. This verb here illustrates once more how English teaching in Khayelitsha is not an activity where teachers mediate between two nomolanguages (Standard Xhosa and Standard English) but rather between a statist repertoire (Standard English) and classroom languaging, between a nomolanguage and languaging. Between these two poles, the teacher relanguages, ordering the classroom repertoire by sometimes restricting and homogenising it, to then open it up again, taking advantage of heterogeneous possibilities. In her engagement with these two learners' contributions, this push-and-pull becomes especially evident as in their responses they make use of linguistic possibilities from the classroom repertoire that lie outside of Standard English and the teacher then relanguages them to fit the homogenised repertoire. So far, the relanguaging model between heterogeneity and homogeneity therefore seems to work quite well. But this sequence, on closer inspection, teaches the analyst a lesson in this regard.

4.5.6 Stopping to see like a state

What this learner has to say about the story far exceeds what would be possible with the Standard English resources accessible for him at this stage. As the teacher modelled with the example of Tarzan, he transfers the insights from the story to his own life. The metaphorical expression 'ngokwenyama' (lit. *as flesh*) helps him to distinguish between changing completely – i.e. changing one's essence – and merely changing superficially while retaining an inner certainty about one's identity. To bring across even a roughly similar meaning to that of 'ngokwenyama', one could use the Standard English adverb 'physically' or maybe 'superficially', both resources that would be inaccessible for the majority of learners and also wouldn't capture the metaphor of a person changing 'in flesh' but not 'in essence'.

The learner expresses this certainty about his essence or core identity via 'ndiyazazi ndingubani' (*I know who I am*). If we recall how the teacher argued that 'what you are' would be confusing for learners, because 'what' doesn't fulfil its more familiar function as a question word (in Section 4.5.4), we can see why 'who I am' would probably be just as difficult for learners to produce and to make meaning of.

When the teacher relanguages this part of the learner's contribution, she first provides this version: 'He can always remember who he is' (F7–F8). But further down, she returns to her own statement, seemingly *sorting out* 'who he is' as a potential source of confusion by using direct speech: 'At the back of his mind he will always remember that: "I am Akhona..."' (F8–F10), and similarly again: 'He will always know that: "I am Akhona and it will never be easy to change me"' (F10–F11). This is an example where relanguaging is *not* used to mediate between linguistic heterogeneity and homogeneity but where the teacher uses it within a homogenised classroom repertoire to replace inaccessible with more easily accessible Standard English resources. It could be argued, of course, that englishing itself is a heterogeneous practice that, in turn, gets sorted into the homogenised textbook-style Standard English. Yet, what I want to emphasise here is that *from the perspective that sets the heterogeneity of classroom languaging as the norm*, which is the perspective I am explicitly striving for here, the repertoire that the teacher moves in now is homogeneous, since all resources that do not count as Standard English have been sorted out. In this view then, relanguaging is here instantiated as an ordering practice within the confines of the statist repertoire, *sorting out* Standard English resources according to their likelihood of accessibility for learners and bringing together the difficult and likely not accessible Standard English resources brought in by the story with more likely accessible resources from the classroom repertoire – that nevertheless still count as Standard English. To illustrate this case, the relanguaging circle can be modified to look like this:

Circle X

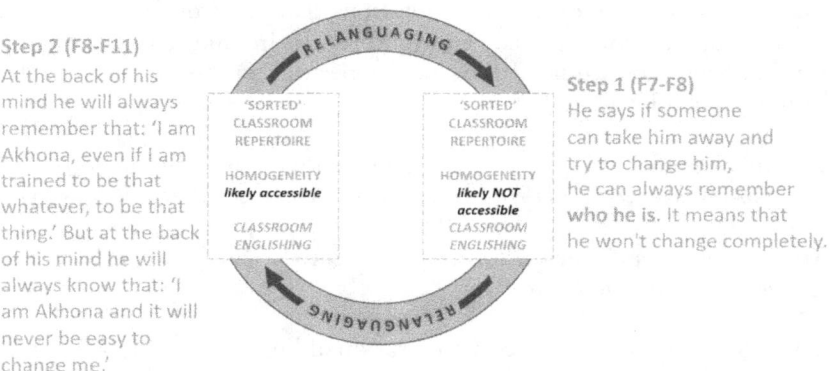

Step 2 (F8-F11)
At the back of his mind he will always remember that: 'I am Akhona, even if I am trained to be that whatever, to be that thing.' But at the back of his mind he will always know that: 'I am Akhona and it will never be easy to change me.'

Step 1 (F7-F8)
He says if someone can take him away and try to change him, he can always remember who he is. It means that he won't change completely.

From Step 1 to Step 2, 'who he is' gets sorted out. This is the point where the convenient binary between linguistic heterogeneity and homogeneity – along which I had first conceptualised relanguaging (Section 2.4) – breaks down, because also in her relanguaged language the teacher is watchful towards the boundaries of Standard English – which then in itself becomes a heterogeneous repertoire to be sorted out. The breakdown of this dichotomy shows that by spatially looking for relanguaging, we can go beyond linguistically seeing like a state, because in fact the very distinction between linguistic heterogeneity and homogeneity is produced by the statist vision. If we stop seeing like a state and take individual linguistic features seriously, it becomes clear that linguistic homogeneity or heterogeneity doesn't necessarily signify different languaging or teaching strategies – indeed the two don't necessarily form a binary that legitimises separate analyses of one or the other. This is what happens if we take 'who' – and by extension linguistic features in their own right – seriously and this then is the radical counter perspective to the categorising, simplifying logic of the state that works via homogenisation and 'grouping together'. I will return to this conceptual point throughout this book.

Coming back to the concrete instance of the teacher relanguaging the learner's response, I argue that besides removing 'who he is' as a potential stumbling block, letting Akhona speak himself in direct speech also shows him that his contribution is taken seriously and acknowledged as uniquely his. Instead of being penalised for not englishing, his response is picked up by the teacher who models for the class what it could sound like when englished. In this lesson, she therefore not only manages to give her learners voice by allowing them to have their contributions heard, but she also uses their responses as an opportunity for teaching the whole class to english.

Summing up this chapter in terms of relanguaging we can say that – excluding little episodes of classroom management – the teacher is engaged in this sorting practice throughout this lesson. It is only during the last five minutes of learners' questions that she stops to relanguage – giving up control over the classroom repertoire and letting it emerge freely. Such an unregulated classroom repertoire in this case looked, for example, like this:

L: Ukuba impuku itya ipoison ieagle itye impuku kwenzeke ntoni kuyo? (*If a mouse eats poison and then the eagle eats the mouse, what happens to the eagle?*)

T: Uhh that is very difficult. Singaneeda iscientist to answer that (*We would need a scientist to answer that*).

This exchange shows the free actualisation of linguistic possibilities from a spatial repertoire where Standard English and Khayelitshan resources are folded into each other in the learner's question as well as in the teacher's response. We see no attempt by the teacher to sort out the linguistic features the learner used or to restrict herself to Standard English resources in her own response. There is no relanguaging – no need to order the classroom repertoire before actualising it – but just relaxed languaging as the lesson slowly comes to an end.

4.6 Chapter Discussion

Through the pronounced focus on small linguistic details in this chapter, I have tried to provide a counter perspective to the categorising and simplifying statist vision that usually manifests itself in linguistic analyses of classroom practices. I have, therefore, to some degree asked different questions to those prevalent in code-switching and translanguaging studies. I didn't inquire why resources associated with different nomolanguages were used at particular points – a strategy that betrays a continuous conflation of linguistic features and nomolanguages. Rather, I have grappled with dissolving this conflation and attempted to analytically link linguistic features to space instead. I trained the spotlight on the fine grain of these features as elements of languaging as a spatial practice emerging from, and constituting, spatial repertoires. This provoked new questions that guided my inquiry and that were raised in the interviews with teachers:

- Are 'ukhozi' (Section 4.2.1), '-fuya' (Section 4.2.3) and 'because' (Section 4.3.8) Khayelitshan resources?
- What can 'Ayiselulo ukhozi' do that 'It is no longer an eagle' cannot do? (Section 4.3.5)
- Why does 'ma-' occur so frequently in this particular sequence? (Section 4.3.3)
- Why does the teacher use '-qeqeshile', 'trained' and '-trainile' in that order? (Section 4.4)
- Would the learners understand 'What you are…' without 'into oyiyo'? (Section 4.5.4)

Through the pursuit of these questions, some of the particular linguistic possibilities of the Khayelitshan English classroom became visible that distinguish it, for example, from ex-Model C classrooms and of which I will here repeat only a few:

- A rich tense and aspect morphology that facilitates the creation of a clear timeline to guide learners through a complicated story (e.g. Section 4.3.2).
- The particle 'ma-', which helped to make explicit a voice of authority that remained a subtle undertone in the Standard English story (e.g. Section 4.3.3).
- A system of noun class agreement morphology that facilitates reference tracking in a story that is otherwise likely to sound 'like a poem' to learners (e.g. Section 4.3.6).

Understanding these particular affordances – those normally either overlooked or regarded as disturbances – could help in developing locally more appropriate English curricula and assessments. I will substantiate this argument further throughout this book.

The teacher's remarks in reaction to our specific questions, such as: 'It was going to sound like a poem maybe' (Section 4.3.1); 'Something would go wrong there if I didn't explain it to them' (Section 4.3.5); or 'Because of the word "what" to them it will appear as a question' (Section 4.5.4), have revealed the local knowledge, motivation and expertise that guide her classroom language practices. The teacher provided us with insightful accounts about her experiences with her learners. For example, by asking her about '-qeqeshile', '-trainile' and 'trained' (and the Grade 4 teacher about 'meanisha'), we learned how teachers view their learners as able to treat Khayelitshan morphology as separable and mobile and to productively dis- and reassemble it – or 'to sort it out' – for example when accessing Standard English vocabulary (Section 4.4.3). These teachers therefore treat their learners as experienced in handling and shaping linguistic heterogeneity, quite different from educational administrations that categorise the same learners as monolingual speakers of Standard Xhosa, according to the logic of seeing like a state (Section 1.3).

This chapter has shown how this statist logic that assigns codified and standardised nomolanguages to territories and population groups – here Standard Xhosa to Khayelitsha – is indeed thwarted by the linguistic heterogeneity in the township. Based, for example, on looking closely at animal names (Section 4.2.1) and on tracing conjunctions like 'because' (Section 4.3.8) or verbs like 'train' (Section 4.4.2) through different spaces, I argued that what constitutes learners' familiar language practices can easily be misconstrued when seeing in nomolanguages. This then means, for example, *not to see* the morphology assembling skills that teachers ascribe to their learners and that some display in their writing (Chapter 6).

Taking Khayelitshan linguistic heterogeneity and fluidity seriously, my analyses have further demonstrated that being an English teacher in Khayelitsha doesn't mean to mediate between a named home language and a foreign language, or between an L1 and an L2 in the classroom. It means to negotiate linguistic heterogeneity and fluidity on the one hand, and linguistic homogeneity and fixity on the other. This negotiation is instantiated in the process of relanguaging, via which the teacher orders the classroom repertoire and that I have illustrated with various examples while 'going along' with this lesson. The advantage of this methodological principle of 'going along' was that I could illustrate how relanguaging means and accomplishes different things at different points of the classroom activity. This is best summarised by dividing the lesson into three phases:

Phase 1: Reading activity

The first half of the lesson was taken up by reading and relanguaging the Standard English story. The spatial repertoire tilted back and forth between Standard English – as instantiated in its most homogenised form in the textbook language – and the heterogeneous linguistic resources of the full, unsorted classroom repertoire. The teacher reliably relanguages almost every sentence of the story, *bringing together* a variety of resources into *in situ* assemblages that promise to help her learners understand.

Regarding relanguaging as *sorting out*, the textbook plays the major role in this phase, as the balancing of the classroom repertoire towards homogeneity is mostly achieved through reading from the story. There are, however, instances (e.g. Sections 4.3.8 and 4.4.4) where the teacher becomes the main agent and sorts out the Khayelitshan resources from her own classroom languaging, demonstrating how to english. The example of 'why' and 'because' has in this context illustrated how part of the English teacher's task is to clarify that already familiar resources can count as Standard English in other spaces and that it is part of learning to english in Khayelitsha to understand this (Section 4.3.8). I have argued that relanguaging as *sorting out* is then not only a mechanism that helps teachers to make this point but also a skill that learners have to acquire, because learning to english (and to xhosa) in Khayelitsha always means to learn to relanguage – to sort out heterogeneous spatial repertoires to produce homogenised, statist ones (Section 4.4.4).

Phase 2: Preparing for discussion

When the language of the story retreats into the background after the reading activity, we saw the teacher summarising parts of it again and drawing parallels, for example, with the story of Tarzan (Section 4.5.3). During this phase there are chunks of englishing where, for stretches of talk, the teacher is oriented almost exclusively towards Standard English. Such englishing is the result of relanguaging as a homogenising move of *sorting out* all Khayelitshan resources from the classroom repertoire and actualising only the Standard English ones. This move becomes more prominent here, I argue, because she is no longer tied to directly mediating the rather dense and difficult Standard English from the story but can select freely those Standard English resources she deems not only accessible but also challenging enough for learners. Having to integrate the specific resources from the story seems more likely to induce relanguaging as a heterogenising move, as we have seen in abundance during the reading activity.

Phase 3: Engaging with learners' contributions

Towards the end, the teacher engaged with learners' contributions and questions. She allowed them to draw on the full classroom repertoire and then relanguaged their responses into classroom englishing. Here, we saw relanguaging again as *sorting out*, a process starting from the heterogeneous classroom repertoire – in this case instantiated by the learners' responses – and moving towards englishing (Sections 4.5.3, 4.5.5 and 4.5.6). Up to now, throughout the lesson the teacher was therefore shown to always mediate between heterogeneity and homogeneity – constantly either *sorting out* or *bringing together* Standard English and Khayelitshan resources. But we have then also seen that linguistic heterogeneity and homogeneity aren't necessarily the relevant categories that form the threshold at which relanguaging emerges. Instead, it also occurred at the threshold for learners' likely inaccessible and likely accessible Standard English resources, as became clear when the teacher sorted out 'who he is' as a potential stumbling block for learners in Section 4.5.6. The mechanism remained the same but normally remains invisible, because no statist nomolanguage boundaries are crossed. I have argued that the point where linguistic heterogeneity and homogeneity are no longer necessarily an analytically relevant dichotomy marks the point where analysts stop seeing like a state and begin to really take seriously individual linguistic features. This is something that I have learned along the way in this experiment and that I will try to continue to do throughout this book, because this way it seems that we can arrive at more complex accounts of classroom language practices that aren't stuck on either side of the alleged languaging and nomolanguages dichotomy.

I argued that, while translanguaging as a linguistic descriptor reproduces this dichotomy – where heterogeneous languaging is analysed separately from homogenised practices – relanguaging accommodates both dimensions of language and allows us to conceptualise them conjunctively. This has led to the insight that relanguaging often brings forth a didactics of explicitness that is at play in the English classroom indiscriminately of heterogeneous classroom languaging or homogenised classroom englishing (e.g. Sections 4.3.4 and 4.3.8). This didactics of explicitness makes implicit information explicit and inaccessible Standard English resources accessible. It will become even more tangible in Chapter 5, where I turn to classroom activities that include the relanguaging of a task instruction from a textbook and of a formal, departmental assessment task. Especially the latter scenario produces a space where the pressure for English-only is significant and brings forth a differently balanced classroom repertoire.

5 Complexities around Uing and Testing in Khayelitsha

5.1 Before Beginning to U and to Test

5.1.1 Moving into different relanguaging scenarios

Chapter 4 gave insight into the reading and relanguaging of a story that led to an open discussion in class. The activity was directed at encouraging learners to understand, relate to and engage with the story orally, and at teaching them some new vocabulary along the way. We now move into classroom activities with different goals where additional factors are at play.

First, I analyse how the Grade 4 teacher relanguages a textbook task that requires learners to respond in writing. The teacher then walks around checking their written responses. It is therefore essential that they gain not just a tentative but an exact understanding of the Standard English instruction, because whether they have understood or not would become apparent in their responses in their workbooks. Those workbooks become material instantiations of learners' proficiency in Standard Written English (SWE) that are occasionally investigated by parents or educational authorities. Teachers told me that departmental subject advisors on their school visits do check learners' classroom workbooks. Therefore, more is at stake for teachers and learners in classroom activities directed at written outcomes and this sometimes influences teachers' language practices. I will, for example, show how relanguaging in these activities can become a mechanism to prepare learners – i.e. to give them the agency – to produce SWE in their responses.

This aim of relanguaging is also central to the second part of this chapter, where even more is at stake when Grade 5 learners write a formal departmental assessment task, about which it says in the Curriculum Assessment Policy Statements (CAPS) for English as a first additional language (EFAL):

> All assessment tasks that make up a formal programme of assessment for the year are regarded as Formal Assessment. Formal assessment tasks are marked and formally recorded by the teacher for progression and

certification purposes. All Formal Assessment tasks are subject to moderation for the purpose of quality assurance and to ensure that appropriate standards are maintained. (Department of Basic Education, 2011: 88)

Such moderation by the Department of Basic Education (DBE) and, as teachers told me, sometimes also in school internally by the head of department, means that the teachers' practices can be scrutinised with regard to how well they make their learners perform in these tests. Therefore, the analysis of this relatively high-stakes classroom activity in conjunction with assessment-related statements the teacher makes in the interview, tells a story that goes far beyond the classroom, pointing to the influence that the demands, and the sometimes inaccessible texts, of a centralised assessment system have on the linguistic strategies that teachers develop. Such strategies serve to negotiate the expectations of Standard English monolingualism in the institutional space of the English classroom, and the local, heterogeneous languaging realities of Khayelitshan learners.

5.1.2 They are new to English and can't read

We start in the Grade 4 English classroom. The Grade 4 teacher is in her late fifties and has been teaching mostly English and life skills[1] at Khayelitsha Primary since 1997.

She has a strict air about her, clearly holds senior status at the school and has a good relationship with school management and the principal. Her strictness shows in her teaching, where she regularly reprimands learners for overstepping her rules of proper behaviour. Nevertheless, a sense of humour often shines through, with which she lightens up her sometimes quite loud and authoritative teaching style. Learners seem to validate her authority, remaining rather quiet when she speaks but laughing heartily at her jokes.

She is as strict with herself as she was with her learners. In interviews, when asked about her languaging in class, she often commented along the lines of 'It's wrong of me to say...' or 'I'm supposed to say...' (Interview Grade 4 Teacher).[2] It took a while for us to clarify that we were not criticising her practices but were interested in her analytical perspective on her languaging in class. She did then open up and, also in interviews, never lacked a sense of humour, laughing at what struck her as the oddity of her own languaging. What in turn struck me about this teacher is her confidence in her learners' ability to master Standard English even under these linguistically complicated circumstances. She said: 'The children learn language easily'. What their success depends on, in her view, are the right resources and appropriate teaching strategies. We will learn from her below what some of these strategies look like, but first she introduces us to the complexities of teaching English in Grade 4.

In this grade, learners' day-to-day schooling experiences as well as testing situations change significantly. They are adjusting not only to different teachers (from Grade 1 to Grade 3 the same teacher had been teaching them all subjects) but also to the new official language of learning and teaching (LoLT): Standard English. Where teachers and learners usually had to orient towards Standard Xhosa, they now have to turn towards Standard English in all classroom activities (Section 1.3). A side effect of this early-transition language policy model is that formal English teaching was a low priority in Grades 1–3, because the focus was on practicing Standard Xhosa (Section 1.4). English teaching in Grade 4 is therefore an especially complex undertaking, as the teacher has to play catch-up to meet the EFAL curriculum demands while working with learners who are new to englishing – be it written or spoken – as well as comparatively new to activities typical for a language classroom, such as metalanguaging that is used to talk *about* linguistic features.

The teachers describes this grade as particularly challenging linguistically for learners, because 'the language [English] is not... it's new to them' (Interview Grade 4 Teacher). Later, she comments extensively on her language use in class and why she finds it necessary to subvert the policy of speaking English-only:

Interview Excerpt f	
T = Teacher	R1 = Researcher 1 (Lara Krause, author) R2 = Researcher 2 (Tessa Dowling, supervisor)

1 T: We are speaking English right through. We only speak Xhosa when it is Xhosa
2   period. As the... as it is required that we mustn't teach English and mix Xhosa.
3   That is not allowed. But we do it there in Grade 4, because they are new to these
4   subjects, you know. Most of the time they were taught in Xhosa. All the subjects.
5   Only in Grade 4 where they start now, learning about English all the subjects. So
6   at least we do that switching over [into Xhosa].

At first it seems as though she is defending herself and her colleagues against the common stigma of township teachers 'mixing' nomolanguages when teaching English or 'teaching English in Xhosa' (Maile, 2004; Ndimande, 2012). She then, however, explains why abiding by the language policy in Grade 4 is not practical (see also Probyn, 2001: 263). Her 'switching over' is analysed in detail in this chapter, using an example from one of her lessons. Before that, another excerpt from the same interview is of interest, as the teacher here comments on how it is particularly difficult for learners to read and understand instructions. This adds some background to the following analysis of data from her classroom, which revolves around a written task instruction, and is also relevant for the analysis of how the Grade 5 teacher later in this chapter mediates the instructions in assessment tasks.

Interview Excerpt g	
T = Teacher	R1 = Researcher 1 (Lara Krause, author) R2 = Researcher 2 (Tessa Dowling, supervisor)

1 R1: And how do your learners cope with written examinations?
2 T: They, they find it difficult, like you know to read instructions. You are supposed
3   to, if it says 'Circle the correct answer', so they must know what 'circle' means
4   [laughs]. Yah it's circle, ohhh.
5 R1: Is it specifically the instructions that are difficult?
6 T: It's the instructions and reading. Reading. They can't read. They can't cope
7   answering questions.
8 R1: So what do you do if you have an examination and you stand there, you…
9 T: You stand there, you give them papers but with the Grade 4's we used to at least
10   read with them. Some can understand when you read.
11 R1: Mhm when they…
12 T: Yah when you read for them. When you read, then they can understand but they
13   cannot read.

In g2–g4, this teacher refers specifically to instructional vocabulary (like the imperative verb form 'circle') that is often unfamiliar to learners but essential in this context. She also observes more generally that 'They can't read' (g6). That learners have trouble reading SWE and need significant support, is consensus among the English teachers at Khayelitsha Primary as I have hinted at in Section 4.1.3, where the Grade 5 teacher explained the importance of reading and speaking slowly. I have indeed not observed any quiet reading activities during my time at the school. Teachers seem to agree that turning SWE into oral englishing makes it more accessible for learners. This is also how the Grade 4 teacher here deals with this problem: She reads with, or for her learners (g12–g13), tilting the balance of the classroom repertoire towards the oral.

To understand these complications around reading, we have to consider that up to Grade 4 learners practiced reading almost exclusively with Standard Written Xhosa (SWX). The example of 'circle' that the teacher gives (g3–g4) illustrates how this is an important fact to consider if we want to understand why learners struggle with reading SWE. The orthographic conventions of SWX are very different from those of SWE. The letter 'c' in SWX, for example, always represents a dental click, whereas in SWE – as 'circle' shows perfectly – it can represent [s] (circle) or [k] (circle). This possible 'double-booking' of one letter to represent two different sounds is not part of the orthographic conventions these learners are used to. In SWX, one letter occurring on its own generally only stands for one phoneme. Also, a consonant cluster like 'rcl' wouldn't occur in SWX, where consonants are mostly separated by vowels.[3] If one is familiar with SWX orthography only, then it would make sense for a word that sounds like 'circle' [ˈsɜːkl] to be spelled like this: 'sekile'. Therefore, while many learners would know 'circle' from oral classroom languaging, or from Khayelitshan languaging even, seeing it written as 'circle' wouldn't jog any memory.

In Chapter 6, I talk in more detail about the differences between the two orthographic conventions that Khayelitshan learners have to juggle. Here, it suffices to say that turning SWE into oral englishing by reading instructions out to learners is likely to help their understanding, which might be severely limited if it hinged exclusively on deciphering SWE on their own. Against this background, let's see how the Grade 4 teacher mediates a task instruction in one of her English lessons.

5.1.3 Reading and relanguaging a story in Grade 4

In a lesson on 8 February 2016, the teacher read the following story to the learners while they were looking at it in their departmental EFAL books:

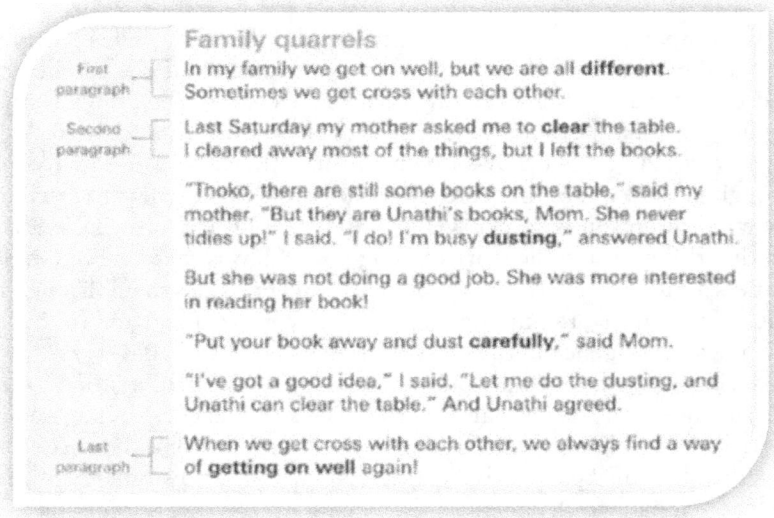

Picture 3 Family quarrels
Source: Baker et al. (2012b: 4)

She begins by reading – turning the written text into presumably more accessible oral englishing – and breaking up the narrative into pieces, similar to what the Grade 5 teacher did in Chapter 4. Even though this is not the focus here, I give a short insight into her relanguaging of part of this story to illustrate some parallels and differences in the two teachers' practices.

Lesson Transcript G		
T = Teacher C = Class	**bold print** normal print *(italics)*	= language as read from the story = classroom languaging/englishing = *(englishing added by the author)*

1   T: I cleared away most of the things but I left the books. She cleared everything but
2   she left the books.
3   C: books. [class joining in]
4   T: Akazisusa iibook *(She didn't remove the books)*. Clearisha yonke *(Clear away*
5   *everything)*. 'To clear' that is 'to clean'. Clean. You used to hear me saying:
6   'Clean your desk! Clear your desk!' Siyavana? *(Do we understand each other?)*
7   C: Yes. [some learners quietly]
8   T: It means you must collect and clean your desk.
9   C: desk. [class joining in]
10 T: Right. Thoko. Are you there? 'Thoko', where is that, where is that sentence?
11   [waiting for learners to point to the relevant sentence in their books] **'Thoko,**
12   **there are still some books on the table', said mother.**

In comparison to the reading activity in Chapter 4, where learners routinely participated by repeating every sentence that the teacher had read from the story, here only the teacher reads. She integrates learners through what has been described as 'cued elicitation' (Chick, 1996; McKinney *et al.*, 2015). She slows down towards the end of a sentence and, through prosodic cues, indicates that she wants the learners to speak the last word in unison with her (G1–G3 and G8–G9) (see also Beck, 2016). Another difference to the story reading in Grade 5 is that here in Grade 4 learners aren't as well 'trained'[4] yet. This teacher guides them through the practice of reading, reminding them that they have to find and follow the now relevant sentence in the story with their fingers (G10–G11).

Seeing how she mediates the Standard English of the story for the learners, however, we see parallels to the Grade 5 teacher's relanguaging. In G1–G2, she changes what is framed as a first-person utterance in the story into the third person, indicating that Unathi is now talked *about*. In G4, she relanguages '… she left the books' into 'Akazisusa iibook' *(She didn't remove the books)* and 'Clearisha yonke' *(Clear away everything)*, then frames the focus word 'clear' in the form of a heterogeneous classroom instruction to 'clear away everything'. After having drawn on the full classroom repertoire, she once again homogenises it, *sorting out* the Khayelitshan resources and bringing her explanation of 'clear' back to Standard English resources (G5–G8).

The linguistic details of this sequence and its pedagogical implications are discussed in Dowling and Krause (2018), where this Grade 4 teacher's classroom practices are in focus. Here, I merely want to point out that the practice of relanguaging – of ordering the classroom repertoire to allow for heterogeneity and then to sort it out again through focusing on Standard English resources – is a prevalent push-and-pull across teachers. 'Akazisusa iibook' and 'Clearisha yonke' aren't switches into a different, pre-existing code, neither do they display the transcendence of linguistic fixity as translanguaging scholars would describe it. Rather, they are *in situ* assemblages (Canagarajah, 2018) of Standard English resources from the text with Khayelitshan affordances, forming heterogeneous classroom languaging that mediates access to Standard English resources. Describing this as translanguaging would suggest that in assembling these forms the teacher is transcending nomolanguages. But in this space – the English classroom – I argue that she is using Khayelitshan morphology to shed light on Standard English and is therefore *re*languaging rather than *trans*languaging linguistic homogeneity.

I now turn to how the teacher relanguages a task instruction that relates to this story. The focus is on 'u-', a morphological device that – so I argue – is a great help in mediating access to the SWE of this instruction. The analyses are particularly microscopic and elaborate, but this deep-dive into the linguistic fine grain will make visible the various affordances of this small feature that is a typical – and central – element of the Khayelitshan English classrooms and has so far remained hidden from analysts who were looking for translanguaging or code-switching.

Following 'u-' will illustrate how Khayelitshan English teachers take advantage of the particular affordances of heterogeneous linguistic resources for metalinguistic and analytical purposes. But seeing what 'u-' can do then also begs a question that helps to further unsettle common-sense assumptions about language: What is 'u-'? A Khayelitshan resource? A Standard Xhosa resource? An englishing device? Let's see.

5.2 What Can U Do?

5.2.1 Relanguaging the instruction

The task from the book is focused on learning 'vocabulary in context' (Picture 4). We focus here on task number 1.

> **Vocabulary in context**
> Find the first and last paragraph of the story.
> 1. In the first paragraph find a word that means angry.
> 2. In the last paragraph find three words that mean being friends.

Picture 4 Task Instruction Grade 4
Source: Baker *et al.* (2012b: 5)

The learners have to identify 'cross' in the first paragraph (Picture 3) as a synonym for 'angry'. Keeping in mind how 'English is new' to the learners in Grade 4 and their struggles to read and understand instructions, we now turn to the teacher's relanguaging of this instruction. The following transcript shows how she first introduces the task to the whole class. After this short sequence, the teacher walks around for about six minutes, clarifying the task to different groups of learners. A task that, according to the curriculum, learners should just read and do by themselves. Because I am aiming at a very detailed analysis, I here focus only on her first introduction of the task to the whole class.

Lesson Transcript H	
T = Teacher	normal print = classroom languaging/englishing (italics) = (englishing added by the author)

1 T: Look on the first paragraph. Look for the word which has the same meaning as
2   angry. Uangry, meaning ipha kwifirst paragraph. Ngubani? *('Angry', the meaning*
3   *is there in the first paragraph. What is it?)* Write 'angry'. Ndifuna imeaning
4   yakhe' *(I want its meaning).*

While the pink colouring of 'angry' (Picture 4) helps to identify it as the focus word, the teacher still seems to deem it unlikely for learners to understand the instruction, seeing that she mediates it in such detail. We now look into how she relanguages the task and the familiar circle is helpful in this regard:

Circle XI

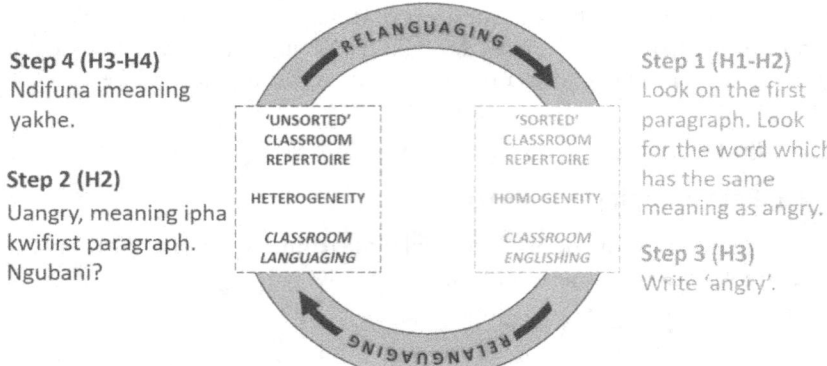

Step 4 (H3-H4)
Ndifuna imeaning yakhe.

Step 2 (H2)
Uangry, meaning ipha kwifirst paragraph. Ngubani?

Step 1 (H1-H2)
Look on the first paragraph. Look for the word which has the same meaning as angry.

Step 3 (H3)
Write 'angry'.

In Step 1, the teacher homogenises the classroom repertoire by orienting towards the written instruction. However, she doesn't read it out but already Englishes a rephrased variant of it. In Step 2, she brings together resources from the instruction with Khayelitshan resources from the classroom repertoire, producing heterogeneous classroom languaging. This leads her, for example, to refer to the word 'angry' as *u*angry by actualising a grammar affordance that will take centre stage in the analyses to follow: the noun class prefix 'u-' (class 1a). Step 3 then marks an important move of sorting 'u-' out again (details in Section 5.2.6). In Step 4, the teacher brings various resources together, with effects also discussed in Section 5.2.6. For now, we focus on what 'u-' can do.

Code-switching studies of South African classroom settings similar to this one show how linguistic forms like 'uangry' have been described so far. Probyn (2001) and de Klerk (2006) both observe that 'Xhosa' prefixes are being used in front of 'English' words (e.g. i-water molecules). Probyn (2001: 263) hypothesises that this 'Xhosalisation' of words by using 'mother tongue prefixes' is used to 'to overcome the strangeness of the English terminology, to appropriate it and make it less alienating'. De Klerk (2006: 136–137) concludes similarly 'that teachers use this device [the "Xhosa" prefix] in order to make foreign or scientific concepts sound more familiar or accessible to the Xhosa learners'.

In translanguaging research in a UK complementary school, Creese and Blackledge (2010: 110, emphasis in the original) refer to similar linguistic forms as 'heteroglossic terms' like *'junglema* "in the jungle", *bookma* "in the book", *yearma* "in the last year"'. Creese and Blackledge (2010: 110) refuse to describe these terms with reference to nomolanguages – 'as either Gujarati or English or as English with a Gujarati suffix' – and instead call them 'heteroglossic'. This sets them apart from the code-switching studies (in my case here, de Klerk, 2006; Probyn, 2001) that talk about 'Xhosa' prefixes in front of 'English' words. However, these authors also allocate a very general function to these forms: teachers use them 'to keep the task moving forward' (Creese & Blackledge, 2010: 110).

The underlying assumption in all three studies seems to be that these linguistic forms are *per se* interesting because they contradict a monolingual norm. They don't fall into line with the statist vision. This makes them stand out and also makes it possible to assign quite general functions to them without considering the specific details of their individual occurrences and the affordances that their morphology might offer in its own right. If we walk the other way – from languaging to nomolanguages – and see heterogeneity as the norm, we cannot get away with assigning a general function to a word just because it looks non-monolingual. Non-monolingual is our normal. It is our starting point. On our new route, details suddenly become important. In the case of this relanguaged Grade 4 task instruction, we therefore also asked the teacher very detailed questions in an interview.

Repetition Lesson Transcript H		
T = Teacher	normal print (italics)	= classroom languaging/englishing = (englishing added by the author)

1 T: Look on the first paragraph. Look for the word which has the same meaning as
2   angry. Uangry, meaning ipha kwifirst paragraph. Ngubani? *('Angry', the meaning*
3   *is there in the first paragraph. What is it?)* Write 'angry'. Ndifuna imeaning yakhe
4   *(I want its meaning).*

After playing this sequence for her, we asked if 'angry' could also be referred to as '*i*angry' here (like '*i*meaning' in H3), or if 'u-' (class 1a) and 'i-' (class 9) aren't interchangeable.

Interview Excerpt h	
T = Teacher	R1 = Researcher 1 (Lara Krause, author) R2 = Researcher 2 (Tessa Dowling, supervisor)

1	R1:	If I would say: 'Faka iangry apha' *(Fill in 'angry' here)*. Does that sound right?
2	T:	Faka uangry *(Fill in 'angry')*. That means: 'Fill in eli gama, uangry' *(Fill in this
3		word: 'angry')*.
4	R1:	Mhm, but you would never say: 'Fakela iangry', you would always say: 'Fakela
5		uangry?'
6	R2:	Xa uthetha... (When you speak...)
7	T:	Yes xa... fakela uangry (Yes when... fill in 'angry').
8	R2:	Xa ubacacisela (When you explain to them).
9	T:	Yah xa ubacacisela *(Yes when you explain to them)*, when you explain it you will
10		say to them: 'Fakela uangry apha' *(Fill in 'angry' here)*.

When I suggest in h1 to say 'iangry' instead of 'uangry', the teacher responds by repeating how she would say it, namely as 'Faka uangry!'. She also explains that 'Faka uangry' conveys the same meaning as 'Fill in eli gama, uangry' *(Fill in this word, 'angry')*. I then repeat a variant of the same question to make absolutely sure the teacher had picked up that we were interested in whether 'iangry' would also be an option (h4–h5). She repeats that it has to be 'uangry' (h7 and h10); 'i-' doesn't seem to afford her the same as what 'u-' does in this scenario. Again, existing code-switching studies don't mention the possibility of different prefixes doing different things but summarise all of them as 'Xhosalisations' that make words sound more familiar. Being more differentiated requires following those different prefixes not only through classrooms but also through the literature that discusses them.

While much has been written by Bantu linguists about class 9 ('i-') being the 'default class' for 'loanwords' (Demuth, 2000; Ngcobo, 2013), not much exists about noun class 1a with the prefix 'u-', except for the fact that it accommodates all kinship terms and proper names in the Bantu nomolanguages it occurs in (Contini-Morava, 2008), Standard Xhosa being one of them. Recent research shows how 'u-' is also used to refer to social media platforms (e.g. uWhatsApp; uFacebook) and names of companies (e.g. uMercedes Benz) (Futuse, 2018). But to illuminate what 'u-' does in front of 'angry' in our instruction, one observation is particularly important: the class 1a prefix is also used to refer to grammatical morphemes and phonemes. See for example: 'u-thatha akamelwe na kukubhalwa nje: thabatha?' *(Shouldn't 'thatha' be written 'thabatha'?)* (Pahl *et al.*, 1978: 14). In their grammar of Standard Xhosa (that is written in SWX), Pahl et al. also use class 1a frequently in their grammatical metalanguaging. For example, when explaining the present tense formative '-ya-' they write: 'U-ya wakha imo ende yexesha langoku' *('-ya-' builds the long form of the present tense)* (Pahl *et al.*, 1971: 95). An excursion into the other English classrooms at the school indeed shows the prevalence of 'u-' as such a metalanguaging device and helps to clarify the exact work it is doing in the instruction in focus here.

5.2.2 Tracing u through other English classrooms

All three English teachers at the school used 'u-' when talking about Standard English words. Below are a few examples from different classrooms:

Grade 5   In a lesson about direct and indirect speech the teacher discusses the sentence: 'Anelisa says: "I want to go to the centre"'. A learner then asks if the 'Anelisa says' part could also be at the end of the construction. The teacher asks to clarify:

  T: Umzekelo *(for example)* if the sentence was like '"I want to go to the centre", says Anelisa'. Do you mean it like that?
  L: Yes.
  T: If usays Anelisa was at the end?
  L: Yes.

  (Grade 5 English Lesson 18.05.2016)

Here, with 'usays Anelisa' the teacher recruits 'u-' to refer to the relevant piece of language, abstracting it from its normal context into metalanguage. For this abstraction, Standard English would only offer quotation marks, which are written and only audible by way of difference in emphasis, which is likely to escape learners who are 'new to english'. Also, the typical body languaging of showing quotation marks with fingers in the air is not available in this space – or at least I have never seen any teacher do it. With 'u-' as a morphological quotation marker, the teacher can here unambiguously identify 'Anelisa says' as a particular linguistic item, one mobile chunk whose position in the sentence can now be discussed.

Grade 6   Reminding learners about conjunctions (or joining words), the teacher says: 'So ubecause, uotherwise, ubut, we call them what? Joining words' (Grade 6 English Lesson 03.02.2016). Note again that without 'u-' the teacher's metalinguistic discussion of the conjunctions exclusively via Standard English resources would look (and sound) like this: 'So because, otherwise, but, we call them what? Joining words'.

Without the 'u-' the words would become ordinary lexical items, not metalinguistic ones. 'Because' and the other conjunctions would run the risk of sounding exactly like when used as conjunctions in Standard English or in Khayelitshan languaging, since such words are certainly part of the Khayelitshan repertoire (Section 4.3.8). But the classroom repertoire offers 'u-' to forego such potential confusion: the morphological version of quotation marks that is familiar and easy to recognise for Khayelitshan learners. With 'u-' the teacher clearly objectifies and identifies the conjunctions as Standard English linguistic items abstracted from their normal context of use, making them objects of metalinguistic discussion. *In this space it is then a Khayelitshan morpheme that marks 'because' and 'but' as Standard English resources.* This shows the capability of Khayelitshan English teachers to enrol heterogeneous language resources that don't exist in Standard English for analytical purposes. Let's follow 'u-' into one more classroom before drawing further, maybe slightly counterintuitive, conclusions.

Grade 7   The same teacher who also teaches Grade 6 explains the make-up of the construction 'white shirt' like this: 'Uwhite is an adjective and then now ushirt is a what? Is a verb? We say it's not a verb, we say what? It's a noun' (Grade 7 English Lesson 11.04.2016). Again, 'u-' makes clearly audible that the teacher is not using 'white' and 'shirt' in their respective syntactic functions as adjective and noun but is talking about them as Standard English linguistic items.

In Chapter 4, the teacher often explained that she chooses particular languaging resources, because otherwise 'things would go wrong' (e.g. Section 4.3.5) – i.e. learners wouldn't understand or misunderstand what is meant. I argue that 'u-' is such a sedimented part of the classroom repertoire of all English classrooms and so frequently used, because it is an extremely efficient metalanguaging device that helps teachers forego potential confusion, saving them a lot of time otherwise spent on explanations and talk *about* language. It can also – as the case of 'because' and 'but' shows – mark linguistic items that could be both Standard English or Khayelitshan resources, as used with watchfulness towards Standard English. What does this make 'u-'? Clearly, in this space it is not a Standard Xhosa resource, because the entanglement of morphology with a fixed set of Standard Xhosa linguistic features like lexemes (Section 2.1.1) is unsettled in 'uangry'. Neither can 'u-' suddenly become part of a statist, codified repertoire like Standard English. Instead, the observations prompt the counterintuitive insight that 'u-' might be productively understood as an *englishing device* used to mark Khayelitshan words as Standard English in the classroom. A point to be developed further while we follow 'u-' a little longer.

5.2.3 Tracing u through teacher interviews

Sometimes in interview, teachers would also use the prefix 'u-'. For example, the Grade 4 teacher explains her use of the suffix –*ish-a*[5] (see Koopman, 1999, for an explanation of this suffix) on the verb 'mean' (in mean*isha*) by saying that when she uses the verb form '-mean*isha*', 'they [the learners] get the word "mean". *U*sha they know it's isiXhosa' (Interview Grade 4 Teacher). Even though in the interview she mostly adjusts her languaging to us as the interviewers and mostly Englishes, she still recruits 'u-' to refer to '–sha' when explaining the use of this grammatical morpheme. So yes, maybe we should consider 'u-' to be not just a Khayelitshan languaging but also as a potential englishing resource – depending on the space.

The Grade 6 teacher – asked about his use of 'ubut' in class – responds apologetically: 'I'm mixing English and a Xhosa, which is a wrong thing', and later adds: '"u-" is what, is not what we call, is not a language that we use in English' (Interview Grade 6 Teacher). Besides the point made by many scholars that teachers in and beyond South Africa feel bad about not adhering to official prescriptions of monolingualism in class (Probyn, 2009; Setati *et al.*, 2002; Zentella, 1981), I find interesting here that he refers to 'u-' as 'a language', a morpheme that is not supposed to pop up in Standard English and if it does, it is a disturbance, not an additional resource. A more positive comment on his classroom languaging could go like this: '"u-" is not a language that Standard English offers us but we can take it from Khayelitsha and English with it'.

So far, 'u-' has been shown to facilitate the quoting of linguistic features on a metalinguistic level, to emphasise their mobility and in some cases even to mark potential Khayelitshan resources as Standard English ones. It is therefore a highly productive metalanguaging device that is accessible for teachers and learners. The particular agency of 'u-' is likely to remain hidden in analyses that look for code-switching or translanguaging (see Section 5.2.1). Here, the fact that a prefix 'associated with one language' is used in front of a word 'associated with another language' would be the linguistic event that attracts attention and that gets assigned some general function – an analytical remnant of the conflation of linguistic features and nomolanguages, of seeing 'in conformity to how the state sees' (Silverstein, 2014: 18). I don't argue against forms like 'uangry' and 'imeaning' having a certain familiarising function (de Klerk, 2006; Probyn, 2001) or 'moving the task forward' (Creese & Blackledge, 2010: 110). Yet, in light of what we saw above about 'u-' alone, these conclusions appear undercomplex.

Upon reflection, walking the other way and taking detours around established vocabulary helped to normalise heterogeneous languaging. I was less distracted by assertions of language belonging or transcendence and more curious about the linguistic fine grain of 'u-' in its own right. Following the morpheme through different spaces has made visible what exactly it affords teachers and learners in these Khayelitshan English classrooms.

Against the background of what uing accomplishes across different English teachers, we now return to our particular case: the Grade 4 task instruction from the beginning of this chapter.

5.2.4 Avoiding potential pitfalls with u

Chapter 4 has shown that teachers often anticipate which languaging resources could cause confusion or misunderstandings. Through relanguaging, they attempt to *sort out* such potential disturbances in advance. To understand the role that 'u-' plays in the original task instruction in Grade 4 (Picture 3), it is firstly useful to think about the potential pitfalls this instruction could have posed without 'u-'.

Repetition Lesson Transcript H	
T = Teacher	normal print = classroom languaging/englishing (italics) = (englishing added by the author)

1 T: Look on the first paragraph. Look for the word which has the same meaning as
2   angry. Uangry, meaning ipha kwifirst paragraph. Ngubani? *('Angry', the meaning*
3   *is there in the first paragraph. What is it?)* Write 'angry'. Ndifuna imeaning yakhe
4   *(I want its meaning).*

Learners are likely to have encountered the word 'angry' most frequently together with a pronoun or a subject concord, for example in Khayelitsha, where it is often recruited as an adjective for utterances like: 'Ndiangry' *(I am angry)*. From classroom englishing at this level, learners might be familiar with expressions like 'I am angry', where 'angry' is preceded by a form of the verb 'to be'. But in this instruction, 'angry' appears in a less predictable construction, preceded by 'means' ('...find a word that means "angry"'), which is unusual outside of language classrooms, because 'means' points to a metalinguistic level.

Under these circumstances, I argue that learners could easily miss that 'angry' is in this instruction not used in its more conventional function as an adjective but highlighted as a linguistic item for which they are supposed to find a synonym. Without 'u-', the form of 'angry' would sound identical when used as an adjective in 'I am angry', and in '...find the word that means "angry"'. Fluent Englishers could infer these different meanings from differences in emphasis ('hearing the inverted commas') and context, but the Grade 4 learners here might be easily confused by these different uses of 'angry'. Interpreting 'angry' as a linguistic item that they have to work with or get information from is, however, essential for understanding this task instruction. In light of what we have seen 'u-' do in other classrooms and in the interviews, I argue that the use of *u*angry accomplishes the following here: it removes the adjective from its usual semantic context and makes it recognisable as an object of analysis.

This highlighting of Standard English items by recruiting 'u-' proves to be a strategy conventionalised across the English teachers in this study and is established independently in their respective classrooms. The morpheme 'u-' has certainly found its niche in the language classroom. It is a useful tool that allows teachers to forego confusion by seamlessly opening up a metalevel on which linguistic features can be discussed in the abstract. Because 'u-' is accessible for learners, since they know it from Khayelitshan languaging and are beginning to hear it from teachers in certain classroom contexts, it is a metalanguaging device that doesn't have to be explained. Instead, teachers can trust in learners being familiar with 'u-' and can use it for analytical purposes.

The affordances of 'u-' in the task instruction are still only incompletely described. Relations of morphological noun class agreement across this instruction paint a more detailed picture of how the Grade 4 teacher nudges learners into understanding this task. Therefore, we now turn to how she makes 'uangry' work together with other associated features from class 1a, and also how class 9 plays a role in her new version of the instruction.

5.2.5 From uangry to ucross by aligning other features with u

Repetition of Lesson Transcript H
1 T: Look on the first paragraph. Look for the word which has the same meaning as
2   angry. Uangry, meaning ipha kwifirst paragraph. Ngubani? *('Angry', the meaning*
3   *is there in the first paragraph. What is it?)* Write 'angry'. Ndifuna imeaning yakhe
4   *(I want its meaning).*

After 'uangry' in H2, the teacher goes on to say that the meaning — we must interpret 'meaning' here as 'synonym' — of 'angry' is in the first paragraph (Picture 3), and then asks: 'Ngubani?', morphologically made up like this:

ngu-   -bani
COP1a   who   *(Who is it?)*

Compared to the Standard English option 'What is it?' where 'it' could refer to any noun, the 'ngu-' in 'Ngubani?' is a copulative used only with reference to a noun in class 1 or 1a. The teacher, by using this particular form, indicates that the anticipated answer — the 'who' — is also a word that would fall into the same noun class as 'uangry', in this case 'cross' or 'ucross'. Thus, the teacher mobilises the affordances of Khayelitshan languaging — such as referential tracking (Section 4.3.6) — with the result that the morphological agreement between 'uangry' and 'ngubani' gives learners another hint to understand the task, namely that they are looking for one particular word in the first paragraph. To reinvoke the teacher's interview comment, the learners now know that they are searching for 'eli gama' *(this word)* (h2, p. 132) that has the same meaning as 'angry'.

Looking at 'uangry' and 'Ngubani?' in conjunction helps us to see how the mobilisation of 'u-' in 'uangry' induces other referential tracking devices like 'ngu-' that help in keeping tabs on 'angry' throughout the instruction. Below, we will see more such devices that lead back to 'angry'.

5.2.6 Sorting out 'u-' and choosing 'yakhe' over 'it'

But what about this word that the learners are looking for? How does it relate to 'angry' and what are they supposed to do with it? The way the teacher clarifies this is best explained by returning to the relanguaging circle:

Repetition of Circle XI

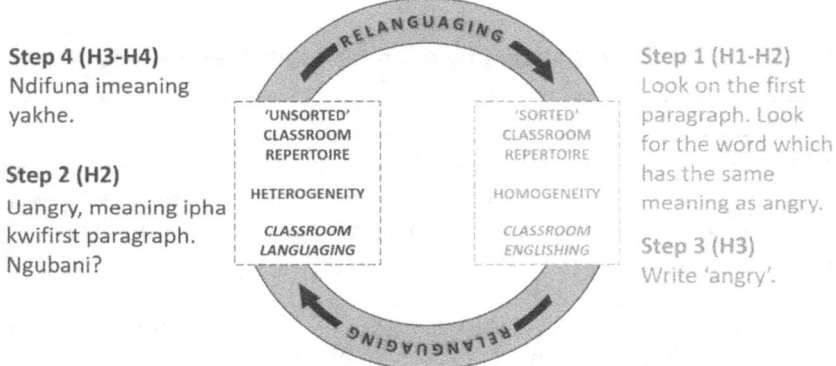

Step 4 (H3-H4)
Ndifuna imeaning yakhe.

Step 2 (H2)
Uangry, meaning ipha kwifirst paragraph. Ngubani?

Step 1 (H1-H2)
Look on the first paragraph. Look for the word which has the same meaning as angry.

Step 3 (H3)
Write 'angry'.

In Step 3, the teacher says: 'Write "angry"', because she wants the learners to write the word into their workbooks first and then write its synonym 'cross' next to it, once they have found it in the text. Essential here is the relanguaging move from Step 2 to Step 3. Notably, the teacher doesn't say 'Write *u*angry'. Instead, she sorts out 'u-' and says 'Write "angry"', arguably because in this context 'u-' would be a potential source of confusion rather than clarification. Some learners might end up literally writing 'uangry' instead of 'angry'. 'u-' would be out of place in their English workbooks, because, as the Grade 6 teacher said: '"u-" is not a language that we use in English'. And indeed, while 'u-' can be an englishing device in oral metalanguaging, it is not 'a language that we use in (Standard Written) English'. Therefore, the homogenising relanguaging move from Step 2 to Step 3 can be understood as a strategy to model what the learners have to do to produce the expected written language: sort out all resources that don't count as SWE. I argue that the anticipation of a writing task directly influences the teacher's choice of languaging resources – from the smallest morpheme. We will see this more pronounced when the Grade 5 teacher mediates a departmental test paper, needing to equip her learners with the agency to answer the test questions in writing.

Back to 'angry' in Grade 4: after instructing the learners to write 'angry', Step 4 instantiates the outcome of relanguaging as *bringing together* various resources from the classroom repertoire again: 'Ndifuna imeaning yakhe' *(I want its meaning)*. This assemblage of linguistic features increases the odds for learners to precisely track that she is talking about the meaning of 'angry'. This becomes clear when looking at the morphological make-up of 'imeaning yakhe':

i-	-meaning	ya-	-khe	
NPx9	meaning	POSS9	POSSSTEM1a	*(its meaning)*

The possessive construction 'yakhe' combines two parts:

(1) the possessive concord 'ya-', linking it to a noun in class 9 as the noun being possessed, here: 'imeaning';
(2) the possessive stem '-khe', making clear that the possessor is a noun in class 1 or 1a, here: 'uangry' (1a).

'Ndifuna imeaning yakhe' conveniently narrows down possible referents as becomes clear when we compare it to imaginable Standard English alternatives like 'I want its meaning' or, less literal, something like 'I want to know what it means', which don't feature at all in the teacher's almost six-minute long mediation via classroom languaging and englishing when walking from table to table. While she Englishes a lot in this sequence, the conventional pronoun 'it' appears only once in these six minutes when she says:

'Write it: "angry"! Here is "angry"!' [pointing to 'angry' in one learner's book]

By following 'it' up with 'angry' and also pointing to 'angry', she immediately clarifies what 'it' refers to, foregoing potential referential confusion. Such confusion is likely, because the deictic pronoun 'its' or 'it' is far less specific with regard to noun reference than 'yakhe'; 'its' could refer to any noun of neutral gender, while 'yakhe' clearly shows that something in class 9 belongs to something in class 1a, namely 'imeaning' belongs to 'uangry'.

Another reason for the teacher to avoid 'its' in a formulation like 'I want its meaning', is that it can be ambiguous for learners, because it could be taken to stand for 'it is' *(it's)*. Additionally, 'its' and 'it' often produce phonological ambiguity with 'eats' and 'eat' in Khayelitshan classrooms, as the Grade 5 teacher mentions. During a lesson on 18 May 2016, she spelled out the pronoun 'it' for her learners. Asked why she did so she said:

>Because sometimes they do confuse the spelling. We have *eat* [pronounces [ɪt] instead of standard IPA [iːt]] that means 'to eat' and the *it* [also pronounces [ɪt]] that means some, 'a thing', 'something'. So sometimes I do have to spell it out to them. (Interview Grade 5 Teacher)

In their classroom englishing, teachers and learners often draw on familiar patterns of vowel pronunciation from Khayelitshan languaging. Such pronunciation patterns have been described as a 'lack of vowel length distinctions' present in many Bantu languages and in turn reflected in 'most African Englishes' (Mesthrie, 2005: 147). Where difference in vowel length in Standard English indicates a difference in meaning, there emerges a potential source of confusion. The teacher knows that risk and has developed a strategy for such cases: spelling words out loud. This shows again how teachers often base their classroom languaging and teaching strategies on their local expertise in anticipating which language resources could cause problems for their learners. Challenges emerging from present and absent vowel length distinctions will feature more in Chapter 6. Here, the point is that another advantage of using 'imeaning yakhe' is that it avoids potential sources of confusion like 'it' or 'its' with regard to not only their referential but also their phonological ambiguity in this context. Relanguaging can therefore entail sorting out potential linguistic stumbling blocks before actualising linguistic possibilities. As discussed in Section 4.5.6, linguistic heterogeneity and homogeneity then aren't necessarily relevant categories but high and low likelihood to cause confusion among learners might be the relevant concerns.

Regarding the Grade 4 task instruction in focus here, the unambiguous agreement markers of the noun classes in 'Ndifuna imeaning yakhe' help the teacher to illuminate the syntax and semantics of a Standard English instruction while foregoing many potential sources for not only referential, but also phonological confusion.

5.2.7 Towards a digestible but resistant instruction

Otheguy *et al.* (2015: 285) describe speakers as cooks 'who can prepare attractive, exciting, delicious, intriguing meals' with what is at their disposal, no matter how heterogeneous the ingredients and how formerly unknown their combination. The dish – i.e. the new version of the task instruction – that this Grade 4 teacher has created is certainly attractive in that it consists of more easily digestible ingredients for her learners. Morphologies from Khayelitshan languaging, especially noun class prefixes and corresponding agreement markers, are particularly useful ingredients. They are mobilised as metalanguaging devices (like the 'u-' in 'uangry') and shed light on referential patterns in unfamiliar syntax (see also Dowling & Krause, 2018). Cooking as a spatial practice can offer useful metaphors to emphasise how teachers are relanguaging the classroom repertoire by strategically bringing various spatial elements 'into alignment with each other' (Pennycook, 2014: 1). The teacher's choice of linguistic ingredients increases the odds of her learners ending up with the synonyms 'angry' and 'cross' in their workbooks – without a written trace of all the other linguistic features that went into 'cooking this up'.

But we are not in a kitchen. In an institutional space where languaging that exploits the full range of linguistic ingredients on offer is officially 'not allowed' (Interview Grade 4 Teacher), it is not merely about what tastes good or works well but also about what does and doesn't adhere to prescriptions of monolingualism in classrooms. Teachers' awareness of how they often overstep the monolingual norms that govern the space of South African schooling is illustrated well by bringing together parts of two interview excerpts (f and d), one from the Grade 4 and one from the Grade 5 teacher, both quoted earlier:

Interview Excerpt f: f2–f6 Grade 4 Teacher (see also p. 125)	Interview Excerpt d: d22–d26 Grade 5 Teacher (see also p. 98)
It is required that we mustn't teach English and mix Xhosa. That is not allowed. But we do it there in Grade 4, because they are new to these subjects, you know. Most of the time they were taught in Xhosa. All the subjects. Only in Grade 4 where they start now, learning about English all the subjects. So at least we do that switching over.	At school [teacher training college] they said that when you teach English you mustn't do code-switching. But to me it came that here this is not a Model C School. Some children speak English full time, at home, the more that they used [sic]. The people that work there are Xhosa. When they go to buy they speak Xhosa when they pay at the till. So I just change it myself.

Both provide strong rationales for their heterogeneous classroom languaging – one relating to the early-transition language policy model and one to the limited access to Standard English that Khayelitshan learners have compared to children at ex-Model C schools. In this light, their heterogeneous classroom language practices become informed acts of local resistance, because teachers knowingly subvert dominant ideologies of monolingual (English) teaching. This also means that while linguistic heterogeneity and homogeneity are not necessary conditions for relanguaging, they certainly often form the threshold at which it emerges. Teachers know that seeing like a state entails the prescription of monolingualism and the scrutiny of linguistic heterogeneity, and they also know when their linguistic practices contradict the homogenising logic of that statist vision. These things considered, the instruction that was in focus in this first half of the chapter is not only a relanguaged, but also a resistant one. 'u-', 'i-', 'ya-' and '-khe' are local tools to build such resistance.

It gets more subversive below, as I turn again to the Grade 5 teacher, this time in a lesson where a formal assessment task (FAT) is written.

5.3 Assessment Relanguaged to Make the System Work

5.3.1 The department is after you

The Grade 5 teacher was most supportive of my research and very open to having me in class in every situation. I was therefore able to observe this formal assessment activity on 11 May 2016. The test paper is a FAT provided by the Western Cape Department of Education (Appendix E) as part of the CAPS curriculum and therefore reflects departmental expectations regarding the Standard English resources of Grade 5 learners at this stage.

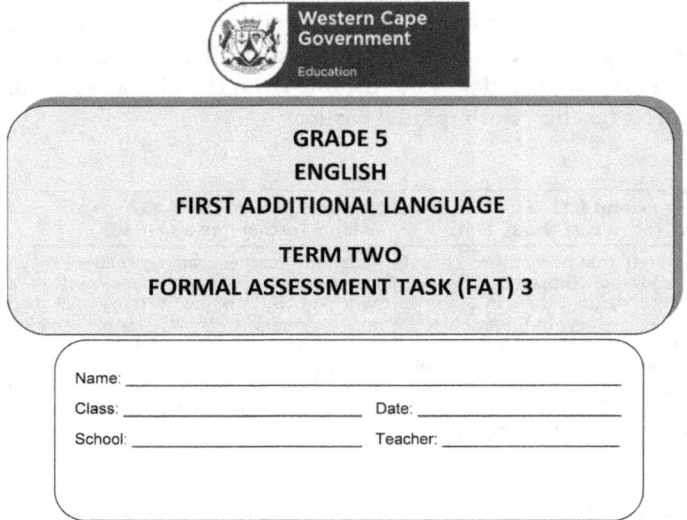

Picture 5 Cover Page FAT

These FATs are marked by the respective teachers and the marks are formally recorded (Section 5.1.1). Test outcomes are subject to moderation at the school and also through the DBE. FATs consist of several separate tasks, each designed to test parts of one of the CAPS curriculum's four focus areas: 'listening and speaking', 'reading', 'writing' and 'language structures and conventions' (Department of Basic Education, 2011: 12). The task in focus here relates to 'listening and speaking'. The comprehension story is supposed to be read out in class by the teacher and then learners have to answer questions about it in writing to test their listening skills.

Picture 5 shows a section from the cover page of the FAT, which brings together various pieces of traceable information. The emblem of the Western Cape Government is symbolic for the increased presence of the state, i.e. for how official curriculum expectations, and the pressure for monolingualism that comes with them, assert their presence more strongly in a formal testing activity. The spaces for the name of the school, the learner and the teacher make these papers clearly associable with particular individuals. The departmental subject advisors checking them can then also infer how good a job teachers are doing in preparing their learners for these assessments, i.e. how good a teacher they are. This information helps to understand the pressure this teacher is under to make her learners pass the test, as she will explain herself below.

I look at the teacher's relanguaging of the Standard English test paper in her quest to make it accessible and answerable for her learners. As in the foregoing analyses, I refer to several transcribed sequences of the test lesson and analyse them in conjunction with assessment-related statements the teacher made in interviews. The story is best told by beginning with one of those statements.

At the start of both assessment lessons that I was able to observe (only one will be discussed here), the teacher remarked – slightly irritated with learners who were unsure about the content of the test's comprehension story – that they had already read the story three or four times in class and that she wondered why they still didn't understand. This caught my attention. I had assumed that learners wouldn't get to see or hear about the details of the assessment tasks before the day they were to write it. I therefore pointed to these statements in the interview:

Interview Excerpt i	
T = Teacher	R1 = Researcher 1 (Lara Krause, author) R2 = Researcher 2 (Tessa Dowling, supervisor)

1 R1: Sometimes I've heard you say that you've said: 'We've read this story four times,
2   two or three times, before we're writing the exam and you still don't understand'.
3 T: Yes.
4 R1: So when did you do that reading?
5 T: When the paper comes, when I receive the paper on Friday, then I make the copy
6   of the story. We'll read the paper during the reading time.
7 R1: On a Monday?
8 T: On the same day. Then we read it again on Monday.
9 R1: And again on Tuesday.
10 T: And again on Tuesday, before we write it.
11 R1: And the department wants you to do that?
12 T: No, I chose to do it. No-one told me that I can do that. I just thought I must give
13   them a chance to understand the story more, to see the words, to be able to
14   understand. Because if you can come with the paper today, they are seeing the
15   story for the first time, they will write nothing. They won't understand at all.

Such test coaching points to a rupture in the logic of a centralised curriculum and assessment system and the teacher's techniques to repair it. She is aware that the designers of FATs expect that they will be administered uniformly across sites and all learners will write them immediately on seeing them for the first time (i12–i15). But she resists these departmental expectations and reshapes the testing activity by tailoring it to what she thinks her class will be able to cope with. She is convinced that if the learners were simply confronted with the test without such preparation, 'they will write nothing. They won't understand at all' (i15). On the same point a bit later, she says that without her coaching 'they would have written something that is totally out of the question' (Interview Grade 5 Teacher). Her description indicates that the Standard English resources in these FATs are often completely new to the learners. Accordingly, in order to 'give them a chance' (i12–i13) to answer the questions, she feels compelled to take actions that subvert departmental and governmental expectations (i11–i12) in order to prepare learners to satisfy these very same expectations. She feels real pressure to take such action, as the following excerpt shows:

Interview Excerpt j	
T = Teacher	R1 = Researcher 1 (Lara Krause, author) R2 = Researcher 2 (Tessa Dowling, supervisor)

1	T:	I become scared because the more learners that fail, the department is after you.
2		So you need to try by all means, you must be able to explain the case. Because
3		when we do the class work, the learner does good.
4	R1:	Do you know what will happen if, let's say, the department would 'come after
5		you' as you said?
6	T:	I don't know really, but I know that they need the learners to pass. You must make
7		sure that you don't get the high number of failures.

Here, the teacher describes some of the institutional dynamics around testing and grading that apply to township schools. Even though all assessment in the Intermediate Phase is school internal and the FATs from the department are marked by the teachers themselves, departmental subject advisors get insight into the marked papers. She hints at this in j1–j3 when saying she would come under pressure from the department if, for example, learners who normally perform well in class (as their workbooks would betray) would fail the test. Therefore, she is pushed into developing mechanisms to give her learners the agency to show their capabilities – which they might well display in their 'class work' (j3) – in the test, despite the inaccessibility of the material. Learners' agency to answer the test questions then simultaneously gives the teacher agency to make educational authorities 'see' her as a well-performing teacher and to not 'come after her'. We now turn to the relanguaging techniques via which the teacher mitigates this performance pressure on her and the learners.

5.3.2 Oliver Twist and a complexified relanguaging circle

The part of the FAT in focus here revolves around a comprehension story about Oliver Twist. This story is set in 19th-century England and has 'indeed travelled far in space-time and across socio-cultural contexts to become a test item here' (Prinsloo & Krause, 2019b: 2).

Comprehension Story in the Formal Assessment Task (Transcript I)[6]

This is how the story text appears on the test paper (see Appendix E, line numbering added here):

OLIVER ASKS FOR MORE

Instructions:

Listen as your teacher reads the story to you.

1 Oliver was even less happy in the workhouse than he had been with Mrs Mann. He
2 now had to work, which made him even hungrier. He was only given three meals of
3 thin watery soup a day, with an onion twice a week and half a small loaf of bread on
4 Sundays.

5 The room in which the boys were fed was a large stone hall. At one end a servant stood
6 and helped by one or two women, served the soup at meal times from a large pot. Each
7 boy had one small bowl and no more. The bowls never needed washing. The boys
8 polished them with their spoons till they shone. When they had done this, which never
9 took very long, they would sit staring with wide eyes at the pot, as if they could have
10 eaten even the metal of which it was made. They would also suck their fingers most
11 carefully to catch any splashes of soup that might have fallen on them

12 Oliver Twist and his companions suffered the pains of slow starvation for three
13 months. At last they got so wild with hunger that one boy, who was tall for his age told
14 the others that unless he had another bowl of soup daily, he was afraid he might eat
15 the boy who slept next to him. He had a wild, hungry eye, and they fully believed him.
16 A council was held and one boy was picked to walk up to the servant after supper and
17 ask for more. The chosen boy was Oliver Twist.

18 The evening arrived and the boys took their places. The servant placed himself by the
19 pot, his assistants stood behind him and the soup was served out. It soon disappeared.
20 The boys whispered to each other and made signs at Oliver while his neighbours
21 pushed him. Child though he was, his hunger gave him courage. He rose from the table
22 and advanced towards the servant, bowl in hand.

23 "Please, sir, I want some more," he said.

24 The servant was a fat, healthy man but he turned very pale. He looked in
25 astonishment on the small rebel for some seconds.

26 "What!" he said at length in a faint voice.

27   "Please, sir, I want some more."

28   The servant aimed a blow at Oliver's head with his wooden spoon, then seized him
29   in his arms and cried aloud for help.

30   Mr Bumble rushed into the room and was told of Oliver's crime.

31   "Asked for more!" he exclaimed. "That boy will live to be hanged!"

32   Oliver was locked up at once. The workhouse officials discussed his case. As a result,
33   a notice was next morning fixed outside of the gate, offering a reward of five pounds
34   to anybody who would take Oliver Twist. In other words, five pounds and Oliver Twist
35   would be given to any man or woman who wanted an apprentice to any trade or
36   business.

Source: Charles Dickens – *Oliver Twist*

I first look into three sequences of the teacher's relanguaged version of the story itself – one from the beginning and two from the main part. I then turn to how the teacher deals with the test questions. This last part makes it necessary to refer back to different parts of the narrative, in order to point out how the teacher might or might not have adjusted her choice of languaging resources during the earlier reading activity to prepare learners for the upcoming questions. With regard to the ordering of the classroom repertoire, we will see not only more relanguaging *within* Standard English throughout this testing activity but also instances of classroom languaging where Khayelitshan resources play a role. A complexified circle can help to visualise the main relanguaging moves and directions that are central to this testing activity.

Circle XII

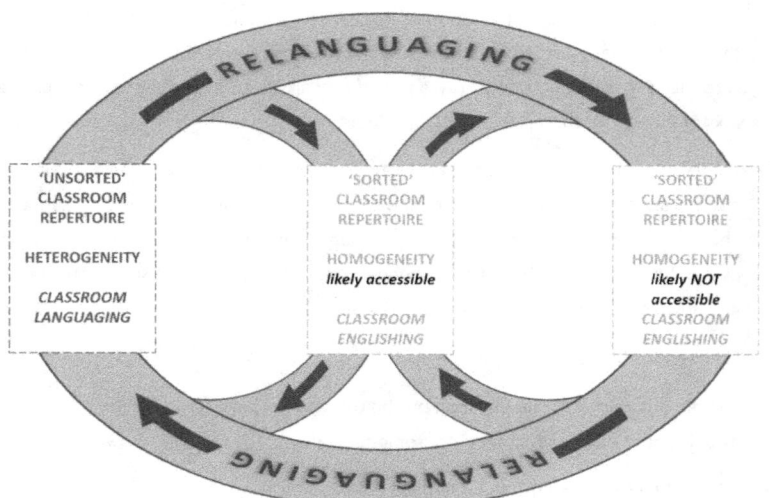

The analytical starting point is again the unsorted classroom repertoire on the left, instantiated in heterogeneous classroom languaging. On the very right, we have the homogenised repertoire instantiated in the SWE as the teacher reads it from the story, producing classroom englishing. In its original complexity this is likely inaccessible for learners. Between those two poles, we then find less complex englishing that is homogeneous but more accessible. We will see a lot of relanguaging that circles within the sorted statist repertoire of Standard English, between likely accessible and likely *not* accessible resources (grey boxes). I argue that this reflects the teacher's increased watchfulness towards the statist repertoire during this formal testing activity. This links to the fact that official demands for monolingualism assert their presence more strongly when written outcomes are at stake that will be marked and become visible to educational stakeholders beyond the classroom walls, documenting learners' – and by extension also teachers' – performance. Not only does the teacher need to ensure that learners follow the lesson, but she also feels pressure to make them produce SWE responses that satisfy the demands of state education. Demonstrating englishing to her learners and thereby preparing them for writing in SWE is therefore a central concern in this assessment activity.

Where the teacher goes full circle in her relanguaging and includes Khayelitshan resources to produce classroom languaging (black box), her focus seems to be more on satisfying the needs of her learners than on adhering to statist prescriptions. From left to right, we can therefore also read this complexified circle as going from Khayelitshan learners (classroom languaging) via classroom englishing that tries to accommodate statist demands for homogeneity and the needs of learners simultaneously, to the linguistic expectations of state administrations and their agents as materialised in the SWE in the test paper. This is, therefore, a relanguaging circle that spans from Khayelitsha to the state.

This schematic account will show more complexity throughout the rest of the chapter as I dive into the detail of the linguistic features involved. I begin by looking into how the teacher approaches, handles and shapes the opening sequence of the exam story (I1–I2) via relanguaging.

5.3.3 From no work to work and from a trans- to a re- perspective

Lesson Transcript J			
T = Teacher	**bold print**	=	**language as read from the story**
	normal print	=	classroom languaging/englishing
	(italics)	=	*(englishing added by the author)*

1 T: **Oliver was even less happy in the workhouse than he had been with Mrs Mann.**

2 **He now had to work, which made him even hungrier.** It means that before Oliver

3   went to stay at the workhouse, he first stayed with Mrs Mann. And in Mrs
4   Mann's house he didn't have to work, but now, since he is staying at the
5   workhouse, in the workhouse Oliver has to work now. It makes him even more
6   hungrier. Imlambisa ngakumbi into yokusebenza *(It makes him especially hungry
7   this thing of working)*.

Circle XIII

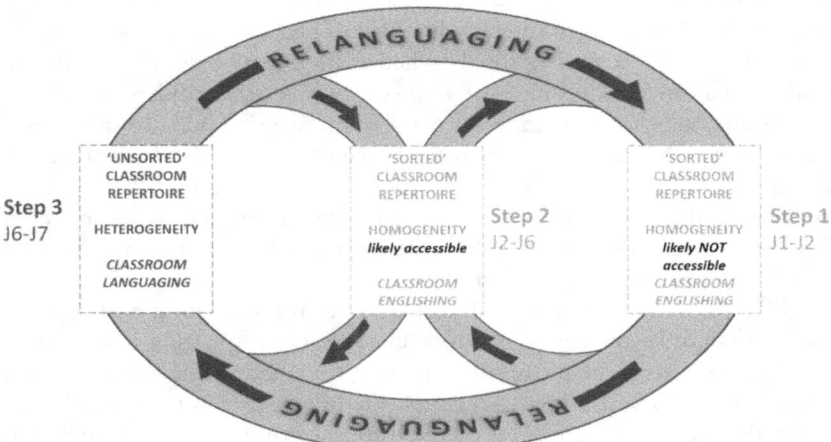

Because trying to represent the complete transcript within the complexified relanguaging circle becomes cluttered, I only refer to the relevant line numbers when illustrating the relanguaging moves:

Step 1 shows the homogenisation of the classroom repertoire via reading from the story. In Step 2, the teacher brings the resources from the story together with others from the classroom repertoire but remains watchful towards the confines of Standard English. In Step 3, the teacher then steps outside of the statist repertoire with 'Imlambisa ngakumbi into yokusebenza' to ensure her learners understand one of the central points from this passage.

Dissecting the original story text in J1–J2 reveals this little passage as grammatically dense and complex. Interpreting past tenses, comparative adjectives and a relative clause is necessary to decipher its meaning. Being able to interpret the shift from simple past ('was') to past perfect ('had been') in J1 is important for understanding the sequence of events that Oliver *first* lived with Mrs Mann and *then* went to live in the workhouse. The teacher relanguages this sequence by *bringing together* the resources from the text with others from the classroom repertoire, but she stays within an already homogenised classroom repertoire. She *sorts out* the complex past tenses from the original passage and brings the resources from the story together with simple past forms and the likely familiar Standard English adverbs of time: 'before', 'first' (J3) and 'now' (J4–J5), illustrating the sequence of events. The importance of clarifying the order in which events occur in complex stories is illustrated throughout Section 4.3, where this same teacher elaborately relanguaged Standard English verb forms in different past tenses via Khayelitshan tense and aspect morphology. Here, she abandons such morphology and instead actualises possibilities that are familiar enough to learners but that simultaneously count as Standard English ('before', 'first', 'now') for the same purpose. With the resources she chooses, she therefore not only sheds light on the content of the test but also demonstrates englishing, which the learners will need in their written responses.

Conceptually, it is central to point out again that the relanguaging mechanism of *sorting out* and *bringing together* is the same as it was in Section 4.3.2 and also in the task instruction with 'uangry'. This communality, however, normally remains invisible, because no statist nomolanguage boundaries are crossed in the case of the exam opening here. An instance like this would therefore conventionally be described as 'rephrasing' while, as soon as nomolanguage boundaries are crossed, studies would speak of translanguaging or code-switching. This distinction only occurs if we fundamentally rely on the statist vision of language and therefore conflate linguistic features and nomolanguages. This view hides relanguaging as the common, underlying linguistic ordering and sorting mechanism that is at work in homogenised as well as in heterogeneous spatial repertoires.

Back to the exam: Besides the complex past tenses, in Step 2 the teacher also attends to another part of this passage where it states that Oliver is now 'even less happy in the workhouse', because his hunger is worsened by having to work (J1–J2). This implies that he didn't have to work at Mrs Mann's house, where he lived before. From J4 to J5, the teacher makes this information explicit by saying: 'And in Mrs Mann's house he didn't have to work, but now, since he is staying at the workhouse, in the workhouse Oliver has to work now'. The teacher doesn't rely on her learners to infer this information from the original text. Also in those lines, she repeatedly mentions the words 'work' and 'workhouse', emphasising 'work' as an important theme. We saw this teacher making implicit information and subtle undertones explicit before, for example in her use of the hortative 'ma-' (Section 4.3.4). We see the same didactics of explicitness here, just within the statist confines of Standard English.

Also here, looking for *re-* instead of *trans*languaging allows us to see the parallels between these explicit-making strategies. On the look out for a transcendence of nomolanguages, we can only discover the didactics of explicitness in Chapter 4, because 'mayibe yichicken' strikes us as made up of resources associated with different nomolanguages. In contrast to that, *re-* makes us look into the before and after, into different ways of saying things, into the dynamics of a linguistic space. Spatially looking for relanguaging doesn't confine us to seeing like a state. It doesn't allow us a convenient 'either-or' focus on homogeneity or heterogeneity. Then we see the parallels between 'mayibe yichicken' and 'in Mrs Mann's house he didn't have to work', which, from a *trans*-perspective, would fall into two completely different categories of language use – one translingual and one monolingual – and would not be analysed conjunctively at all. *Re-* helps us see homogeneity and heterogeneity at the same time, *trans-* tempts us to leave one behind and remain dependent on the statist vision. Only through the statist lens do these strategies look different, because it makes us see in nomolanguages. If we see heterogeneity and languaging as the norm, we see all the ways in which such strategies of explicit-making are actually the same. Through a resolutely applied relanguaging lens, therefore, heterogeneous languaging and homogenised nomolanguages stop looking qualitatively different from one another. In Chapter 6, I show why it is essential to dissolve this alleged binary between languaging and nomolanguages, as it opens up new possibilities of adapting language tests to take into account the particular linguistic skills in spaces like Khayelitsha.

Coming back from these conceptual excursions, we now follow the teacher when she clarifies the causal connection between the fact that Oliver has to work now and that he is becoming hungrier.

5.3.4 Making Oliver hungrier via noun class agreement

Repetition Lesson Transcript J	
T = Teacher	**bold print** = language as read from the story normal print = classroom languaging/englishing *(italics)* = *(englishing added by the author)*

1	T:	**Oliver was even less happy in the workhouse than he had been with Mrs Mann.**
2		**He now had to work, which made him even hungrier.** It means that before Oliver
3		went to stay at the workhouse, he first stayed with Mrs Mann. And in Mrs
4		Mann's house he didn't have to work, but now, since he is staying at the
5		workhouse, in the workhouse Oliver has to work now. It makes him even more
6		hungrier. Imlambisa ngakumbi into yokusebenza *(It makes him especially hungry*
7		*this thing of working).*

Repetition of Circle XIII

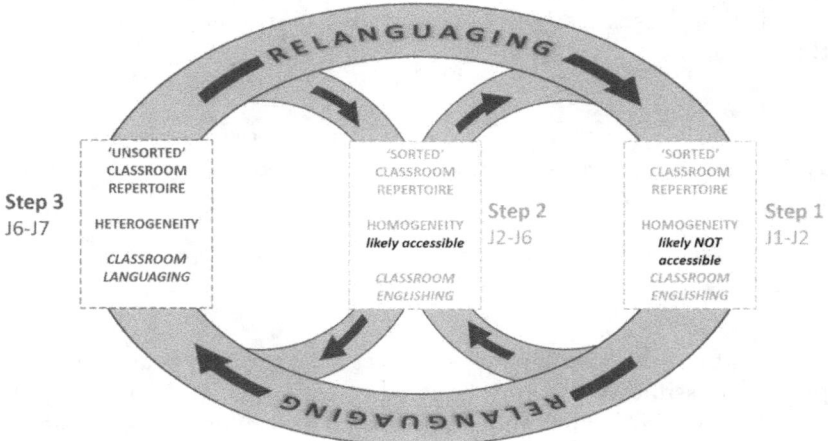

The connection between working and becoming hungrier is described like this: 'He now had to work, which made him even hungrier' (J1–J2). This is a complex relative construction where the relative pronoun 'which' refers to a situation – Oliver having to work. Relanguaging the relative clause into more accessible classroom englishing (Step 2), the teacher first disentangles it from the main clause 'He now had to work'. She relanguages this main clause first into: '…but now, since he is staying at the workhouse, in the workhouse Oliver has to work now' (J4–J5). She repeatedly emphasises the connection between Oliver staying in the workhouse and him having to work now.

Starting in J5, she now turns to '…which made him even hungrier' (J2) and relanguages this relative clause twice into:

(1) It makes him even more hungrier (Step 2, J5–J6).
(2) Imlambisa ngakumbi into yokusebenza (Step 3, J6).

In the first version, she clarifies the comparative aspect of 'even hungrier' by adding 'more'. This creates an unconventional phrase 'even more hungrier', but 'more' gives learners a useful hint at the meaning of the comparative adjective form 'hungrier'.

The teacher now also uses 'it' as an anaphoric pronoun to refer to 'the working' that makes Oliver even hungrier. As discussed in Sections 4.3.6 and 5.2.6, 'it' is not a very clear reference tracking device for Khayelitshan learners, because of the multiplicity of its possible referents in a situation where a thorough understanding of the context cannot be presumed. When the teacher then goes full circle (Step 3) and includes Khayelitshan resources, she facilitates clearer reference tracking by drawing on the often-mentioned noun class agreement. This is best illustrated by looking into the morphological make-up of this passage:

i-	-m-	-lamb-	-is-	-a	ngakumbi	in-	-to
SM9	OM1a	become hungry	CAUS	FV	especially	NPx9	thing

ya-	-uku-	-sebenz-	-a	*(It makes him especially hungry this thing of working.)*			
POSS9	INFIN	work	FV				

The familiar languaging resources the teacher draws on here prevent possible confusion about what causes Oliver's hunger. The initial 'i-' (SM9) in 'imlambisa' *(it makes him hungry)* signals agreement with a noun in class 9, here: 'into' *(the thing)*, followed by the qualification 'yokusebenza' *(of working)*. The agreement markers of class 9 clarify that *the work* causes Oliver – here represented by '-m-' as the OM1a for 'uOliver' in class 1a – to become hungrier. This critical understanding of causality would have likely been lost on many learners when having to be inferred from the story alone. With regard to clarifying referential relationships in this space, Khayelitshan morphology proves again to be a particularly useful set of linguistic possibilities in a didactics that makes these relationships more explicit than what Standard English would allow for. The fact that the teacher actualises them here, rather than continuously confining herself to Standard English, also shows that she now prioritises a clear understanding on the part of her learners over adherence to statist prescriptions of monolingualism. She orients more towards her learners (left side of the relanguaging circle) than towards the state (right side). The fact that both orientations are open to her illustrates again how she is the pivot between her learners' linguistic realities and the official demands for Standard English (see also Section 4.5.2) and how that pivotal position maps onto her language practices.

I now undertake a little excursion into territory that is not the analytical focus of this book, which overall remains mostly concerned with traditionally *linguistic* elements of the classroom repertoire. In this particular lesson, however, where the teacher is dealing with a socially, spatially and historically very distant story in a testing activity, it seems important to consider how she tries to make what happens in the text relatable for her learners. The morphemes and lexemes she uses cannot alone account for that. We will see in the next section how she enrolls other resources from the spatial repertoire and her own body into the activity.

5.3.5 Opening language up and bringing Oliver Twist to Khayelitsha

In what follows, it seems that the teacher attempts to make it possible for learners to imagine Oliver Twist and his companions as real people with whom they can relate. We jump forward in the test story to where the boys – especially one of them – begin to show their anger about being hungry at the workhouse (I13–I15, p. 145):

Lesson Transcript K	
T = Teacher	**bold print** = language as read from the story normal print = classroom languaging/englishing *(italics)* = *(englishing added by the author)* [underlined] = [body languaging]

1 T: **At last, they got so wild with hunger that one boy, who was tall for his age, told**
2   **the others that unless he had another bowl of soup daily, he was afraid he might**
3   **eat the boy who slept next to him.** Oh: **At last that they got so wild with hunger**
4   **that one boy, who was tall for his age,** I think that boy was like Likho [turning
5   towards and looking at Likho, a boy in class sitting in front to the left of the
6   teacher]. Likho is eleven years old like all of you guys but he's a little bit bigger
7   and tall for his age. They say one boy that was ahm tall for his age, **told the others**
8   **that unless he had another bowl of soup daily, he was afraid he might eat the boy**
9   **who slept next to him.** It means that that boy was so hungry, that he wanted, or he
10   was thinking of eating one boy, whatever boy, that will sleep next to him. He was
11   threatening the boys that: 'No, unless I get more soup, I'm afraid that I'm going
12   to eat anyone that is going to sleep next to him'. Can you imagine? Someone
13   telling you that he's going to eat you! You will stay awake for the whole night,
14   you won't sleep, you'd be afraid that: 'Maybe I won't see tomorrow'. Let's see
15   what happens then.

When the teacher in K4–K7 attends to the idiomatic expression 'being tall for one's age', this time it is not familiar words or morphemes that take centre stage in her relanguaged version of it, but a familiar body signified by a familiar name: Likho. Likho is a tall, rather strongly built boy and he and his tall-for-his-age body are part of the classroom repertoire on this day during this assessment activity. By naming him and turning towards him, the teacher makes him and his body relevant to the activity (Kusters *et al.*, 2017) and uses him as a meaning-making resource. This is reminiscent of Pennycook and Otsuji's (2015: 8) observation about food items and their role in market interactions. They say that 'items such as yellow zucchini (the food rather than the linguistic form) play a mediating role in the metrolingual action'. Here, it is also Likho as a body and a Khayelitshan boy whom the teacher makes relevant as a resource to clarify the expression 'being tall for one's age'.

Advantageously, the notion of spatial repertoire can account for the fact that 'virtually anything in our world can be enlisted to signify' (Baynham & Lee, 2019: 108). I argue that in the space of the English classroom, where activities are quite language focused, we could look at objects or bodies like Likho's as languaging resources in fact not much different from the morpheme 'u-' (Section 5.2). We saw how 'u-' was enrolled (by being uttered) to make the inverted commas around 'angry' *audible*. In this case, Likho's body is enrolled (by being pointed at) to make the tall boy in the story *visible* in the classroom and also to relanguage the expression 'being tall for one's age' into a bodily presence. Both 'u-' and 'Likho's body' are part of the classroom repertoire and thus potential languaging resources for this activity. Only the necessary processes of enrolment are different: 'u-' has to be uttered, while 'Likho's body' can be turned towards or pointed at. Once enrolled, however, 'u-' and 'Likho's body' carry their semantics into the activity and co-constitute, for example, a relanguaged story.

In his physical presence, however, Likho's body can do more than just help to illustrate and clarify the expression 'being tall for one's age'. By making Likho relevant, the teacher transports a story character into the classroom, contracting the distance in space–time between the Oliver Twist story and the learners' present realities. From K11 to K12, the teacher now lets Likho (or the tall boy from the story?) speak directly to the learners by relanguaging parts of the complicated indirect speech (K2–K3) into direct speech, quoting the tall boy (or Likho from the classroom?). This direct speech version firstly simplifies the language, as for example the conditional forms 'had' and 'might' are *sorted out*, and secondly it also turns her learners into potential addressees of the tall boy's threat, involving them emotionally and blurring the line between this old, faraway story and the here and now. Starting in K12, she builds on that by asking her learners directly: 'Can you imagine?', prompting them to put themselves into the shoes of the characters, imagining sleepless nights scared to be eaten by the tall boy (or by Likho?).

With the direct speech interludes and her recruitment of Likho, the teacher relanguages this part of the story into a stage play of sorts – rather unexpected in a formal assessment scenario. The following sequence shows this theatrical character even more clearly. At this point, the boys had held a council and decided that Oliver, after this evening's soup, must go to the servant and ask for more food. This transcript sets in when the boys had just finished their dinner (I20–I21, p. 145).

Lesson Transcript L	
T = Teacher	**bold print** = language as read from the story normal print = classroom languaging/englishing *(italics)* = *(englishing added by the author)* [underlined] = [body languaging]

1	T:	The boys whispered to each other and made the[7] signs at Oliver, while his
2		neighbours pushed him. The, I think the boys were like this [moving her mouth

3	as if whispering, waving and making signs at the learners in class, imitating what
4	the boys do to Oliver]. Some guys were even pushing him [stepping forward
5	toward the learners, hands stretched out, pretending to push one of them], telling
6	him to go to the servant and ask for more soup.

Here, the teacher relanguages the description of whispering, sign-making and pushing into a stage play–like performance. After her short introduction (second language [L2]), she relanguages the verb forms 'whispered' and 'made signs' into imitating mouth movements and waving at the learners as if sending them off somewhere. She also performs the action of pushing while verbally relanguaging the past tense form 'pushed' into the past continuous 'were pushing', emphasising the procedural character of the action that she is performing with her body. Linguistic resources here co-produce meaning with the actions that the teacher's body is modelling – very similar to what Baynham and Lee observed about the verbal and embodied practices of a capoeira instructor during one of his sessions. The 'elements fluently brought together' (Baynham & Lee, 2019: 112) are language and bodily movements.

Such fluent assembling of language and movements as a teaching strategy is described by the Grade 4 teacher when we asked her what advice she would give a new English teacher starting at Khayelitsha Primary with regard to how language is best used in the classroom. She said:

They must speak English and have actions, use gestures. Then if you say: 'The boy falls [pretending to fall off her chair]', you know you must use that. (Interview Grade 4 Teacher)

Even though we asked her specifically about advice for 'language use', she naturally includes embodied actions and gestures as essential elements of meaning-making, pointing to a restrictive and artificial conceptual divide between language and other modalities (Kusters *et al.*, 2017). This is well illustrated by the Grade 5 teacher in this test lesson, who draws on languaging resources from morphemes to words, to bodies, via gestures to turning towards, naming and mimicking when relanguaging the test story into accessible languaging. The teacher appears like an actor or storyteller who performs by means of heterogeneous spatial elements that she assembles from the classroom repertoire into a 'skillfully timed sequencing of reanimated words and reanimated actions' with the effect that 'for a few lines, the audience can sustain the brief illusion of being witness to the actual event' (Streeck, 2009: 147).

Speaking about how she uses language and her body when mediating between a story and the learners, this teacher says:

They [the learners] love it a lot. They enjoy it. They pay more attention. Can you imagine coming to class you just read the story. No body language, no facial expressions. It won't be interesting to the learners. It won't at all. They need to see that and I like it generally. Even if I'm not in class, even in my home, I like to play with my face and all that. The learners like it. (Interview Grade 5 Teacher)

Despite my general focus on the traditionally linguistic elements of the classroom repertoire, what I have tried to demonstrate with the above examples is that the repertoire is not limited to such. Instead, in her quest to make Oliver Twist and his companions more present in the Khayelitshan classroom, the teacher also recruits from and contributes to the classroom repertoire resources that don't conventionally count as language.

Spatial repertoires allow us to account for the fact that when teachers use 'resources available at particular times and in particular spaces, they don't separate the linguistic from the embodied, but make meaning through repertoires of signs which integrate verbal and body action' (Blackledge & Creese, 2017: 255). Maybe, under these circumstances, it makes sense to describe the classroom repertoire as being 'resemiotized' (Baynham & Lee, 2019: 160) into a different order rather than relanguaged. Or we could describe these repertoires of signs instead as *repertoires of heterogeneous languaging resources*, opening up the notion of language and the discipline of linguistics to include the conventionally non-linguistic – a line of argument I will not pursue further at this point.

With these rather entertaining elements of the teacher's efforts, one could almost forget that we are in the middle of a formal testing activity. The teacher is still under pressure to ensure that most of her learners pass the test. Looking at one of the test questions below – in connection with how the teacher relanguages the story – shows a highly strategic intervention to prepare learners to answer this question.

5.3.6 Approaching the questions through relanguaging as test coaching

Below, we see Question 1.4 from the test paper. For the correct answer, learners would get one point.

1.4 Why did the bowls never need washing? (1)
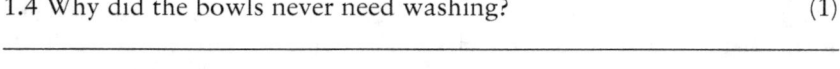

It refers to how the children in the workhouse get so little food that they polish their bowls in order to get as much soup out of them as they possibly can (I7–I12, p. 145). Therefore, the bowls don't need washing because they have already been polished clean. Looking more closely into the teacher's relanguaged version of I7–I12 reveals how she seamlessly includes an answer – or at least very detailed hints towards an answer – to Question 1.4 into the relanguaged story.

Lesson Transcript M	
T = Teacher	bold print = language as read from the story normal print = classroom languaging/englishing (italics) = (englishing added by the author)

1	T:	**The bowls never needed washing.** We don't know why. We are still going to find
2		out. **The boys polished them with their spoons till they shone. When they had**
3		**done this, which never took very long, they would sit staring with their wide eyes**
4		**at the pot as if they could have eaten even the metal of which it was made.** Ahm
5		the, the bowls didn't need washing. Zazinganeedi kuvaswa *(They didn't need to*
6		*be washed)*. Why? Because the boys polished them with their spoons. They wiped
7		them with their spoons. They wiped them so hard they, they didn't even want to
8		leave a drop of soup. They wanted to take away everything, to try and fill their
9		stomach. They say that soup in their bowls didn't take too long to eat, because it
10		was small. And their bowl never needed washing, because they were wiped with
11		the spoons. Who wiped the bowls? It was the boys. Why? They never got enough.
12		They wanted to get each and every drop of soup from that bowl.

With the complexified relanguaging circle we can visualise what the teacher is doing here:

Circle XIV

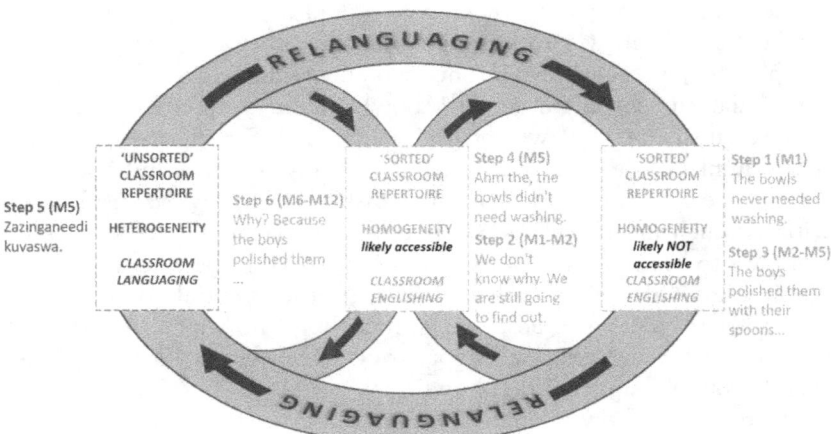

Step 1 (M1) is the reading of the sentence that the test question refers to: 'The bowls never needed washing'. Step 2 (M1–M2) is an Englished interlude with which the teacher already prompts her learners to think

about why the bowls never needed washing and makes them anticipate an answer to that question in the course of the story. In Step 3 (M2–M5), she then reads two more highly complex sentences, featuring the irregular past tense verb 'shone' and opaque constructions like 'would sit staring with their wide eyes' (M2–M5). But she doesn't attend to them much in her mediation. Instead, in Step 4 (M5) the teacher reverts back to 'The bowls never needed washing', by relanguaging it into 'The bowls didn't need washing'. The next relanguaging move then leaves the middle box via the arrow at the bottom left, bringing the teacher full circle to the inclusion of Khayelitshan resources in Step 5 (M5).

'Zazinganeedi kuvaswa' underpins a point made in Section 4.4.2, namely that the same verb can be a Khayelitshan as well as a Standard English resource. The verb root '-need-' regularly features in Khayelitshan languaging. I have often heard people say – or I have said myself – 'Hayi, andiyineedi' *(No, I don't need it)*. In this case, however, because the verb 'need' appears in the original text (**'The bowls never needed washing'**) and in the first relanguaged version ('The bowls didn't need washing'), it seems more accurate to describe 'zazinganeedi' as an *in situ* assemblage of 'need' as a resource from the story with some Khayelitshan morphology.

My focus is on Step 6 (M6–M12), where the teacher has sorted out the Khayelitshan resources again and – in accessible classroom englishing – follows 'Zazinganeedi kuvaswa' up with 'Why?', to then basically model the answer to Question 1.4 with: 'Because they polished them with their spoons'. Why-questions inducing because-answers are a recurring pattern in the English classroom and the teacher here brings it to her learners' minds, preparing them, as I would argue, to produce a very similar because-answer to Question 1.4 when they get there. From the complex sentences in M2–M5, she then only relanguages a few points in her mediation, leaving out how the bowls 'shone' or that the boys 'could have eaten the metal of which they were made'. She therefore *sorts out* some chunks of the story that are linguistically complex and not immediately relevant to the test questions. Instead, she provides her learners with as much inspiration as possible for approaching the test question from M6 to M12. In the last two lines (M11–M12), she even simulates a question-and-answer game that summarises the essential points learners need to remember for Question 1.4, namely: 'Who wiped the bowls? It was the boys. Why? They never got enough. They wanted to get each and every[8] drop of soup from that bowl'.

Here, we see how relanguaging, often a practice that attends to the linguistic strengths and struggles of learners and is oriented towards making them understand Standard English, can also be the basis for a test coaching strategy aimed at making learners satisfy the demands of educational authorities instantiated in the test paper. The teacher's focus is not on making learners understand *each and every* detail of what is going on in the story (as in Chapter 4), but on modelling exactly those Standard English resources that they will need to answer the question. This also explains why the teacher so stringently homogenises the classroom repertoire in this sequence and uses almost no Khayelitshan resources. I argue that she is setting the tone – or ordering the repertoire – for the writing activity to follow, which will require a homogenised code: SWE. Here lies a parallel to what the Grade 4 teacher did with regard to 'uangry' (see Section 5.2.6), where she used the morpheme as a metalanguaging device but *sorted it out* as soon as she instructed the learners on what to write. Relanguaging, therefore – also here in the testing scenario – is regularly used to prepare learners for the production of SWE in their responses.

In contrast to work that emphasises how state language policies don't reach spaces like Khayelitsha and how learners and teachers there are cut-off from standard linguistic norms (Blommaert *et al.*, 2005), I argue that teachers' linguistic choices in the classroom and their relanguaging strategies show that language policy pressures do reach them. Their practices – especially in classroom activities directed at writing – show that they are aware of the need to focus on seeing language like a state (as bounded, separate and homogeneous) in order to give their learners the agency to comply with the linguistic demands of educational administrators in writing. Relanguaging therefore accomplishes different things in a classroom space where writing is involved or aimed at and where statist demands therefore assert their presence more strongly than when this is not the case (as in Chapter 4). The details of this linguistic sorting practice therefore unfold relative to space.

Let's return to the testing activity. After she is done coaching the test story, the teacher reads and relanguages the test questions, giving the learners time to write their answer after each question. Here is what she does when she gets to the much-mentioned Question 1.4:

Transcript of Test Question 1.4		
T = Teacher	**bold print** normal print *(italics)*	= language as read from the story = classroom languaging/englishing = *(englishing added by the author)*

T: **1.4 Why did the bowls never need washing?** Yintoni ebangela ukuba ezaa zitya zabo zingadingi kuvaswa? *(What is it that causes those bowls of theirs not to need washing?)* **Why did the bowls never need washing?**

It stands out that when the teacher gets to the test question, she relanguages it completely via Khayelitshan resources before she sorts them out again and repeats the original Standard English question. This may have to do with the fact that, while she had already read the Oliver Twist story several times in class, the learners probably don't know the questions yet. Additionally, as we have heard from the Grade 4 teacher (Section 5.1.2), learners struggle with the language used in instructions and questions.

Teachers are therefore likely to use all resources at their disposal to ensure understanding, especially in a testing activity where learners' answers will be marked and can become visible beyond the classroom walls. Relanguaging as heterogenisation – as the *bringing together* of Standard English and Khayelitshan resources – therefore becomes more important again as the teacher is oriented towards the linguistic needs of her learners when approaching the test questions.

Returning to Question 1.4, a Khayelitshan languaging version that stays closer to the original could have looked like this: 'Kutheni ezaa zitya zingadingi kuvaswa?' *(Why do the bowls not need washing?).* However, the teacher makes use of 'yintoni' *(what is it),* an interrogative that would be answered by identifying something. Here it is followed by the relative clause 'ebangela' *(that causes).*[9] Together these languaging resources emphasise – more than the simple interrogative 'why' or 'kutheni' – that the learners need to identify something that has actively caused the bowls not to need washing. The teacher then repeats the original question again, ending with 'Why did the bowls never need washing?' – a retreat into the confines of Standard English with 'why' signalling that a because-answer is wanted.

To sum up: compared to the eagle story (Chapter 4), where the teacher gave very nuanced insights into every single sentence, the test questions make her relanguaging more selective here. She is evading some parts of the story (M3–M4), even though they are unlikely to be understood by the majority in class. In turn, she rather invests more time into story parts that learners will be asked about later. She also integrates prefabricated question-and-answer games (e.g. 'Why? Because the boys polished them with their spoons' [M6]; 'Who wiped the bowls? It was the boys. Why? They never got enough' [M11]), giving attentive learners the chance to simply copy what she is saying as the answer to a test question. She therefore significantly increases the odds of them mastering the test.

5.3.7 Reading a question in a way that is similar to the answer

By helping her learners to produce something that educational authorities recognise as valid SWE answers, the teacher undermines the way in which assessment is thought out to work as a measure of learners' ability to engage autonomously with testing material. This becomes even clearer when we look at the final question, Question 1.7. It differs from Question 1.4, to which the answer could be drawn more or less literally from the story. This enables the teacher to model a possible answer to the question while relanguaging the story itself. She doesn't, however, repeat this possible answer when it is time for the learners to answer Question 1.4. This shows that, to some extent, she does take seriously that this is a testing activity and therefore she doesn't make it too easy for the learners.

However, in Question 1.7, the learners are asked to reflect upon their own life in comparison to that of Oliver Twist:

1.7 Explain how your life is different to Oliver's life. (2)

_____
_____
_____

Here, the teacher cannot sneak the answer into the relanguaged story, because there the learners' lives play no role. Rather, an answer to this question has to build on a more abstract understanding of Oliver's circumstances as narrated in the story, because Khayelitshan learners have to find a way of comparing their own lives to his. Even though in Section 5.3.5 I have shown that the teacher has done quite a bit to create a certain connection between her learners and the story characters, what she does with Question 1.7 shows that she still doubts that they could master this task by themselves. Not only does she relanguage the question, but she arguably also answers it in large parts for her learners.

Lesson Transcript N of Test Question 1.7	
T = Teacher	**bold print** = **language as read from the story** normal print = classroom languaging/englishing *(italics)* = *(englishing added by the author)*

1 T: **1.7. Explain how your life is different to Oliver's life.** Chaza ukuba ubomi bakho
2   bohlukeka njani kokaOliver *(Explain how your life differs from that of Oliver).* Remember,
3   uOliver used to stay from one house or one place to another. To me that on… that statement
4   says that Oliver didn't have the parents. Because at the beginning of the story they say, he
5   used to stay with Mrs Mann. From Mrs Mann's house he went to stay in the
6   workhouse where he was starving for three full months. Now the question is, explain how
7   your life is different to Oliver's life.

Using several examples, I have demonstrated how the Khayelitshan languaging resources in N1–N2 facilitate reference tracking for learners with regard to whose life is different from whose life. Here, I focus on the rest of the teacher's explanation. First, she recaps how Oliver was always moving from place to place (N3). The 'u-' in 'uOliver' is again the noun class prefix from class 1a (discussed extensively in Section 5.2), here in its use before proper nouns (Contini-Morava, 2008; Futuse, 2018). Referring to Oliver as 'uOliver' – the Khayelitshan way – pulls the British boy into the Khayelitshan classroom, making him a child like any other there (uLikho, uAkhona, etc.). Establishing this parallel helps in approaching a test question that asks Khayelitshan learners to compare their lives to that of Oliver.

The teacher's description of how Oliver is constantly moving to different places is then a hint for those learners who aren't constantly on the move, to quote this fact as a difference between their lives and Oliver's life when answering the question. She then goes on to explain that Oliver's varying places of residence indicate that he doesn't have parents, adding information that is not contained in the story and doing the job of thinking beyond what is immediately evident in the text for her learners. She also repeats that Oliver was starving for three months, as if to remind the class that this is another factor that makes Oliver's life different. It also stands out that she only englishes from N3 to N7, modelling the homogenised, sorted classroom repertoire learners have to actualise in their writing.

Because the teacher's hints at possible answers are quite obvious, we played this sequence for her in the interview. In response, she first explains that she has a mix of very weak, mediocre and well-performing learners in one class and goes on to say:

> But because we lack time to divide the class into two when they are writing the examination, we end up, especially me, I end up ah reading a question in a way that is similar to the answer sometimes. That is very close to the answer. (Interview G5 Teacher)

Asked if things could work without such help, she says: 'If I can just read the questions, without making even one example, then half of the class will fail' (Interview Grade 5 Teacher). Even though she is aware, as she also points out, that her practices skew the test results, she sees no other way. This shows again how there is a rupture between the curriculum demands and what learners can reasonably master in Khayelitshan Grade 5 English classrooms. This rupture firstly has to do with testing material being developed based on the assumption that learners received a lot of English teaching in the Foundation Phase – which is not usually the case (Section 1.4). Secondly, in the schooling space of Khayelitsha Primary, learners have to acquire two statist repertoires (Standard Xhosa and Standard English) early on. Arriving with heterogeneous Khayelitshan languaging, they therefore have plenty of linguistic *sorting out* to do that is also not taken into account in the development of teaching and testing materials. This is exactly because the heterogeneity of Khayelitshan languaging and therefore the particular predicament this two-nomolanguage policy produces is rendered invisible in the statist vision.

However, instead of making this rupture between official linguistic expectations and local realities visible to departmental authorities via the learners' marks (by actually letting 'half the class fail'), this teacher has developed test coaching strategies that help learners produce at least some of the expected SWE responses – enough for most of them to pass. This leads back to what she said earlier (Section 5.3.1):

Repetition of Interview Excerpt j (p. 171)	
T = Teacher	R1 = Researcher 1 (Lara Krause, author)
	R2 = Researcher 2 (Tessa Dowling, supervisor)

```
1   T:   I become scared because the more learners that fail, the department is after you.
2        So you need to try by all means, you must be able to explain the case. Because
3        when we do the class work, the learner does good.
4   R1:  Do you know what will happen if, let's say, the department would 'come after
5        you', as you said?
6   T:   I don't know really, but I know that they need the learners to pass. You must make
7        sure that you don't get the high number of failures. Her statement shows how she
8        thinks that if she wouldn't coach the test and actually let a lot of learners fail, the
9        department wouldn't take this as a hint that something might be wrong with the
10       curriculum or centralised, standardised assessment. Rather, the blame would be
11       put on her as the teacher and departmental authorities would 'come after her',
12       because 'they need the learners to pass'.
```

Looking at what I have discussed in the introduction regarding the widespread tendency to make township teachers the scapegoats for the underperformance of their learners (Section 1.5), this teacher is likely right in suspecting that she would be blamed by the department. The official narrative in South Africa is that ongoing educational inequality, which materialises in large differences between the results of learners in township and rural schools compared to ex-Model C schools, 'is not the fault of the curriculum, but the result of systemic non-curriculum causes', one of them allegedly 'weak educator knowledge capacity' (Department of Education, 2017: 22).

With the prospect of having her competency questioned more readily than the administrative system that she is a part of, the teacher prefers to make it look as if she and her learners are coping with the curriculum demands instead of risking any attention. With the arrival of the test paper, relanguaging can therefore turn into a mechanism that facilitates a test coaching practice. It then becomes the pivotal process that allows the teacher to give her learners the agency to pass tests. Relanguaging is then no longer much of a didactics that helps her learners gain access to Standard English but rather a tool to repair the rupture between curriculum expectations and the Khayelitshan linguistic and educational realities.

In light of what I have discussed up to now, it is clear that *relanguaging and what it accomplishes is always relative to space and needs to be described accordingly*. Assertions of the general functions of heterogeneous language practices (Ferguson, 2009; García & Leiva, 2014; Probyn, 2015), be they described as code-switching or translanguaging, aren't helpful to gain insight into the details of what matters when teaching and testing English in Khayelitsha. Instead, the spatial assemblage – here changed drastically by the test paper – is central for identifying the functions of particular language practices in classrooms and other spaces for that matter.

5.4 Chapter Discussion

5.4.1 Looking closely at u and Likho

I have spent much of this chapter tracing the morpheme 'u-' through classrooms, teacher interviews and also through Bantu linguists' work. These methods helped in making visible why exactly 'u-' is so useful here. Uing is an example of how Khayelitshan teachers enrol heterogeneous languaging resources that are absent from Standard English for analytical purposes (Section 5.2.2). 'u-' is used by all three English teachers in this study. It facilitates the quoting of linguistic elements in metalanguaging and can act as an englishing device that marks resources that might either be used as Khayelitshan or Standard English ones to be enrolled as the latter in a particular space. Such insights into what appear to be minute details are valuable because they unsettle common-sense assumptions about language. The Grade 6 teacher said '"u-" is not a language that we use in English', but actually it is sometimes exactly that: *An englishing device, a resource that is not codified as Standard English but used in watchfulness towards the boundaries and rules of that code* (Section 5.2.3). Such an observation can only be made if consistently walking the other way. Any analysis that accepts – either explicitly or in a subtler, hidden premise – the conflation of linguistic features and nomolanguages will categorise 'u-' (again im- or explicitly) as a Xhosa prefix. This, in turn, makes the insight that 'u-' can be an englishing device – literally a marker of Englishness – theoretically impossible.

The possibility of seeing 'u-' as an englishing device is a result of taking detours that led to a *re-* rather than a *trans*-perspective. This perspective produces such detailed accounts of individual linguistic features, because it doesn't allow us to jump to conclusions about types of words or languaging based on surface-level identifications. Code-switching or translanguaging accounts, in which this conflation is not thoroughly dissolved, then remain undercomplex compared to the insights we can gain when spatially looking for relanguaging and taking the accomplishments of linguistic detail seriously (Section 5.2.3). But what counts as *linguistic* detail was not always clear. Considering the importance that teachers ascribe to body languaging in their English classrooms and the role it played in the test mediation (Section 5.3.5), there is certainly a need to extend ideas like relanguaging to accommodate resources that are conventionally not associated with language and linguistics – such as gestures, body movements, bodies themselves, etc. I have argued here that conventional *linguistic* features might not be that different from such embodied resources, as the only thing that differentiates a morpheme like 'u-' from a body like Likho's is the way in which it is recruited into the meaning-making activity. So, depending on how much we are willing to open up the notion of 'language' and the discipline of linguistics and to see heterogeneity as the norm, we could describe both, Likho's body and 'u-', as *languaging resources* (Section 5.3.5). It is, therefore, not only about disentangling the association of linguistic features with nomolanguages. Asking what counts as a languaging resource sheds light on a further entanglement that might need to be loosened in order to adequately analyse (classroom) languaging – that of languaging with those resources that can be uttered or written and the outsourcing of resources that require other recruitment processes into different modalities. While it remains a side note here, important work in this regard is being done in studies that employ the concept of spatial repertoires, exploiting its full potential to account for interactional resources beyond but not separate from more traditionally linguistic ones (Baynham & Lee, 2019; Blackledge & Creese, 2017; Canagarajah, 2018; Pennycook & Otsuji, 2015).

5.4.2 Relanguaging and (test) writing

In terms of relanguaging, the example of the Grade 4 reading activity (Section 5.1.3) and the close investigation of the instructions (Section 5.2) have shown that the mechanism is not only established in the Grade 5 classroom in focus in Chapter 4, but also in the Grade 4 classroom. By zooming in on constructions like 'Ndifuna imeaning yakhe', it became clear that relanguaging can also mean *sorting out* potential stumbling blocks before actualising linguistic possibilities (see also Section 4.5.6). Asking what 'yakhe' can do that 'it' cannot do and following 'it' into another classroom scenario (where the Grade 5 teacher spelled it out to her learners) showed how sorting out 'it' or 'its meaning' and choosing instead 'imeaning yakhe' avoid the potential referential and phonological ambiguity that comes with relying on 'it' in this space (Section 5.2.6). The point about the referential confusion often caused by Standard English third-person pronouns will be further substantiated in Chapter 6.

Using the example of (u)angry in the relanguaged instruction, I have also argued that teachers use relanguaging to systematically prepare learners for writing. Through *sorting out* Khayelitshan resources (from 'uangry' to 'Write "angry"') and balancing the classroom repertoire towards homogeneity, they set the tone for learners to produce homogenised SWE in their workbooks (Section 5.2.6). So, when writing is aimed at in an activity, this influences how we have to interpret certain relanguaging moves and what they accomplish. Another layer of complexity is added when the aim of writing is part of a comparably high-stakes testing activity (Section 5.3). Here, I have argued that the increased departmental pressure to comply with official expectations for linguistic homogeneity has the classroom repertoire often balanced towards homogeneity with the teacher only rarely including Khayelitshan resources in heterogenising moves. I have illustrated this scenario with a complexified relanguaging circle that includes:

...the teacher's orientation towards Khayelitshan learners via classroom languaging,	her attempt to accommodate statist demands for homogeneity and the needs of her learners simultaneously via accessible classroom englishing	and the linguistic expectations of state administrations and their agents as instantiated in the SWE in the test paper (Section 5.3.2).

Within this circle, we have seen relanguaging unfold as a mechanism that facilitates a test coaching practice. The teacher, for example, sorted out those parts of the story that were linguistically complicated and not immediately relevant to the test questions – making relanguaging much more selective than it was in Chapter 4, where the goal was to make learners understand but not to make them pass a test. Via accessible classroom englishing, the teacher also provided elaborate hints at the answers to the test questions, equipping her learners with the agency to respond in SWE (Sections 5.3.6 and 5.3.7). She rarely went full circle to include Khayelitshan resources in her mediation, keeping the classroom repertoire mostly balanced towards homogeneity. This way, I have argued, she modelled the type of language use learners would need for their test answers.

The above are techniques with which the teacher increases the odds for her learners to master the test. Simultaneously, she avoids having her own reputation put into (even more) jeopardy by keeping the number of learners who fail to a minimum, thereby reducing the likelihood of attracting negative departmental attention (Section 5.3.7). Via complex processes of relanguaging, she therefore keeps one eye on the children's future and the other on her own career as an employee of the state in education.

5.4.3 Subverting the system to keep it working

English teachers at Khayelitsha Primary know that practices like heterogeneous classroom languaging and preparatory test coaching are 'not allowed' (compare Interview Excerpt f, p. 125) but they 'just change the rules themselves' (compare Interview Excerpt d, p. 98). With strong stigmatisation from all sides, this is, in fact, an act of courage and initiative that subvert the rules of a system that teachers have identified as unfair. They aren't convinced that sameness across contexts equals fairness in South African education and so they change the rules of the game to make teaching, learning and passing tests possible. However, their practices of local resistance against statist prescriptions of monolingualism and against ideas of how assessment is supposed to work (Sections 5.2 and 5.3) are simultaneously also acts of compliance, because the only way to make learners meet the demands of the system is to subvert its rules. The formal curriculum and assessment system survives only because of how Khayelitshan teachers locally reshape it with one eye on their learners' linguistic skills and struggles and the other on the demands of state education.

Township teachers have relanguaging techniques at their disposal that range from pedagogically productive (when they are oriented towards the linguistic skills and struggles of their learners) to politically defensive (when they are oriented towards satisfying the demands of state education) and cover everything in between. Because they don't expect any real understanding from departmental authorities of the circumstances under which they teach, they'd rather not take the risk of letting their learners fail. So, while they are experts at facilitating learning under linguistically highly complicated conditions co-produced by an unfair system, they are also experts at continuously making the same system work. In Scott's words, we can summarise South African education as a system imposing a formal order that is, like any such order,

> always and to some considerable degree parasitic on informal processes, which the formal scheme doesn't recognise, without which it couldn't exist, and which it alone cannot create or maintain. (Scott, 1998: 390)

It is the teachers' agency that keeps the formal scheme running. They have knowledge of official linguistic expectations as well as of their learners' skills and struggles and they juggle these two poles – often via relanguaging. Education officials and many linguists who 'see like a state' cannot see this juggling, because they either look at homogeneous nomolanguages or heterogeneous languaging but not at both together. Therefore, they overlook how township teachers keep things together and make the system work via their complementary vision: township teachers have one eye on Khayelitsha and one eye on the state.

What we can learn for (South African) education from township teachers will be discussed in the conclusion. Before that, I turn away from teachers and, in Chapter 6, put Khayelitshan learners centre stage as they negotiate local linguistic complexities in a writing activity that gives them more freedom than usual.

6 Rewriting Nomolanguages

6.1 The Idea for a Writing Task

6.1.1 OK: Code-switching

This chapter discusses a writing task that allowed learners to describe a picture story, drawing on the full ensemble of the linguistic possibilities of the classroom, without conventional restrictions to nomolanguages. The idea for this task came about during a lesson recorded on 30 May 2016 in the Grade 5 teacher's English class. It was different from all the other lessons I had observed at the school.

On this day, the Grade 5 teacher walks into the classroom, greets the learners and instructs the whole class to stand up. She then says:

> Today I want you to try by all means to answer in English only. No Xhosa today, just English. No code-switching today, just simply English. You aren't given a chance to sit down, not unless you say something. Not unless you give me an answer. Then you'll be given an opportunity to sit down. But if you don't give me anything you will remain standing until the end of English period. (Grade 5 English Lesson 30.05.2016)

This is the only lesson I observed where a teacher explicitly announced a strict language policy for the whole lesson and even enforced it via physical means. The teacher disciplines the learners by giving Standard English, with its linguistic features and grammatical rules, immediate physical impact. Englished responses are rewarded with the comfort of sitting down, while taking different languaging routes is prohibited and silence is punished with the continuous discomfort of standing. Being among the last ones standing also puts learners in a shameful state, because their alleged inability to speak English-only is now instantiated physically and put on display via their upright bodies.

Throughout this unconventional lesson, the teacher herself englishes without exception, not enrolling any of the Khayelitshan resources from the classroom repertoire. She models what she expects from her learners in their oral responses: English-only. The core activity in this lesson is again the reading of a story but this time the learners just listen (while standing), without the text in front of them. The teacher relanguages most parts of the story about a thirsty crow trying to get water out of a jug. Her relanguaging, however, exclusively produces classroom englishing as she confines herself to Standard English resources, (re)producing a homogeneous repertoire – homogeneous from the perspective that sets the heterogeneity of the classroom repertoire as the norm (see Section 4.5.6) – during this activity. The relanguaging circle therefore looks like this in this lesson:

Circle XV

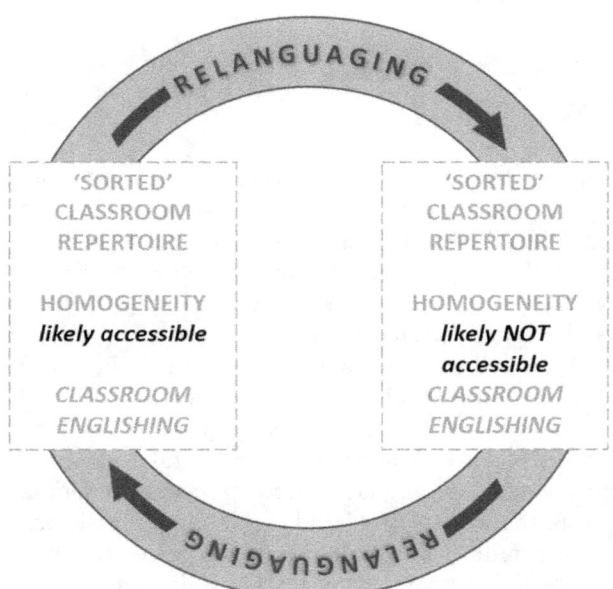

After reading and relanguaging, she then encourages learners to contribute, sometimes by asking them to explain the meaning of a word or with statements like: 'Tell me anything that you have heard in the story', 'Summarise the story' or 'Retell the story'. Learners hesitate, but one after another, they English short contributions and are allowed to sit down. Towards the end of the lesson, the teacher is left with seven learners who are still standing and whom she cannot get to utter even one word, despite repeated encouragement. That is when – after 50 minutes of englishing – she says:

Lesson Transcript O		
T = Teacher L = Learner (individual)	normal print = *(italics)* =	classroom languaging/englishing *(englishing added by the author)*

1   T: Ok, code-switching. Khawusibalisele eli bali ngesiXhosa *(Please tell us this story*
2   *in Xhosa)*. Odwa, ube namagama owafakayo weEnglish *(Odwa,... with words*
3   *that you put in English)*. Khawusibalisele ibali. Ngolwimi lwakho ke ngoku,

4		ngesiXhosa *(Please tell us the story. In your language now, in Xhosa).*
5	L:	Intaka yayibhabha... *(The bird was flying ...)*
6	T:	Icrow.
7	L:	Icrow.
8	T:	Icrow yayibhabha kwifield *(The crow was flying in the field).* I want few English
9		words.
10	L:	Icrow yayibhabha kwifields and she was seeing a jug down into...
11	T:	Mhlaba (Earth/ground).
12	L:	Into mhlaba (Into the earth/ground).
13	T:	Yes.
14	L:	And she couldn't open the jug.
15	T:	Good.

I will not give a detailed analysis of this sequence here but only summarise the points relevant for this chapter:

After her official announcement of a change in the language policy of the lesson ('OK, code-switching'), in O2 the teacher first explains that by code-switching she means speaking 'Xhosa' but putting in some 'English' words. Then she repeats the instruction to retell or summarise the story from O3 to O4 and says that the learner should 'tell the story "in her language", in "Xhosa"', but what she means is not Standard Xhosa. When the learner she addressed begins to speak in O5, using resources that would also count as Standard Xhosa ('Intaka yayibhabha...'), the teacher interrupts and relanguages her response by assembling vocabulary items from the story ('crow' and 'fields') into classroom languaging that draws on familiar morphology but integrates the targeted words 'crow' and 'field'. Assembled with Khayelitshan morphology they become 'icrow' (O6) and 'kwifield' (O8). Her comment 'I want few English words' (O8–O9), that goes along with it, shows not only that 'Xhosa' is not Standard Xhosa here, but also that 'icrow' and 'kwifields' count as sufficiently big steps towards Standard English. The teacher makes these forms count as englishing, we could say. They are assembled with watchfulness towards – even though not in complete keeping with – the boundaries of Standard English.

The learner repeats this sentence (O10) and continues with 'and she was seeing a jug down into...', having now sorted out all Khayelitshan resources from her englishing. She is then struggling to express a locative prepositional phrase like 'down on the ground'. Beginning instead with 'down into', she doesn't know how to go on. The teacher helps her to complete the sentence into an unusual assemblage of resources with the noun 'mhlaba' *(earth/ground)* (O11), which the learner repeats (O12). In O14, the learner then englishes all by herself – in complete keeping with the boundaries of Standard English – saying: 'And she could not open the jug'. She is allowed to sit down because she succeeded in *sorting things out* (relanguaging), and was therefore able to english.

This example shows how the very relaxation of the strict language policy, the 'making available' of the full classroom repertoire, seems to have encouraged the learner to try and english. Resources that she actually did know how to assemble in compliance with Standard English (e.g. 'And she could not open the jug') remained hidden under strictly enforced monolingualism but became visible as soon as this policy was relaxed. When the learner was given a chance to relanguage in cooperation with her teacher – to *bring together* ('icrow', 'kwifields') and then to *sort out* the languaging resources she had access to – she eventually produced the homogenised target repertoire of the lesson.

So what does this have to do with a chapter about learners' writing practices? Writing activities at Khayelitsha Primary are governed by strictly policed monolingualism. But what if this strictly enforced Standard English monolingualism in writing does the same as in the oral example above: hiding what learners could make of the linguistic possibilities of the English classroom – also in terms of englishing – if they were given more freedom to openly engage in linguistic sorting processes? These questions prompted me to create a writing exercise where learners would be free to draw on the full classroom repertoire. I wanted to know what language practices would emerge in such an unrestricted writing space. More particularly, I was interested in the englishing competencies that might become visible in writing tasks that allow for linguistic heterogeneity. Because, as the opening example from the oral classroom activity has demonstrated and as I have argued throughout this book, linguistic heterogeneity and homogeneity aren't mutually exclusive: the fact that learners are allowed to 'code-switch' doesn't mean that they will not also try to english. *Therefore, it is possible to find englishing in heterogeneous writing, we just haven't been looking for it yet.*

Because I conceptualise languaging as a spatial practice, any analysis has to begin by defining the constitution of the linguistic space in question. So, what constitutes the Khayelitshan English classroom as a writing space? During the oral activities that were in focus up to now, the classroom repertoire folded the Khayelitshan and the statist repertoire into one another. This complexifies during this writing activity for learners.

6.1.2 A writing space at Khayelitsha Primary

As shown in Chapters 4 and 5, orally, teachers constantly engage in strategically homogenising and heterogenising the classroom repertoire through relanguaging – modelling not always englishing-only but often instantiating the push-and-pull between extending and limiting linguistic possibilities in their teaching. Learners, as shown in Chapter 4, are also often allowed to draw on the full classroom repertoire in their contributions. The strictly enforced policy of monolingualism that characterised the above-described lesson for up to 50 minutes is therefore the exception. Importantly, however, it is the unchallenged rule when it comes to writing. If this rule isn't followed, contributions get marked as 'wrong', as this interview excerpt from a Grade 4 Xhosa and Geography teacher at the same school underlines. He first talks about how he uses language fluidly in class to not lose learners along the way, but then, about written tests, he says:

T: In Geography there must be, all the things must be in English.
R1: Mhm so when they answer in Xhosa you gonna mark it wrong?
T: Yes.
R1: So even the content, if it's correct?
T: It's correct but it's, it's wrong.

(Krause & Prinsloo, 2016: 353)

Throughout my research, I have never heard teachers encourage learners to write anywhere beyond the confines of Standard English and I have also never seen them model such writing practices in the classroom.[1] When it comes to writing, a practice central to the establishment and imperial endeavours of the nation state (Anderson, 1983; Errington, 2008) with its simplifying and categorising mechanisms and an emphasis on measurability (Scott, 1998), the logic of seeing like a state asserts itself more strongly in Khayelitshan classrooms than when activities are oral. We have seen some hints of this already in Chapter 5: as soon as activities were aimed at writing, the classroom repertoire would be tilted towards homogeneity by the teachers more often.

It is through writing that learners ultimately make their performance legible to educational authorities, and these authorities only accept nomolanguages and not languaging. Stein summarises that

> in mainstream classrooms, certain forms of representation are dominant and valued, like standard forms of written language. Students who don't perform 'to standard', for whatever reasons, are labelled as 'deficient'. (Stein, 2008: 3)

Different from oral classroom languaging, writing activities are therefore always tied to a standard nomolanguage (Blommaert, 2013; Horner *et al.*, 2011), a formal 'established code' (Canagarajah, 2006: 595). Performing to that standard or not makes the difference between a learner being judged as deficient or successful. Only Standard English resources may be written, disentangled from other languaging resources offered by the classroom repertoire, and relanguaging, the *bringing together* and *sorting out* that goes into the production of this homogenised code, is not allowed to become visible.

Although some teachers are generally open to the idea of letting their learners write heterogeneously and were quite excited when I showed them some of the writing pieces I will discuss below, opening up linguistic possibilities outside Standard English for writing activities is still not something they do in their classrooms. For one, this is because ideologies of linguistic purity assert themselves more strongly with regard to written language, which is historically seen as 'illustrative of the "essence" of the language' (Blommaert, 2008: 305) with its less fleeting and more 'artefactual' character compared to speech. Secondly, we also have to consider that teachers' oral heterogeneous classroom language practices are already subverting dominant monolingual ideologies (see, for example, Section 5.2.7). But because of their oral nature, these subversive practices can, at least to a certain extent, remain hidden behind classroom walls. Everyone knows they happen but there is no tangible proof, no resulting, visible artefacts. Letting learners write heterogeneously, however, would make such subversive practices visible, be it for parents, the principal or departmental subject advisors. The latter not only moderate tests but also check learners' ordinary classroom workbooks (Section 5.1.1). Finding heterogeneous writing across workbooks would show that teachers validate such practices in their teaching. For that – considering the dominant ideology of monolingualism in South African education – they would quite certainly be harshly criticised.

Scholars of translanguaging argue that 'teachers can incorporate translanguaging strategies by opening up the spaces that will allow the recursive process of writing to interplay between the languages a student has' (Velasco & García, 2014: 21). For teachers at Khayelitsha Primary, it is not that easy to open up such spaces without feeling like they are putting their own careers in jeopardy. Such political predicaments that teachers find themselves in must be taken seriously when advocating for linguistic fluidity and heterogeneity in school writing practices.

From the above, it follows that learners never practice heterogeneous writing at school and the routinised, formal practices that they bring into writing spaces are entangled with nomolanguages. While linguistic fluidity is an option most of the time in oral activities, for writing the code is always fixed. On top of that, due to the early-transition language policy model, the standard nomolanguage they were oriented towards in their writing had until recently still been Standard Xhosa. So, while from Grade 4 'all things must be in English' (Grade 4 Teacher quoted in Krause & Prinsloo, 2016: 353) in writing, from Grades 1 to 3 all things had to be in Standard Xhosa. This code also excludes – as I have shown at different points throughout this book – many of the Khayelitshan resources with which learners are familiar. This is illustrated by a quote from a Foundation Phase teacher interviewed during my MA research. She mentioned in an interview that when teaching maths in the early grades, she often realised that learners knew certain words 'in English', for example numbers. I then asked if they would be allowed to write those numbers 'in English' during Xhosa mathematic lessons. She replied: 'They have to write "inye"[2] but when they talk they say "one"' (Interview Foundation Phase Teacher Khayelitsha Primary 2014).[3]

So, for the first three years of schooling the rule was not that all things had to be in 'English' or otherwise they were marked wrong, but that all things had to be in 'Xhosa' or otherwise they would have been marked wrong. So, the linguistic confinement in writing for these learners has changed from Standard Written Xhosa (SWX), one set of combinatory grammatical, syntactical and orthographic[4] rules tied to a delimited set of lexical and morphological features, to Standard Written English (SWE) as another such set with very different rules. It is important to emphasise these points about Khayelitshan learners' particular schooling histories in terms of nomolanguages in writing as a background for understanding the writing pieces that emerge in this space. Furthermore, if we take seriously the idea that people's linguistic trajectories influence the spatial repertoires they draw on and contribute to, then this radical break from SWX to SWE must be expected to influence the ensemble of linguistic possibilities in the classroom space during writing activities.

So far, I have shown that Standard Xhosa is not a relevant ordering principle during oral classroom languaging as it is neither policed nor consistently approximated by teachers or learners (Section 4.5.3). I argued that it doesn't make sense to speak of the resources used as Standard Xhosa resources, because overall neither teachers nor learners are watchful towards the principles of that statist repertoire as such – much in contrast to Standard English, which is the very target of teaching in this case. Accordingly, I consistently spoke about Khayelitshan resources, even when they also looked like Standard Xhosa ones.

When learners write, however, given their particular schooling history, they might well orient towards SWX – be it consistently or partially – because they had to adhere to the principles of this code throughout their first three years of schooling. Therefore, another statist repertoire is now folded into the classroom repertoire as a potential principle to orient towards: Standard Xhosa. Because a lot of Khayelitshan resources can also be Standard Xhosa resources, it is often impossible to clearly say whether learners are orienting towards the day-to-day Khayelitshan repertoire in their writing or towards Standard Xhosa. I will discuss different possibilities in the data analysis. For example, sometimes we might be looking at what Canagarajah (2015: 41) calls 'a hybrid form of literacy activity combining oral and literate resources', where learners put Khayelitshan resources into writing via codified orthographies. Other times, learners might be orienting mainly towards SWX. Given the complexity of the spatial repertoire of this writing space, folding into each other potential Khayelitshan, Standard English and Standard Xhosa resources, as well as the orthographic norms associated with SWX and SWE, learners have to be sophisticated relanguagers. Being able to order and sort out this folded repertoire in multiple directions before actualising parts of it in writing is an essential skill. Some of these directions will become clear throughout the analyses.

I will focus on writing pieces in which learners exploit the possibility of fluidity – meaning where they don't confine themselves to one of the nomolanguages in their writing. They write heterogeneously (if our point of reference is their usually homogenised school writing practices). Few studies look at such writing practices. Those that do normally use the term translingual writing or literacy (Canagarajah, 2013; de los Ríos & Seltzer, 2017; Velasco & García, 2014), but I prefer to talk about *heterogeneous writing*, because the *trans-* prefix suggests a transcendence of nomolanguages rather than their negotiation. I therefore detour from translanguaging also in this chapter. I will show that rules associated with nomolanguages play an important role in the learners' practices, so suggesting that they use *whichever* resources are at their disposal and *transcend* nomolanguages doesn't seem appropriate.

I am interested in the writing strategies that become visible if I zoom into the linguistic details of these pieces in the same manner I zoomed into the details of teachers' oral classroom languaging. I assume that, like their teachers, learners have their own strategies to navigate the particular challenges of school writing. By making those strategies visible, teaching and testing could build more on learners' existing writing expertise.

Below, I give some insight into the nature of the task and how I introduced it to the learners. Then, we move onto the analysis of some concrete examples.

6.1.3 A relanguaging researcher

Picture Story 6

I decided to structure the writing task around a picture story, because teachers spoke about pictures as important elements in their teaching, which can significantly enhance learner engagement in class. Pictures as input have the advantage of not putting words (and nomolanguages) into learners' mouths and are therefore well suited for my interest: Which languaging resources would learners choose if the writing space was as unrestricted as possible?

This particular picture story seemed suitable because it is quite versatile. The picture content is accessible and can invite a fairly simple picture-by-picture description that mainly focuses on the isolated actions of a boy. However, for more advanced learners it is also possible to connect the pictures with a more intricate story of dreaming about swimming in the sea while actually lying in a bath tub. This story would therefore neither overwhelm Grade 4 learners, nor be too simple or boring for Grades 5 and 6. I introduced the task by elaborating on the instruction above the picture story, which says:

Tell us what you see on these pictures. You can write in isiXhosa[5], English or Code-Switching.

I decided to work with conventional nomolanguages for pragmatic reasons and also to use 'code-switching' as the familiar term for learners at the school to refer to heterogeneous language practices. A shortcoming in the formulation of the instruction that I became aware of while explaining the task in the first classroom is that it leaves out a host of other languaging resources that learners might have access to – a few learners, for example, asked whether they can also use 'Sotho' or 'Afrikaans'. I then added to my oral explanation: 'Ningasebenzisa zonke iilwimi enizaziyo' *(You can use all the languages that you know)*.

During my research, I have learned a little from teachers about how to make sure that learners understand written task instructions (e.g. Section 5.2). Accordingly, I found myself relanguaging my very own instruction in a way that I deemed digestible for the learners. The result approximated to this:

Jongani kwipage yesibini, likhona ibali with iipictures eziyifour. There is a picture story there. Khanibhale le story. Kodwa ikhona into ebalulekileyo kakhulu: Xa nibhala, ningakhetha ulwimi. Ningabhala ngesiXhosa, ningabhala ngesiNgesi[6] okanye ningamixa iilwimi. Ningayenza icode-switching, ok? (Author Khayelitsha Primary September 2016)

Look at the second page, there is a story with four pictures. There is a picture story there. Please write this story. But there is an important thing: When you write, you can chose the language. You can write in Xhosa, you can write in English or you can mix the languages. You can do code-switching, ok?

I deemed this quite explicit mediation of my own task instruction necessary because firstly we know from foregoing discussions that written instructions are often difficult to understand for learners. Secondly, as discussed above, writing in the English classroom is normally only validated when it exclusively features Standard English resources. Even though learners hear heterogeneous languaging constantly, also from authority figures like the teachers and the principal, they would normally not be allowed, let alone encouraged, to imitate such practices in writing. I therefore wanted to make sure that they understood that the task at hand gave them more freedom.

It is important to mention that through this relanguaging of my instruction, I also – similarly to the teachers in the foregoing chapters – set the tone for the writing activity. Only that, in my case, the form and content of my explanation didn't homogenise but heterogenise the classroom repertoire by entangling resources that are normally separated in writing. The language resources I chose therefore modelled, and thereby emphasised, the heterogeneous option. Other than that, however, I didn't explain any further what I meant by 'code-switching' in the instruction because learners are familiar with the notion.

After this relanguaging interlude, I handed out the picture story and waited until all learners had finished the task – this took about 20 minutes in each of the three classrooms (Grades 4–6). I collected 101 descriptions of picture stories this way. In each classroom where I explained the task, a couple of learners were particularly excited about the code-switching option, exclaiming 'Yes!' or whispering excitedly with their neighbours when I announced it. These reactions are reflected in the fact that 44 (44%)[7] of the 101 learners wrote heterogeneously. This in itself is remarkable. Consider, for example, a study on translingual writing in two US secondary school classrooms by de los Ríos and Seltzer. The authors note that, despite teachers' encouragement to use all resources at their disposal, 'students' translanguaging didn't appear in abundance in either classroom' (de los Ríos & Seltzer, 2017: 71), as they mostly chose SWE. In this study, however, without any previous practice, heterogeneous writing did indeed appear in abundance. One reason might be that heterogeneity is these learners' day-to-day oral reality and they are excited to draw on it in their writing for a change. This, however, would also be true for many Spanish–English bilinguals in the US study. Another point is that in secondary school classrooms in the United States, learners mostly have mastered SWE to a point where they can express what they want to say and aren't completely silenced. Also, they are aware of statist expectations of monolingualism, and translanguaging is then a much more politicised and subversive practice, not a game full of experimentation. At Khayelitsha Primary, the much younger learners probably feel the power of statist prescriptions regarding language but are less aware of it. The writing space I could create as a researcher – not worried about putting my career in jeopardy – could therefore become a

Table 6.1 Learners' writing practices across grades

Grade	Heterogeneous	SWX	SWE
Total (101 learners)	44 (44%)	30 (30%)	27 (27%)
4 (28 learners)	7 (25%)*	12 (43%)	9 (32%)
5 (34 learners)	19 (56%)	9 (27%)	6 (18%)
6 (39 learners)	18 (47%)	9 (24%)	12 (31%)

* Percentage of the number of learners per grade, not of the total.

more playful, experimental space. While still within the normative space of the school, reminding learners of the rules of the formal writing game and possibly motivating them to show the formal language rules they already know, this space is nevertheless outside of punitive measures for 'impure' language use. Therefore, learners had the opportunity to play with the resources they can access while showing their (re)languaging and englishing skills. We can now look at how the learners handled and shaped this experimental space. It is insightful to look at the numbers of heterogeneous, SWE and SWX writing pieces in total and broken down per grade (see Table 6.1).

While this sample is certainly too small to be statistically significant, some interesting tendencies can be identified that might inspire further research. Looking, for example, at the number of learners who write within the confines of SWX at the different grade levels, we see a significant number in Grade 4 (43%) which in Grade 5 has dropped to 27% and then to 24% in Grade 6. This seems indicative of the learners' particular schooling histories described above: the further they move away from Grade 3, the less likely they are to restrict themselves to SWX when having the full classroom repertoire at their disposal. This seems to connect to the fact that SWX no longer plays a big role in learners' writing practices at school from Grade 4 onwards, outside of Xhosa as a subject lesson.

The number of learners who choose to orient exclusively towards SWE in their writing doesn't show such a clear trajectory across grades and cannot be explained solely by reference to the schooling spaces that learners have traversed so far. One might, for example, ask whether those learners who already orient towards SWE in Grade 4 might have access to the respective literacy practices in their homes, which would explain a certain familiarity with the relevant resources.

The number of learners who write heterogeneously, not restricting themselves to one of the nomolanguages throughout their description of the picture story, more than doubles from 25% in Grade 4 to 56% in Grade 5 and remains high in Grade 6 with 47%. Learners apparently find some merit in actualising possibilities from the classroom repertoire in less restricted ways and, as hinted at earlier, didn't need any form of guidance to do so.

The first writing piece I analyse reminded me of the relanguaging between SWE teaching material and oral classroom languaging that I have described for teachers' practices. This learner first tries to approximate SWE in her description of the pictures and then rewrites parts of the description via SWX. While my relanguaging perspective primarily drew me to this piece, the detailed analysis uncovers further interesting linguistic aspects that I then trace through other writing pieces and sometimes back to the teacher interviews. This line of investigation determines the structure of this chapter.

6.2 Seeing Writing Differently: From Deficit to Potential

6.2.1 Emergent englishing

The following description of the picture story was produced by a learner in Grade 5.

Example A: Greaming abut sweeming in a betch

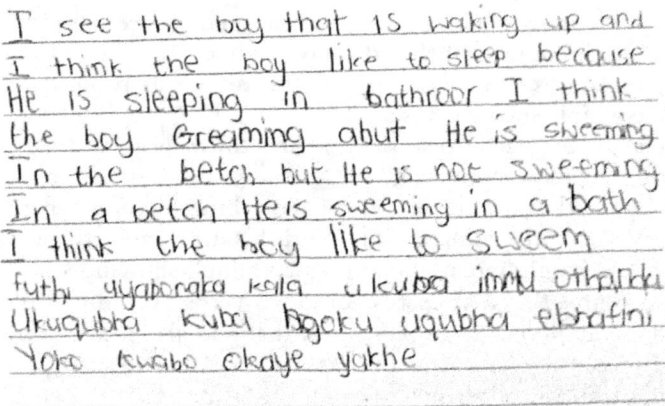

For ease of reference I below type out the writing piece with line numbers:

1	I see the boy that is waking up and
2	I think the boy like to sleep because
3	he is sleeping in bathroor I think
4	the boy Greaming abut He is sweeming
5	In the betch but He is not sweeming
6	In a betch He is sweeming in a bath
7	I think the boy like to sweem
8	futhi uyabonaka kala ukuba imntu othanda
9	Ukuqubha kuba ngoku uqubha ebhafini
10	yoko kwabo okaye yakhe

In the first seven lines, the learner is oriented towards SWE and then rewrites part of her own description via SWX. Before I turn to how and why she might do that, I first want to draw attention to how, despite the fact that she has other, more familiar options at hand, from A1 to A7 the learner orients exclusively towards SWE. Looking at this part of her writing, it is easy to identify points where she doesn't comply with SWE conventions:

- absent punctuation
- unconventional grammar and syntax
- unorthodox spelling
- 'erratic use of capitals' (Blommaert *et al.*, 2005: 386)

However, if we systematically 'see' differently, then there are also competencies to be shown here. For example, in A1 the learner approximates the rules for relative clause formation in 'I see the boy that is waking up'. She is arguably making an unconventional choice with the relative pronoun 'that', but nevertheless displays an understanding of which type of linguistic features she needs to look for in the classroom repertoire in order to assemble such a clause.

The same sentence also shows that she knows how to build the present continuous tense with '-ing' and therefore has access to a grammatical affordance that is very useful for describing pictures where actions are seen as currently going on. She uses this affordance throughout the text with 'sleeping', 'Greaming' and 'sweeming', showing knowledge of how to assemble this tense across different verbs by adding '-ing' to the root. The 'waking up' example shows that she also knows how to use the present continuous within a phrasal verb – verb forms that can cause some confusion when learning to english (Matlock & Heredia, 2002) (see Section 4.5.1). I have observed the assembling of the continuous tense being extensively practiced in Grade 4 and it is an affordance that learners across grades frequently draw on in their writing. In parts, therefore, learners' ability to assemble '-ing' with various verbs (other examples to follow) may be traced back to the successful teaching of this tense in English classrooms.

We aren't bound to read lack and deficit from this example, we can also see potential: an emergent skill on the part of the learner to navigate the syntactic and grammatical landscape of SWE – emergent englishing one might call it. The emphasis on potential rather than lack, and on the presence rather than the absence of resources, sets the tone for the analyses in this chapter. In the next section, I focus on the resources present in the last lines of her description (A8–A10) and how they relate to the rest.

6.2.2 Learning rewriting from learners

The learner gives quite a layered description of the picture story and also presents her own thoughts about the boy enjoying sleeping and swimming. She describes that the boy is sleeping in the bathroom and dreaming about swimming on the beach. From A5 to A7, she explains that the boy is not swimming on the beach but in a bath (tub) and that he likes to swim, as she writes in A6–A7:

> He is sweeming in a bath I think the boy like to sweem.

She then continues from A8 to A10 with:

> futhi uyabonaka kala ukuba imntu othanda Ukuqubha kuba ngoku uqubha ebhafini yoko kwabo okaye yakhe *(And he looks like someone who likes to swim, because now he is swimming in the bath tub at his parents' house or in his bath tub)*.

In terms of content, we see a significant overlap between her SWE (A6–A7) and her SWX approximation (A8–A10). Both parts express the observation that the boy is swimming in a bath (tub) and that he likes to swim. In the second version, however, she adds some information that is absent from the first one (more details below). This learner appears to rewrite her own writing by essentially repeating the content of A6–A7 but with other resources that allow her to express certain things differently and to add more detail. Wolfersberger (2003) describes a similar practice as 'back-translating', which he observes in Japanese–English writing in a study on first language (L1) to second language (L2) strategy transfer. Here, a student negotiates the tension between a complex idea she wants to express and what she can reasonably bring across via SWE. Therefore, even though in this study only one learner rewrites in this way, it might well be a more common strategy for such negotiations – something that large-scale studies of heterogeneous writing would have to confirm.

One useful resource of the learner in her rewritten version is 'uyabonakala ukuba'[8] *(he looks as if)*. While in A7 she simply writes: 'I think the boy like to sweem', with '-bonakala' she uses more analytical language that explains to the reader how she gets to this conclusion – she can therefore share, to some extent, her analysis of the pictures.

The learner goes on to write 'imntu[9] othanda ukuqubha', a main clause plus a relative clause morphologically made up like this:

i-	[ngu]	-m-	-ntu	o-	-thand-	-a	uku-	-qubh-	-a
SM9	COP1	NPx1	person	REL1	like	FV	INFIN	swim	FV

(it is someone who likes to swim)

Familiar morphology here allows this learner to connect elements that she previously presented in disconnected short sentences ('He is sweeming in a bath' and 'I think the boy like to sweem'). With the SM9, she tracks reference to 'the boy', who, in SWX would be referred to as 'inkwenkwe' in class 9. This clarifies that the person she describes as someone who likes to swim is 'the boy' she wrote about earlier. The REL1 'o' is then a class-specific relative pronoun with a clear referent: 'umntu' (class 1), allowing her to connect the description of liking to swim back to 'the someone', the boy.

Relative clauses are an affordance to connect people, activities and events. They allow for more complex meaning-making than adjacent main clauses. I mentioned above that the learner already approximates an SWE relative clause in A1: 'I see the boy that is waking up'. Her unconventional choice of the relative pronoun 'that' instead of the rule-conforming 'who' suggests that she might not yet be oriented well enough within SWE to assemble relative constructions confidently throughout. I argue that familiar patterns of noun class agreement for reference tracking here help her to make these complex connections. Instead of presenting ideas in a disconnected way (as in A6–A7), she can now draw them together in a phrase that approximates: 'He looks as if he is someone who likes to swim', in SWE.

She goes on to write:

kuba ngoku uqubha ebhafini yoko kwabo okaye[10] yakhe *(because now he is swimming in the bath tub at his parents' home or in his [bath tub])*.

When orienting towards SWE, she doesn't specify the location or the owner of the bath tub, but turning towards SWX she integrates this specification with 'yoko kwabo'[11] and 'yakhe'. My bracketed version of the sentence already shows that, to express the same complex meaning via SWE, the learner would need to know how apostrophes are used to express possession on nouns in the plural form (parents'). She would also have to use the gendered possessive pronoun 'his' to track reference back to the boy, making clear that he is the owner of the bath tub. Such reference tracking via Standard English gendered personal and possessive pronouns is, however, often confusing for Khayelitshan learners. I have noticed this, because teachers across classrooms repeatedly remind them of the usage of 'he', 'she', 'it', 'his', 'her' and 'its', respectively (discussed in more detail in Section 6.2.4). At this point, suffice it to say that while this learner in her writing does use the pronoun 'he', she doesn't use the corresponding possessive pronoun 'his'. But she does build reference tracking devices ('yoko kwabo' and 'yakhe') into her rewritten version from A8 to A10. My conjecture is that reference tracking in and across clauses is a grammatical ordering principle that, at this point, she still struggles to implement via Standard English resources alone. Therefore, she enrols from the classroom repertoire devices that instantiate the familiar noun class agreement system (more on reference tracking also in Section 6.2.4).

Overall, with regard to Example A, it stands out that this learner doesn't rewrite the earlier part of her description but only the part from A6 to A7 ('He is sweeming in a bath I think the boy like to sweem'). I suggest that the last part of her writing is not up to her own standards regarding what she wants to express here (see also Wolfersberger, 2003). She therefore exploits the opportunity to draw on the full classroom repertoire to write it again differently, bringing the intended message across more reliably and in more detail. She thereby demonstrates to potential readers that her analytical insights into the picture story do at some points exceed what she feels confident expressing within the confines of SWE.

This piece is one example of what the product of a writing task that allows for heterogeneity can look like. A quite useful product for the purposes of English teaching, as it provides information about elements of SWE that this learner already masters, but simultaneously reveals the complexity of meaning she would like to express and the resources she would need in order to do this via SWE. For example, to express the same complexity she would need to know how apostrophes work in SWE possessive constructions like 'at his parents' home' or she would need access to some useful analytical phrases like 'he looks as if'. Finding out what learners would like to write if they could, can feed into decisions about which SWE resources are immediately relevant to them.

This rewriting technique might therefore have potential for the English classroom. We can learn from learners and take a piece like this as a model from which to abstract task instructions that make all learners practice such rewriting. An option would be to develop an instruction along the lines of

> Describe the pictures in English as well as you can. Then rewrite your description using whichever language resources you want.

Such opportunities for heterogeneous writing tasks and their potential in the English classroom will be discussed further in the conclusion. For now, we look into more interesting aspects from Example A that relate to spelling and orthography and that will lead us into other writing pieces as well.

6.2.3 Lack or oversupply of standard linguistic norms?

Throughout Example A, we see the learner grappling with different orthographic realisations of the long vowel [iː] and its short version [ɪ] in SWE. To understand this phenomenon, we need to situate the following analysis firmly within the context of Khayelitshan English classrooms. Recall that during one of her lessons (18 May 2016), the Grade 5 teacher spelled out the pronoun 'it' for learners. I asked her why she did so. She said:

> Because sometimes they do confuse the spelling. We have eat [pronounces [ɪt] instead of standard IPA [iːt]] that means 'to eat' and the *it*

[also pronounces [ɪt]] that means some, 'a thing', 'something'. So sometimes I do have to spell it out to them. (Interview Grade 5 Teacher)

When she explains this, the teacher herself pronounces 'it' and 'eat' as ɪt – making the words homophones. In classroom englishing, such differences in vowel length often don't feature. This has been analysed in research on Black South African English (BlSAfE) that shows that vowel length distinctions are absent from this way of englishing (Mesthrie, 2005). Thus, learners in schooling spaces with pronunciation patterns approximating more closely to the standard receive a phonetic orientation as to when spelling norms require, for example, a digraph (e.g. 'ea') to represent [i:] or when they have to use the single vowel 'i' to represent [ɪ]. Most learners in Khayelitsha are completely lacking this phonetic clue, because it doesn't feature in the local classroom englishing they hear.

Importantly, also in Khayelitshan languaging and in Standard Xhosa, like in many other Bantu nomolanguages, there is no distinction between long and short vowels (Mesthrie, 2005: 147). Accordingly, because vowel length is not phonemic, there is only one orthographic representation of [i:] and [ɪ] in SWX: the letter 'i'. It cannot be over-emphasised in this context that Khayelitshan learners spent their first three years of primary school learning to write according to this orthography. Looking at how they spell when trying to approximate SWE, we should therefore keep these local particularities in mind.

Let's look into the englished passage from Example A that is the focus of the following excursion into spelling.

Repetition Example A (Lines 1–7)
1   I see the boy that is waking up and
2   I think the boy like to sleep because
3   he is sleeping in bathroor I think
4   the boy Greaming abut He is sweeming
5   In the betch but He is not sweeming
6   In a betch He is sweeming in a bath
7   I think the boy like to sweem

She realises the [i:] in 'see', 'sleep' and 'sleeping' in accordance with SWE orthography with the digraph 'ee'. She also uses 'ee' to represent the [ɪ], producing 'sweeming' (A4 and A5). But 'ee' is not the only digraph that she knows, as her use of 'ea' in 'Greaming' (A4) shows. The examples of 'betch' and 'he' (A5 and A6) point to a negotiation of 'e' as another possible representation of [i:] that in SWE is accepted in 'he' but not in 'betch', where orthography prescribes the digraph 'ea' (beach). While the learner knows that 'ea' plays some role in SWE ('Greaming'), she is not yet sure *where exactly* it fits. In words like 'think', 'is' and 'in', she confidently represents [ɪ] as 'i', which might relate to the fact that these are high frequency words practiced regularly in writing.

Regarding orthographic rules, her writing therefore displays an awareness of different possible representations of [i:] and [ɪ] (which to her probably sound the same in speech) in SWE orthography: 'ee', 'ea', 'e' and 'i'. Note that in SWX orthography, digraphs exist only as combinations of the same letter (e.g. 'ee', 'ii', 'oo') but not as made up of two different letters (like 'ea'). So, while the learner still displays insecurity with regard to where which realisation is called for, she nevertheless shows that she is familiar with some of SWE's orthographic resources for vowel realisation and has been confronted, for example, with different digraphs such as 'ea'. Therefore, she is not simply spelling according to pronunciation – phonetically – or transferring SWX orthography to SWE. Instead, she orders the classroom repertoire in watchfulness towards the boundaries of SWE but within that statist repertoire she is still busy *sorting out* different ways to represent vowels, all of which would be written as 'i' in SWX. In other words, what we see here is not a learner who is clueless about orthographic norms but one who is already englishing – actualising resources from the classroom repertoire while being watchful towards the boundaries and rules of Standard English – while trying to get her bearings with regard to which vowel representation belongs where in SWE.

It is further telling that in her rewritten section at the end, the learner then doesn't use any of these digraphs that are characteristic for SWE to represent the [i:] and [ɪ], but adheres to the rules of SWX orthography to represent the phoneme. She has a clear idea of when she is writing 'in English' and when she is writing 'in Xhosa' and that different orthographic conventions apply to these nomolanguages. She is able to relanguage the heterogeneous classroom repertoire, sorting it out in accordance with the statist view with an orientation towards these two standard codes and their associated orthographies.

Exploring the spelling of [i:] and [ɪ] in other writing pieces reveals similar negotiations of vowel representation. A Grade 6 learner, for example, writes:

It peak up igalo[12] zayo and now is going to a beej
(It picks up its (his) arms and now is going to a beach.)

'It' here refers to the boy – again an illustration of how reference tracking via Standard English pronouns is often confusing for Khayelitshan learners (further discussed in Section 6.2.4). Regarding the representation of [i:], the learner's spelling of 'peak' *(pick)* and 'beej' *(beach)* shows that, while for her there is no difference between [i:] and [ɪ] (as in Example A), she nevertheless knows that different digraphs can be used to represent [i:] and [ɪ] in SWE and juggles them in her writing.

A third example comes from another Grade 6 learner, who writes:

Kwifoto yesi thathu[13] I si the boy is swimming. In photo four I see the boy that is sleeping.

First, she realises the two [iː]/[ɪ] sounds in 'kwifoto yesi thathu' *(in the third picture)* with 'i', according to SWX orthography. Then, in her realisation of 'I see' (SWE) as 'I si', she seems to apply the same orthographic rule, using 'i' to represent [iː] and therefore representing a Standard English resource ('see') via SWX orthography ('si'). But as she continues to write, she glides into SWE orthography, illustrated by 'I see' and 'sleeping' in the next sentence. This example shows most clearly how learners in Khayelitsha acquire not one but two different sets of orthographic principles in their early schooling. Here, we can observe a learner in the immediate process of relanguaging the classroom repertoire by *sorting out* these principles according to an emergent idea of what spelling is asked for in which of the nomolanguages and their associated orthographies:

kwifoto yesi thathu ➡ I si ➡ I see

Relanguaging as a linguistic sorting practice can only become so clearly visible here, because heterogeneous writing is allowed in the first place and resources like 'kwifoto yesithathu' and 'I see' can therefore occur adjacently in the same writing piece.

This emphasis on sorting processes produces an account of learners' spelling in township schools that is radically different from that which Blommaert *et al.* put forward in their influential study on literacy practices in a different Cape Town township school (discussed in Section 1.6). They describe the writing of learners there as heterographic literacy practices that 'don't respond to institutional ortho-graphic norms' (Blommaert *et al.*, 2005: 388). Learners, and also teachers, are described as cut off from such institutional norms, (re)producing their own peripheral normativity. While locally functional, these peripheral norms keep them from learning to approximate the standard nomolanguage and literacy practices valued beyond the township (Blommaert *et al.*, 2005).

In response, I argue that the example of [iː] and [ɪ] has shown how, in their spelling, Khayelitshan learners are, in fact, responding not only to one, but to two sets of institutional orthographic norms that are folded into each other in the Khayelitshan classroom as a writing space. Now, they are in the process of learning how to sort them out, i.e. how to relanguage complex spatial repertoires according to what is expected of them. They already know how to see language like a state, since they recognise the basic categories that structure the statist vision: separate nomolanguages. It is now about sorting the resources accordingly and about learning what goes where in this game of xhosing, englishing and Khayelitshan languaging. While learners certainly still need to improve their bearings, the analyses of these writing pieces show that they are already busy sorting things out. I argue that the challenges Khayelitshan learners face in their spelling aren't the result of a lack of accessibility and orientation towards institutional orthographic norms but rather that of an oversupply of such norms. Learners here are not stuck in peripheral normativity but, local complexities considered, are engaged in a very challenging task. These writing pieces display an awareness of multiple Standard English spellings of [i:] and [ɪ], even if conventions about which belongs where are still unclear. These findings add empirical evidence to what Canagarajah (2015: 35–36) has argued in response to Blommaert *et al.*, namely that 'it is possible then for the local community to be not unaware of (and even not incompetent in) the indexical orders and literacy regimes of other places'. Seeing these competencies in their nuanced detail, I would add, requires close linguistic analyses of languaging (or writing) as a spatial practice that is framed by a careful conceptualisation of the constitution of the linguistic space that is in focus.

The point about the oversupply of standard linguistic norms at Khayelitsha Primary will come up again later. Let's now turn to another topic that has transpired in the analysis of different writing pieces and that I discussed also with regard to teachers' oral language practices: reference tracking via Standard English pronouns in learners' writing.

6.2.4 Learners sorting out Standard English pronouns

I have remarked at different points in the analyses above that reference tracking exclusively via gendered Standard English pronouns seems to pose problems for learners in their writing. They often make unconventional choices, for example: 'He enjoy her day'. Teachers are aware of gendered pronouns being a source of confusion. They regularly remind learners of their appropriate usage. Here is an example from the Grade 4 classroom:

> When we talk about a girl, we use ipronoun enguher, if it is a boy: uhis[14] *(When we talk about a girl we use the pronoun that is 'her', if it is a boy, 'his')*. (Grade 4 English Lesson 08.02.2016)

With reference to this specific example, I later asked the teacher in an interview why she thinks that learners need to be reminded frequently about the gender difference between these Standard English pronouns. She draws a comparison between Standard English and Standard Xhosa to explain why they might struggle:

> In English if I say 'a boy' I will say 'he'. In English. But in Xhosa we'll say 'yena'. In Xhosa. At the same time, if I say in English 'a girl': 'she'. In Xhosa I'll say 'yena'. In Xhosa it's the same but in English you differentiate it: u-he-and-she.[15] (Interview Grade 4 Teacher)

Here, the teacher provides a metalinguistic explanation of why reference tracking in Standard English is hard for learners, because it is based on gender distinctions. She uses the absolute pronoun 'yena' (class 1a/first- and third-person singular) to illustrate that, in their day-to-day language practices, learners can refer to boys and girls with the same pronoun and therefore might get confused by having to choose between different gendered options.

The Grade 5 teacher makes similar remarks about struggles with pronouns in her teaching, prompting us to solicit her opinion on these little words in the interview:

T: In African language we have no pronouns. Umama u-. You will say the same thing when you speak of a male: Utata u-. Or instead of saying 'she', [you say] 'u-'. Instead of saying 'he' [you say] 'u-'. We don't have pronouns.
R1: Mhm so they get confused?
T: Yes. You have to stress it: When I speak of a female person I use 'she', the pronoun, the correct pronoun to use is 'she'. The male person we use 'he'. (Interview Grade 5 Teacher)

The teachers' comments show how their interventions in class are based on an understanding of their learners' struggles with pronoun choice – an often underestimated advantage of the fact that learners and teachers in Khayelitsha share a similar language background. For both teachers, it is clear that learners' struggles result from the fact that gender is an ordering principle for nouns and their pronouns in Standard English, whereas in Khayelitsha and in Standard Xhosa (as well as in many Bantu nomolanguages) females and males are referred to with the same pronoun (Beck, 2003). Third-person gendered pronouns in Standard English are therefore indeed rather confusing for learners.

A connection to establish between the learners' writing and teachers' oral classroom languaging is that, while teachers often remind their learners explicitly about how to use Standard English pronouns, in their actual classroom language practices they often seem to avoid them themselves or relanguage them into Khayelitshan morphology. While this is an efficient resource to make Standard English teaching material accessible for learners (see, for example, Sections 4.3.6 and 5.2.6), it also means that in classroom talk learners get less exposure to the referential order of Standard English.

When it comes to learners' writing, across all pieces, examples similar to 'He enjoy her day' (Grade 6) are plentiful. In addition, another group of writing pieces displays a general avoidance of third-person gendered pronouns. Learners would, for example, constantly repeat the head noun, producing much redundancy in their texts. This redundancy, however, might indicate problem-conscious learners, who have already understood that there is something complicated about choosing the appropriate reference tracker in Standard English.

The observation I want to focus on here is that in this writing task where heterogeneous language use is allowed, quite a few learners use the opportunity to draw on the full classroom repertoire for rather punctual interventions in sentences that otherwise seem to display an orientation to SWE. This often occurs exactly where SWE would require them to use a gendered personal or possessive pronoun for reference tracking. Recall this earlier example from a Grade 6 learner:

> It peak up igalo[16] zayo and now is going to a beej *(It picks up its (his) arms and now is going to a beach)*.

Firstly, 'it' is used here instead of 'he', showing an insecurity in choosing the conventional gendered pronoun to refer to 'the boy'. Then, the learner uses 'i[in]galo zayo', morphologically made up like this:

i[in]-	-galo	za-	-yo	
NPx10	arm	POSS10	REL9	*(his arms)*

While the POSS10 connects the possessive construction to 'i[in]galo' (class 10), the REL9 refers back to 'the boy', often associated with class 9 (inkwenkwe/iboy). By stepping out of the confines of Standard English and actualising the possibilities of an extensive noun class agreement system, she avoids a decision about which possessive pronoun – 'its', 'his' or 'her' – is in order here.

Similarly, a Grade 5 learner seems to elegantly circumvent the pronoun 'he' when writing:

> I see a little boy and uvuka[17] at the bad.

She uses the subject marker 'u-'[18] to refer back to the boy with the construction 'uvuka' where Standard English would prescribe 'he wakes up'. In the same vein, the following example from a Grade 6 learner is interesting:

Example B: I see the child engqengqe ngomqolo

> On these picture I see the child on the bad. I see the child on the see beach. I see the child swimming on the beach. I see the child engqengqe ngomqolo on the bath.

Sensitised to the issue around reference tracking via Standard English gendered pronouns it now stands out that this learner, who restricts herself to SWE throughout most of the description, does in fact not use any third-person pronouns at all. Instead, she always repeats 'the child'. However, in the last sentence she writes:

I see the child engqengqe ngomqolo on the bath.

To produce a similar meaning within the confines of Standard English, this sentence would have had to look something like this:

I see the child relaxing on its back in the bath.

Not only does this sentence feature two prepositional phrases[19] that make it rather complex, but it would also require the possessive pronoun 'its' (or 'his'). In Standard Xhosa as well as when languaging in Khayelitsha, body parts, especially when used together with the instrumental 'nga-' (ngomqolo (nga- + umqolo) = by means of the back), are inalienable – meaning it is clear that they are 'owned' by whoever is described as acting with/by means of them. A possessive construction is therefore usually omitted with body parts. Enrolling 'engqengqe ngomqolo' circumvents the complexities of reference tracking and sequential prepositional phrases she might not yet be able to navigate without compromising on meaning-making when moving exclusively within the confines of Standard English. Rather than not adhering to the conventions of Standard English, she writes up a new grammar and syntax – one that cannot be judged by standard criteria but that is a vehicle for clear and complex meaning in this context.

These examples strengthen my hypothesis that one reason for learners to orient towards the full classroom repertoire is that they struggle to pick the conventional gendered third-person pronoun (e.g. 'she'/'he'/'it') as a device to track reference. With alternatives at hand, they can now sort out the Standard English reference trackers that are still confusing to them and choose more familiar ones. This is reminiscent of the way in which teachers sort out those resources via relanguaging that are potential stumbling blocks for their learners (see, for example, Sections 4.5.6 and 5.2.6).

If this *sorting out* was confirmed by further research, it would also show that those learners who do it are aware of the points at which they might overstep Standard English conventions. Learners who write heterogeneously would therefore sometimes display more advanced englishing skills than learners who write: 'He enjoy her day'. Heterogeneous writing exercises can therefore sometimes tell us more about learners' understanding of how Standard English works than monolingual tasks. Under a policy of monolingualism, learners would *have to* choose one of the gendered pronouns. If they then produced a sentence like: 'He enjoy her day', one wouldn't be able to tell whether they grappled with the choice, or whether they were not problem-conscious at all. The heterogeneous examples shown here seem to suggest an awareness of the complexities around gendered pronouns in Standard English rather than a blindness to them. Instead of choosing 'the wrong pronoun', learners sort out those potential stumbling blocks and turn to other resources, combining them in ways that aren't subject to standard judgements but track reference coherently. Such writing strategies, I argue, in their very heterogeneity display emergent englishing competencies as learners are approaching and sussing out the order of a homogenised statist repertoire.

We can only see this emergent englishing if we closely analyse the details of heterogeneous languaging. Walking the other way by beginning our theorisations from heterogeneity, we might then find traces of nomolanguages in languaging. This is also why I find referring to such writing practices as translingual writing (Velasco & García, 2014) misleading, as the term implies a non-watchfulness to constructed language boundaries (Otheguy *et al.*, 2015). But what we observe here are learners' intense negotiations of statist linguistic fixity rather than its transcendence. They strategically step out of the confines of Standard English to avoid violating the rules of that statist repertoire. In the process, they exploit specific affordances from the rest of the classroom repertoire that includes Standard Xhosa and/or Khayelitshan resources. They relanguage the complex heterogeneous repertoire of this school writing space by ordering it – in accordance with the statist vision – into two nomolanguages and their associated orthographies. They are therefore watchfully adhering to standard linguistic norms and are by no means cut off from them (see also Canagarajah, 2015).

6.2.5 Dis- and reassembling morphology

Example C: A tale of vuking, tshoning and swiming

> In these ~~pic~~ pictures ndibona ~~Inko~~ Inkwenkwe
> kumbonise wokuqala the boy is Vuking
> The boy is tshoning in the river
> in picture 3 the Boy is Swiming
> in picture 4 Inkwenkwe Ihlamba umzimba
> wayo ngokuba ifuna ukuba clean

1   In these ~~puc~~ pictures ndibona ~~Inke~~ Inkwenkwe
2   kumboniso wokuqala the boy is Vuking
3   The boy is tshoning in the river
4   in picture 3 the Boy is swiming
5   in pucture 4 Inkwenkwe Ihlamba umzimba
6   wayo ngokuba ifuna ukuba clean

Overall, this piece is a great illustration of what Khayelitshan languaging could look like in writing. We see a slight insecurity about how to spell 'picture' in the first line where she first writes 'puc' (C1) and then corrects herself, while in C5 she doesn't correct herself and writes 'pucture'. Similarly so with 'Inkwenkwe', where she starts with 'Inke' (C1), but then corrects herself to add in the 'w'. Apart from this and some 'out of place' capitals, she seems confident in juggling SWX as well as SWE orthography, applying each spelling convention to its administratively assigned set of linguistic features. With those resources sorted out and at hand, she is able to take advantage of the possibility of choosing freely from the whole inventory of linguistic possibilities to which she has access.

One of the possibilities she actualises is '-ing' – a feature used frequently and comparably confidently across many SWE and heterogeneous writing pieces in the sample in this study (see also Section 6.2.1). This learner stands out because she seamlessly applies this feature to the verb stem '-vuk-' *(wake up)*, a Khayelitshan and Standard Xhosa resource. She adheres to the same rules that Standard English requires for the inflection of a verb that ends in a vowel – for example 'take' loses its final vowel when inflected into 'taking', just like '-vuka' loses its final vowel when here inflected into 'vuking'. The same strategy is apparent when she builds the continuous tense with the verb stem '-tshon-' *(sink/drown)* (C3). This use of 'vuking' and 'tshoning' reminded me of how teachers in their classroom languaging often rely on their learners to recognise different pieces of morphology as being separable and mobile and to disassemble and sort these features out according to different nomolanguages. I used the example of 'ndiyitrainile' and the Grade 4 teacher's interview comment about her use of 'meanisha' in class to illustrate this point in Section 4.3.3. She said: 'I want them to get the word "mean". U-sha they know is Xhosa' (Interview Grade 4 Teacher). It is exactly this disassembling – but also reassembling – of morphemes that we can observe in this learner's writing. Even though the feature '-ing' is only taught with examples of Standard English verbs in class, the learner here shows that she has understood the rules of the englishing game and can confidently apply them for her own purposes beyond a limited set of verbs. Taking advantage of the freedom provided by this unconventional, heterogenised school writing space, she uses the affordances and the expressive potential of '-ing' without being concerned with the conflation of grammatical features and nomolanguages (Section 2.1.2).

Apart from appearing rather playful and creative, 'vuking' might also help the learner to get around having to use a phrasal verb with '-ing' as in 'the boy is waking up'. The use of 'tshoning' might also be easier than thinking about how to spell 'drowning' with the rather uncommon SWE digraph 'ow'. Those two verb forms might therefore allow the learner to exploit the semantic potential of '-ing' and demonstrate her morphological assembling skills without getting muddled up in phrasal verbs and spelling complications that she might not yet navigate confidently. One has to be careful, however, not to reduce such writing to an avoidance strategy and also consider the possibility that this learner, in fact, simply prefers 'vuking' and 'tshoning' over 'waking up' and 'drowning', because she might want to show off her creative languaging skills or she feels that these forms allow her to express particular shades of meaning that the other forms wouldn't have offered. Her forms might simply be the best choice for what she has to say and/or a way of demonstrating to potential readers what she can do with language.

The following can be inferred from this learner's practices with regard to teaching Standard English in Khayelitsha: Similarly to the abstraction of a task instruction from the learners rewriting in Example A (Section 6.2.2), the 'vuking' and 'tshoning' example can be used to inspire verb-form assembling tasks where learners could test Standard English morphology on Standard Xhosa or Khayelitshan verbs and vice versa. Such exercises would value the resources and languaging skills that learners bring to the classroom and further their metalinguistic awareness of the mobility of morphemes at the same time.

I have not yet attended to the third time this learner assembles the feature '-ing' in her writing (in C4 where she writes 'in picture 3 the Boy is swiming') for reasons I will explain below.

6.2.6 Swiming or swimming? Deficit or potential?

When I first looked at this writing piece, I saw three instances of '-ing': 'vuking', 'tshoning' and 'swiming'. The two discussed above, 'vuking' and 'tshoning', struck me as innovative and skilful, 'swiming' didn't. I saw it as a 'spelling mistake' – a learner trying to write the Standard English form 'swimming' but failing to realise the second '-m-'. Simple. I had, however, committed not to revert to terms like 'mistake' or 'error' in my analyses (Section 1.7), so I had to take a detour and look again.

I realised that I had, in fact, heard people use the verb root '-swim-' in Khayelitshan languaging. There is a beach not too far away, where everyone likes to celebrate Christmas or New Year's Eve. Going to the beach and (not) being able to swim are sometimes topics of conversation. In fact, if I were to explain to someone in Khayelitsha that I like to swim, I would say something like: 'Ndiyathanda ukuswima'. A Google search for the infinitive 'ukuswima' *(to swim)* generates 235 hits in online writing[20] – predominantly on social media – from across South Africa. The verb root '-swim-' is then not only a potential Standard English and Khayelitshan resource, but also seems sedimented in a variety of spatial repertoires in South Africa – including in online spaces.

Walking the other way and then seeing 'swim' as not necessarily a Standard English resource in this space opens a new analytical avenue with regard to Example C: 'swiming' might, in fact, be used no differently from 'vuking' and 'tshoning' – as a Khayelitshan verb root with the present continuous marker '-ing'. This interpretation sheds a different light on the spelling of 'swiming' with one 'm'. Standard Xhosa orthography generally doesn't allow for double consonants[21] and therefore 'ukuswima', even though it ends in a vowel, would still only be spelled with one 'm'. Accordingly, when attaching the vowel-commencing present tense continuous suffix '-ing', the learner also abstains from inserting another 'm'. If we consider the different sets of orthographic conventions that can be folded into the English classroom during a writing activity, then we see that *what we might read as a failure to comply with one set of standard orthographic conventions (SWE) might in fact be a successful orientation towards another such set of standard conventions (SWX)*.

The example of 'swiming' then highlights the difference between reading township school writing with an orientation towards deficit versus one towards potential. This is the difference, I would argue, between seeing like a state and seeing like a Khayelitshan languager. When I saw 'swiming' as a spelling mistake, I was seeing like a state. When I took a detour and considered the option that the verb '-swima' might be involved, I began seeing like a Khayelitshan languager. It is the latter perspective that allowed me to see creativity instead of limitation and emergent englishing instead of deficient Standard English.

6.3 Chapter Discussion

I started this chapter with the hypothesis that a strictly monolingual policy in writing hides part of learners' existing englishing competencies. The latter, then, might only become visible in a space that allows for heterogeneity and experimentation but that is still within the normative space of the school.

englishing in spaces like Khayelitsha, which are constituted by heterogeneous linguistic possibilities, presupposes relanguaging – the *sorting out* of those resources that don't count as Standard English, because they aren't codified as such (see also Section 4.4.4). Once sorted out, the homogenised repertoire can be actualised through englishing. Translanguaging posits that such sorting processes happen in the minds of individual speakers (García & Wei, 2014; Otheguy *et al.*, 2015). This chapter has shown that analyses of heterogeneous writing can indeed make visible such spatialised sorting and choosing processes. Recall the example where we saw a learner in the immediate process of *sorting out* the spelling of [iː] in

> kwifoto yesi thathu ➡ I si ➡ I see

according to an emerging idea of what is asked for in different nomolanguages and their orthographies. Therefore, in the very heterogeneity of some writing pieces, learners' emerging awareness of the workings of SWE in contrast to SWX orthography became visible. Such pieces also push us to pay attention to the demand placed on Khayelitshan learners to handle and get tested via two orthographies in their early schooling careers (Section 1.4). An acute awareness of this fact is necessary, I argue, to assess learners' writing sensibly (discussed further in the conclusion).

Apart from spelling, the examples of reference tracking via third-person gendered pronouns have also shown how heterogeneity can actually speak of a strong orientation towards the rules of Standard English. Learners seem to avoid 'getting English wrong' by *sorting out* those features that confuse them, to then draw on alternative resources. Avoiding such pitfalls through relanguaging means that they have a sense about where they lurk in the first place – very similar to teachers who know when 'something would go wrong' (e.g. Sections 4.3.5 and 4.5.4). This, in turn, means that these learners have an emergent idea of the rules that constitute Standard English – e.g. that different gendered third-person pronouns are required in different scenarios – and actively grapple with them. Reversing the perspective and starting from heterogeneous writing therefore makes visible what learners can do instead of what they cannot do.

The examples of 'vuking' and 'tshoning' display the englishing competency of assembling the present continuous tense across various verbs. Furthermore, we see here reflected the teachers' assumption that their learners can treat morphology as separable and mobile and dis- and reassemble pieces as part of learning to english (discussed in Section 4.4.3 with 'ndiyitrainile' and 'meanisha'). Somewhat unexpectedly, therefore, letting learners write heterogeneously can, in this case, confirm and substantiate the knowledge that teachers have about their learners' languaging skills and the way it guides their teaching. There could be an explicit feedback loop about these emerging skills if learners were allowed to write heterogeneously in English classrooms. But for now this is unthinkable, due the strong ideologies of – and the departmental pressure for – linguistic purity in writing (Section 6.1.2).

The last example illustrated how an unscrutinised statist vision, which only considers nomolanguages as reference points in analyses, doesn't allow us to see anything but a 'spelling mistake' in 'swimming'.[22]

Considering linguistic features as linked to spaces, however, allows us to see '-swima' as a Khayelitshan resource and 'swimming' as derived from that form in adherence to SWX orthography. Unsettling the statist lens and providing alternatives is therefore indeed a matter of educational justice – not because the statist vision has to be altogether discarded, but because it isn't illuminating enough on its own. We need the local languager's vision to complement it, if we are seriously concerned about teaching and assessing the mastery of the principles of Standard English in locally appropriate and fair ways.

This chapter has also shown that we can learn from learners when developing such locally appropriate teaching and assessment of SWE. The learner who rewrote part of her own text (Section 6.2.2) demonstrated how task instructions could be developed that make learners first practice and then rewrite SWE, giving them a chance to express their nuanced understanding of the material via the full spatial repertoire they have access to – without compromising on engagement with the targeted statist repertoire. The 'vuking' and 'tshoning' example inspired thought on verb-form assembling tasks where learners could test Standard English features on Standard Xhosa or Khayelitshan ones and vice versa, to value the resources they bring and to further their metalinguistic awareness of the mobility of morphemes. But rather than being concerned about the concrete shape of tasks that could be developed, I am here advocating a method of abstracting appropriate content for curricula from the situated practices of teachers and learners (discussed more in the conclusion).

In light of these findings, suggestions of a lack of standard linguistic norms in spaces like Khayelitsha, which allegedly keeps learners and teachers stuck in peripheral normativity (Blommaert *et al.*, 2005), have to be strongly rejected. The opposite is more like it: there is an oversupply of standard linguistic norms that learners have to navigate. Due to this oversupply, Khayelitshan learners have to be skilful relanguagers, good at ordering and *sorting out* heterogeneous spatial repertoires according to two nomolanguages. They demonstrate how they can do that in their writing, if given the chance. But if we look through a statist, homogenising lens, we cannot see how they are sorting things out.

While I as an analyst am constantly concerned not to see like a state, this chapter shows learners who have taken on this statist perspective and are learning to order their writing accordingly. Their heterogeneous writing pieces aren't products of translanguaging – a practice associated with a non-watchfulness towards constructed language boundaries (Otheguy *et al.*, 2015). Instead, their writing is a product of relanguaging, of *sorting out* the complex heterogeneous repertoire of this school writing space while being watchful towards – but not yet always a hundred percent in keeping with – standard linguistic norms.

The problem with translanguaging, as I see it, is that – as a linguistic descriptor – it is constructed as inherently different from nomolanguages.

This dichotomy becomes apparent when Otheguy *et al.* (2015) argue that nomolanguages are *never* relevant categories for linguistic analyses under the translanguaging paradigm. So, if we decide to stand on the translanguaging side, then we might no longer see the role of nomolanguages. This explains why translingual writing is mostly described as occurring in the planning and drafting stages of what is later to become a written piece in a standard nomolanguage, or for particular stylistic points in the final product (Velasco & García, 2014). Translingual writing has also been promoted in higher education contexts for students to develop their individual voices and to unsettle linguistic purism in academic writing (Canagarajah, 2013). But translanguaging is not used when testing for competencies in standard nomolanguages because allegedly there are no nomolanguages in translanguaging.

The analyses I provided here, in search for *re-* rather than *trans-* languaging, instead suggest that we can see linguistic heterogeneity as inclusive of – but not limited to – linguistic homogeneity. If we can see writing that displays englishing competencies without being in English-only, then we can see languaging as inclusive of nomolanguages. This has consequences for conceptualisations of language teaching, learning and testing, because it means that there is no need to posit that competency in a standard nomolanguage can only be tested monolingually. englishing competencies can, in this view, indeed be tested beyond the confines of Standard English – a point further discussed in the Conclusion.

7 Conclusion: So What?

7.1 Seeing More

I have argued throughout that existing concepts of language (re)produce blind spots in our analyses of language practices. I illustrated this with the example of Khayelitshan English classrooms, where we see mostly linguistic deficit and the absence of Standard English if we rely on analytical concepts that don't thoroughly unsettle the default conflation of linguistic features and nomolanguages (Section 2.1.2). This relic from classical linguistic thought still finds its way into the application of concepts like code-switching (Section 2.2.2) and even into inchoative ideas like translanguaging (Section 2.2.3) that are meant to free us from being caught in nomolanguages when analysing languaging.

When relying on these concepts, we therefore wouldn't capture what exactly language education in Khayelitsha looks like and whether there is more to discover than linguistic lack and deficit. In this experiment, I have inflicted on myself some serious word-finding difficulties by *sorting out* a range of established analytical descriptors for linguistic analyses (Section 1.7). The resulting quest for new vocabulary has overall proven productive, as it forced me to explore different analytical and descriptive avenues.

Seeing that 'swimming' could be a manifestation of a learner's linguistic sorting skills is a result of my refusal to describe it as a 'spelling mistake'. Shedding light on 'u-' as a metalanguaging tool and an englishing device depended on *not* labelling 'uangry' a 'heteroglossic term' that has some general functions in common with other such non-monolingual terms. Discovering 'train' as (also) a Khayelitshan resource relates to rejecting a default association of linguistic features with nomolanguages and – by conceptualising languaging as a spatial practice – to analytically attaching them to spaces of interaction instead.

Linking linguistic features to space instead of nomolanguages has also produced more detailed questions about these features' individual occurrences; questions we then could ask teachers in interviews. Their detailed responses, combined with the linguistic, ethnographic and conversation analytical approach to the data that took the agency of individual linguistic detail seriously, has revealed Khayelitshan English classrooms to be spaces that offer a wide range of heterogeneous linguistic possibilities. The fact that learners and teachers share the languaging of the township, which is characterised by heterogeneity and flexibility (Section 1.2), means that the ensemble of linguistic possibilities in the English classroom that teachers have at their disposal is extended in different ways compared to that in classrooms at, for example, ex-Model C schools. The latter are the schools where learners and teachers perform well in standardised assessments and are therefore seen (when seeing like a state) as in the lead in South African education. However, useful tools like 'u-' are likely absent from these sought-after classrooms, where teachers generally have only very limited access to the resources that characterise the out-of-school language practices of most of their learners. Neither would their teacher training, which is English centred and doesn't value heterogeneous language practices (see, for example, Sections 4.4.3, 5.1.2 and 5.2.7), introduce them to the intricacies of such morphology, even though a substantial proportion of their learners are likely to come from language backgrounds where the affordances of such morphology play a central role.

When teaching English, Khayelitshan teachers therefore handle and shape classroom repertoires that offer them more linguistic affordances. Simultaneously, they need to put more effort into ordering and sorting out these repertoires, so that they don't lose sight of their mandate to provide learners with access to homogenised Standard English. I have described the practice with which teachers order and sort out linguistic possibilities from the classroom repertoire as relanguaging. Teachers were shown to sort out or bring together linguistic possibilities from the classroom repertoire before actualising them into classroom languaging or englishing.

I had conceptualised relanguaging first as emerging at the threshold of linguistic heterogeneity and homogeneity, systematically preparing either classroom languaging or classroom englishing (Section 2.4). But this convenient binary broke down at certain points throughout the analyses, which I interpreted as a sign that I had stopped linguistically seeing like a state. We then saw relanguaging occur within the Standard English repertoire as well, now at the threshold of what the teacher considered likely accessible and likely inaccessible englishing for her learners – like when she sorted out 'who he is' from 'He can always remember who he is', as a potential stumbling block, replacing it with a direct speech construction (Section 4.5.6). Or when the teacher relanguaged complex passages from the test paper into more accessible englishing that made implicit information explicit. It became clear that, from a perspective that posits heterogeneity as the norm, a binary between homogeneity and heterogeneity cannot be maintained. By zooming in on individual linguistic features and then looking at how they shape the classroom repertoire, 'mayibe yichicken' (Sections 4.3.3 and 4.3.4) and 'in Mrs Mann's house he didn't have to work' (Section 5.3.3) were both shown to be outcomes of relanguaging as an ordering of the spatial repertoire to facilitate a didactics of explicitness.

Linguistic homogeneity or heterogeneity, therefore, doesn't necessarily mark different languaging or teaching strategies – they might in some cases, but not always. Therefore, the two don't form a binary that consistently legitimises analyses of one as separate from the other. Their distinction is not relevant in every space at every point in time – it is only the statist lens that makes us believe that it is (Section 5.3.3). Relanguaging, therefore, cannot always be discovered by spotting non-monolingual language practices in a way reminiscent of the statist vision that posits homogeneity as the norm and heterogeneity as the deviation – or at least as the interesting event. Accordingly, what exactly constitutes relanguaging is always relative to space and the mechanism cannot be spotted at the surface level without conceptualising what constitutes the linguistic space in which it occurs and which it simultaneously produces. This differentiates the term from translanguaging as a linguistic descriptor, which has been applied 'from school to street and beyond' (Lewis *et al.*, 2012: 641) and always tends to signify the same thing: heterogeneous language practices that are *per se* interesting and said to fulfil functions that are different from homogeneous practices.

Relanguaging has the potential to unsettle the binary between nomolanguages and languaging so that we can conceptualise them together, and it might therefore become a useful descriptor for linguistic dynamics in spaces of language teaching. The term describes a complex sorting mechanism that requires further exploration. It needs to be examined, for example, in how far the relanguaging circles I have built are models with illustrative and explanatory potential beyond the data at hand. Here, the circles have helped me to show that relanguaging is more accurately described as emerging at the threshold of teachers' responsibility towards their learners on the one hand, and towards the state – more specifically educational officials – on the other. This threshold sometimes coincides with that between linguistic heterogeneity and homogeneity and other times with that between accessible and inaccessible englishing within a homogenised repertoire (homogenised here again from the perspective that normalises the heterogeneity of classroom languaging [see Section 4.5.6]), but it always reflects teachers' simultaneous orientation towards their learners and towards what is expected by the curriculum. Relanguaging, in the case of Khayelitsha Primary, appears as a pivotal practice that repairs the ruptures between the demands of a centralised curriculum and Khayelitshan linguistic and educational realities, as I will discuss further below.

7.2 Seeing Like a Township Teacher

Being an English teacher at Khayelitsha Primary means to simultaneously see like a Khayelitshan learner and like a state. Teachers have an eye on their learners' needs and an eye on statist demands, which are expressed, for example, in examination papers. They have an eye on local languaging and an eye on Standard English; an eye on Khayelitsha and an eye on the state. Through relanguaging, they integrate these two perspectives into a complementary vision: They sort out the classroom repertoire to satisfy statist demands and bring resources together to speak to the linguistic needs and skills of their learners. Relanguaging, I argue, facilitates what is increasingly found by South African scholars to be 'in many ways an impossible task of teaching children with an inappropriate language policy and a complete lack of language support in textbooks and assessment' (Bua-Lit Collective, 2018: 20).

Plenty of translanguaging literature urges teachers to value the flexible linguistic skills of their learners instead of prioritising monolingualism. The two teachers in focus in this study do both, by thinking linguistic heterogeneity and homogeneity together. They are well aware of what the Department of Education wants (Standard English) and what it doesn't want ('code-switching'), but they still merge the two. This awareness of statist demands for linguistic homogeneity makes relanguaging as *bringing together*, which often results in heterogeneous classroom languaging, a subversive practice with which teachers change the rules of the game and resist official prescriptions for monolingualism. This happens in a quest to eventually make learners adhere to these same prescriptions so they can satisfy the demands of the curriculum (Sections 5.2 and 5.3). Therefore, teachers' subversive practices ultimately support the system that makes such subversion necessary in the first place (Section 5.4.3).

Teachers at Khayelitsha Primary normally manage to combine pedagogically valuable teaching strategies with this aim of system compliance. Yet, if the systemic pressure for English-only becomes too strong, teachers are forced to look more in the direction of the state and teaching strategies can turn into prompting and coaching practices. The analysis of the test lesson illustrated this (Section 5.3). I have argued that the spatial assemblage here is different from everyday classroom activities. The traceable test paper, to be filled with written responses in homogenised Standard Written English (SWE), makes educational officials' demands for English-only more present in the classroom and turns relanguaging from something that prepares pedagogically valuable didactic strategies into the basis for a test coaching practice that trains learners to listen out for answers rather than to engage with the material. Now the teacher is less oriented towards teaching her learners how to english and more towards making them produce what the education system expects of them: Standard English. This orientation towards officialdom becomes visible in a largely homogenised classroom repertoire during the testing activity. Even in that process, however, she still manages to some extent to cater to the needs of her learners, creatively bringing Oliver Twist characters to life in the Khayelitshan classroom, showing us that relanguaging is not limited to what are traditionally considered to be linguistic features (Section 5.3.5). But when it comes to the test questions, the pressure to make her learners pass – so that the department will not 'come after her' – wins, and she uses relanguaging basically to tell her class what to write (Sections 5.3.6 and 5.3.7).

Teachers' knowledge and practices act as the glue that keeps a centralised curriculum – which relies on multiple homogenised standard nomolanguages as vehicles for testing – and local heterogeneous linguistic realities together. Teachers' complementary vision allows them to keep South African education working. They are not peripheral but *central* to the system. In an ironic reversal of the conclusion in the curriculum evaluation report, where 'weak educator knowledge capacity' (Department of Education, 2017: 22) keeps the Curriculum Assessment Policy Statements (CAPS) curriculum from providing equitable education across South Africa, there are indications here that it is the complementary vision instantiated in the relanguaging skills of these very teachers that makes the curriculum implementable in the first place. Without it, 'half of the class would fail' (Section 5.3.7), eagle stories would remain poems (Section 4.3.1) and synonyms for 'angry' would be lost (Section 5.2) in Standard English texts that learners cannot access, because the first three years of schooling they spent almost exclusively on learning how to access Standard Xhosa texts.

The evidence for these intense negotiations of linguistic heterogeneity and homogeneity – and of the needs of their learners and the demands of the state – that are displayed in township teachers' language practices is simultaneously evidence against the argument that teachers and learners are stuck in peripheral normativity and have 'downscaled' education to the level of their local community (Blommaert et al., 2005). Teachers order the classroom repertoire through relanguaging based on detailed knowledge about Standard English and the specific struggles their learners face when trying to access it. In-depth interviews that zoomed in on the use of particular linguistic features have here revealed such knowledge.

Instead of being cut off from standard linguistic norms, teachers at Khayelitsha Primary are entangled in negotiations between languaging and nomolanguages. Relanguaging instantiates these negotiations in the classroom. Forms like 'ndiyitrainile' (Section 4.4) in this space don't reveal a lack of standard linguistic norms or their transcendence but are strategic pointers into Standard English. The morpheme 'u-' can mark words as Standard English rather than transcend linguistic fixity – nomolanguages are in the languaging here, and through a lens that assumes heterogeneity we can identify norms associated with homogenised codes in heterogeneous practices. Thus, there is no lack of standard norms in Khayelitsha, rather we have not been looking for them in the proper place. We have been looking for them as separate from linguistic heterogeneity and fluidity as 'something different'.

Rather than peripheral, teachers at schools like Khayelitsha Primary are, in fact, central to the workings of South African education. Their central role, however, remains invisible in a system that constructs linguistic homogeneity and heterogeneity as strictly separate and posits the former as the norm and the latter as the deviation. Our notion of the standard tends to be too fixed to find traces of it anywhere outside of its own confines and our notion of languaging too fluid to be accommodative of fixed elements. How orientations towards linguistic homogeneity and standard linguistic norms can be found in heterogeneous languaging has also been illustrated in the analyses of learners' writing (Chapter 6).

7.3 Blind Spots Blocking Educational Change

It is not only teachers who have to sort out the classroom repertoire before they actualise linguistic possibilities. Learners have even more intense *sorting out* to do. In order to understand why they are often silenced under a strictly enforced policy of monolingualism, one has to 'see' that language learning at Khayelitsha Primary means beginning from a heterogeneous Khayelitshan repertoire and then having to relanguage it – to sort it out in order to comply with two nomolanguages: Standard Xhosa and Standard English.

When viewing languaging as a spatial practice, this sorting process imposed on Khayelitshan learners is not a consequence of their particularly complex individual repertoires, as translanguaging scholarship with its focus on individual speakers has it (García & Wei, 2014; Otheguy et al., 2015). Rather, the fact that they have to become relanguagers is actively produced by a system that enforces two standard nomolanguages in early schooling that are, both in their own ways, quite removed from Khayelitshan languaging. As a Khayelitshan learner, if you cannot relanguage – i.e. in this case if you cannot sort out a heterogeneous spatial repertoire into nomolanguages – then you can neither xhosa nor english, yet you need both to succeed in primary school. Again, this study has shown that Khayelitshan learners don't confront a lack but an oversupply of standard linguistic norms (Section 6.2.3), as the state brings to bear two homogenised ordering regimes on heterogeneous linguistic realities.

The analyses of the writing pieces revealed that one practice that enables Khayelitshan learners to produce something that fits the Standard English category is indeed relanguaging – the ordering and *sorting out* of heterogeneous spatial repertoires. It is only then that they can english – actualise the sorted, homogenised repertoire. Allowing for heterogeneous writing and analysing it as a spatial practice make visible relanguaging as a complex, multidirectional linguistic sorting practice that can bring forth emergent englishing. This sorting practice became especially visible not only in the spelling trajectory that led from 'kwifoto yesibini' to 'I si' and then to 'I see' (Section 6.2.3), but also in the general juggling of several orthographic norms and the *sorting out* of Standard English gendered pronouns to replace them with familiar morphological reference trackers (Section 6.2.4).

These intense negotiations of linguistic fixity in fluidity, which learners can be shown to engage in when writing heterogeneously are invisible to educational officials. As it stands, seeing like a state in South African education means *not to see* linguistic sorting skills – neither those of teachers nor those of learners. This is because educational administrators get information about learners' and teachers' performance across schools with the help of standardised tests and measurements that rely on categories and scales. With regard to English teaching and learning, the measurement scales begin and end within the confines of Standard English, limiting administrators' eyesight to this statist repertoire. The threshold of heterogeneity and homogeneity – where relanguaging often takes place and englishing emerges – is not part of the unit of measurement and therefore invisible. What is left to be seen is rudimentary Standard English, just enough to pass the tests. Those tests can be passed (barely), because teachers are, to some degree, able to glue over the ruptures in a system that turns learners into professional relanguagers and emergent englishers but, blind to its own product, tests them within the confines of nomolanguages. From the statist perspective, where linguistic homogeneity is the norm, only deficient Standard English – and by extension deficient education – exists in Khayelitsha.

This restricted eyesight also limits available options for educational change. Either education needs to be 'downscaled' in response to alleged local deficiencies, or the status quo must be maintained under the motto that those who work hard enough will make it. These two options are reflected in the 2017 CAPS evaluation report, which brings up the following question:

> Should a 'watered-down' version of CAPS be implemented in rural contexts, or indeed in Quintile 1-3 schools, since, as a group, they are disadvantaged compared with those in Quintiles 4 and 5? (Department of Education 2017: 19)

Educational administrators counter this suggestion with a sameness-equals-fairness argument, according to which the same curriculum ensures that learners across the country have the same chances. Adjusting standards locally is therefore not an option (Department of Education, 2017: 19). The sensible thought of the evaluators to be read from the watering-down suggestion is that curricula might have to be spatially adequate and not the same across the country. As usual, however, this is framed in the powerful discourse of lack and disadvantage within which rural and township schools are constructed in South African education. Here, it is not even enough to depict these schools as peripheral spaces to which the centre would have to look out. Rather, they become subordinate spaces for which standards would have to be watered down because learners and teachers there cannot keep up. Neither option – watering things down nor leaving everything as it is – suggests any scrutiny regarding the dominant deficit perspective on township or lower-quintile schools that would take the particular linguistic skills learners and teachers develop in these spaces into account.

As it stands, the interaction between teachers in these spaces and educational stakeholders seems to be hung up in an unproductive balance. From the perspective of the teachers, it doesn't make sense to speak up about the struggles they have in dealing with 'books with too difficult words' (Section 2.3.2) or in making learners pass English tests. They cannot expect much understanding from departmental officials, in whose eyes 'code-switching' is to be avoided and who might 'come after' teachers if many learners fail tests (Section 5.3.1). With the prospect of having their teaching and their English language competencies – or indeed their very capacity for knowledge – questioned more readily than the structures of the administrative system that they are a part of, it can be assumed that most teachers keep quiet so as not to attract any attention.

In the face of the complexity of English teaching and learning in Khayelitsha, it can be argued that educational stakeholders should consider relanguaging their language when giving accounts of township schools or lower-quintile schools more generally. The contempt towards teachers' English skills and 'knowledge capacity' is oblivious to what it means to keep things together linguistically in Khayelitshan English classrooms. Then again, stakeholders are, in fact, literally blind to relanguaging with which English teachers and learners juggle statist demands. The responsibility for educational change therefore doesn't exclusively lie with educational stakeholders – even though a change in their attitudes must certainly be a big part of the move towards more equitable education – but linguists in education also have to produce analyses that can lead to visible and feasible alternatives. So what could enable officials to see linguistic sorting skills and what would that mean?

7.4 Some Recommended Rethinking

As of now, linguistic homogeneity occupies centre stage and heterogeneity symbolises the periphery – and even subordination – in education in South Africa. It has been noted that there is a 'lack of take up in language in education policy and practice of anti-essentialist and heteroglossic approaches to language from critical applied linguistics and sociolinguistics' (McKinney *et al.*, 2015: 121). In turn, scholars in the country increasingly call for policies that put translanguaging, or languaging-for-learning, centre stage, to do justice to the complex sociolinguistic realities of the majority population that remains marginalised in education (Banda, 2018; Bua-Lit Collective, 2018; Guzula *et al.*, 2016). Translanguaging here has become a powerful language-political term that unites movements and voices advocating for educational change. While I scrutinise and critically evaluate translanguaging as a linguistic descriptor, because it draws attention to surface-level phenomena and makes us overlook details that matter, I nevertheless value the term for its potential for political mobilisation.

Based on my findings, which have revealed Khayelitshan English classrooms as spaces of specific possibilities, I align myself with calls to put these heterogeneous resources and learners' and teachers' existing languaging skills centre stage in South African education. Nevertheless, operating as it stands within the order of the nation state, we need to also be concerned with how the state's demands for legibility and measurability can be sufficiently satisfied if the focus is to shift from a preoccupation with linguistic purity and boundedness towards flexible languaging skills that, by definition, are harder to account for via standardised tests. On the basis of the findings presented here, I wish to contribute to these calls for educational change in South Africa a narrative that relates specifically to the teaching of English – or maybe of nomolanguages more generally – and that might help bridge the gap between educational stakeholders, learners and teachers in Khayelitsha and beyond.

In my view what is needed is an empirically and theoretically well-founded argument that can convince educational stakeholders that linguistic heterogeneity is not inherently different from standard nomolanguages and therefore not detrimental to their teaching and acquisition. Quite the contrary: It needs to be convincingly argued and demonstrated that it is linguistic sorting practices that lead to the acquisition of nomolanguages in spaces like Khayelitsha. These can only become visible when linguistic heterogeneity is also allowed to become visible. Like linguists, state officials and state influencers who work on language policy must learn to 'see' linguistic heterogeneity as the norm and homogeneity as the result of increasingly sophisticated linguistic sorting practices.

This then is firstly a call for a spatially sensitive linguistics that commits to untying the knot of nomolanguages and linguistic features until nomolanguages are no longer analytical default categories. Simultaneously, the claim that nomolanguages are altogether irrelevant categories in linguistics (Otheguy *et al.*, 2015) has to be rejected. This would make linguists blind to scenarios where statist repertoires are, in fact, oriented towards and watchfully adhered to – for example in education. Conceptualising translanguaging as an individual practice that is undistracted by nomolanguages doesn't seem helpful for explaining linguistic dynamics in such spaces. Within the minds of individuals, we have no possibility to detect linguistic sorting processes. We can therefore also not reconcile linguistic heterogeneity and homogeneity, because relanguaging, the mechanism that entangles them, remains hidden. The new wave of translinguistics then runs the risk of reproducing unsustainable and unhelpful binaries, this time making linguistic homogeneity the odd one out, reminiscent of how classical linguistics has systematically shut out linguistic heterogeneity (see also Jaspers, 2019). We can return here to Hymes (as quoted in Section 2.2.1), who said that

> we have to break with the tradition of thought which simply equates one language, one culture, and takes a set of functions for granted. In order to deal with the problems faced by disadvantaged children, and with education in much of the world, we have to begin with the conception of the speech habits, or competencies, of a community or population, and regard the place among them of the resources of historically-derived languages as an empirical question. (Hymes, 1972: 288)

This can be read as a call to put linguistic heterogeneity centre stage but to keep our concepts open for nomolanguages. I argue that progress in this direction can be made by thinking further about what it means to see languaging as a spatial practice and to exploit the inchoative concept of spatial repertoires not only outside of, but also within institutionally regulated linguistic spaces. With the help of the conceptualisation of classroom repertoires as folding into one another linguistic heterogeneity and homogeneity, and the relanguaging model that makes visible the linguistic sorting practices of teachers and learners, it can be argued that standard linguistic norms can be read from heterogeneous practices. If linguistic homogeneity can be conceptualised as the result of sorting processes that begin from a heterogeneous norm, then standard nomolanguages become possible constituents of languaging.

Conjunctive conceptualisations of languaging and nomolanguages can produce new ideas to address problems in (language) education. For English classrooms in Khayelitsha (and arguably beyond) this means that Standard English needs neither to be taught nor tested exclusively within its own confines. Instead, teaching strategies can be formalised that promote the advancement of relanguaging skills – examples are the teachers' vocabulary teaching strategies via Khayelitshan morphology (meanisha; ndiyitrainile) and their oscillation between heterogeneous classroom languaging and the demonstration of englishing.

So maybe, instead of judging how teachers teach and measuring how learners write within a predefined statist repertoire, the degree of advancement of their linguistic sorting skills could be measured, while they are learning exactly what goes where in the game of xhosing, englishing and Khayelitshan languaging. All this would mean to turn English classrooms into englishing classrooms that assume heterogeneity as the baseline condition from which a journey towards Standard English begins. Instead of finding heterogeneous deviations in supposedly homogeneous practices, we can turn the perspective on its head to look for homogeneity in heterogeneity and formalise techniques for gradually eliciting it. I argue that in this process of developing such techniques, illustrations from spaces where teachers have been teaching and learners have been learning how to sort out heterogeneous classroom repertoires all along, can help (see also Bua-Lit Collective, 2018).

Rather than (solely) relying on descriptions and prescriptions of translanguaging strategies from educational settings in the Global North, I suggest we build a knowledge base that consists of detailed descriptions of how English teaching currently functions in spaces like Khayelitsha. We are just beginning to explore the expertise hidden in schools that have traditionally been banned to the periphery. We need more studies that make it visible, render it accessible and make its productive features strategically reproducible. In-depth linguistic ethnographies are essential here and I hope this study has given some insight with regard to what fine-grained enquiry could look like. With an expanding knowledge fund, appropriate content for curricula could be abstracted from situated practices and illustrated with examples from these spaces. Why not formalise strategies of metalanguaging and vocabulary teaching via Bantu morphology? All English teachers in South Africa, who are almost bound to have Bantu language speakers in their classes, could profit from extending their English classrooms' repertoires by knowing how to use 'u-' or other morphological affordances that can facilitate access to Standard English. Why not promote the ability 'turn an English word into a Xhosa word' (compare Interview Excerpt d, p. 92) to help learners access Standard English vocabulary? Is that so far-fetched for teachers at more affluent schools to learn?

When it comes to testing, tasks can be developed that speak to learners' particular linguistic skills and struggles – rewriting and verb form assembling tasks (Sections 6.2.2 and 6.2.5) are examples I here elicited from learners' practices – and scales can be developed that measure learners' progression as they gain increasing access to Standard English and become able to sort out more and more Khayelitshan resources. For example, they might still need the Khayelitshan noun class agreement morphology to unambiguously express referential relationships in their emergent englishing, because reference tracking via only three gendered pronouns has been shown to be especially difficult for these learners in their writing (Section 6.2.4). Teachers have also been shown to avoid Standard English third-person pronouns in their classroom languaging, reducing learners' exposure to such forms. It is imaginable that in writing tasks up to a certain level, the tracking of referents via Khayelitshan morphology in written englishing is legitimate and particular teaching tasks get developed that speak to the difficulties of navigating landscapes of different orders for reference tracking. With regard to spelling, the oversupply of standard orthographic norms that Khayelitshan learners have to negotiate in early schooling needs to be considered in testing. For example, the use of diphthongs within words – whether in complete accordance with the rules of SWE or not – should be considered a major step in the *sorting out* of the different orthographic conventions of Standard Written Xhosa (SWX) and SWE. How far these sorting processes are advanced becomes most visible in heterogeneous rather than homogenised writing, as the example of *sorting out* the spelling of 'I si' into 'I see' (Section 6.2.3) has shown.

These are just some pointers at what we can learn from Khayelitshan learners' heterogeneous writing. Large-scale, survey-like studies could gather writing pieces where learners across the country are unrestricted in their linguistic choices. Do learners in other schools also decide to write heterogeneously in large numbers? What emergent englishing skills and struggles can be read from their writing? What tasks can be developed that speak to these learners' particular needs and skills? Where are the differences and the similarities that are displayed in the linguistic heterogeneity elicited from different classroom spaces across the country? As a more differentiated picture of what constitutes relanguaging and englishing skills emerges, concrete suggestions can be made about how teaching and testing material could recognise and develop these skills.

If findings from this exploratory study can be substantiated, I argue that heterogeneous writing tasks can be used to test emergent englishing skills and that scales can be developed to make linguistic sorting practices visible and measurable for educational officials. This would, in my view, have a twofold effect: On the one hand, stakeholders' – including South African parents' – comprehensible desire to ensure access to Standard English for learners wouldn't be compromised but supported. On the other hand, the notion of what Standard English *is* or *has to be* would become more flexible as it would have to be questioned in the process of developing tasks that make it visible within linguistic heterogeneity. What Davila (2016) has called the discursively constructed 'inevitability of "Standard" English' in education and beyond is difficult to declare irrelevant or mistaken in a country like South Africa where access to what elites and state administrators recognise as this code strongly influences people's life trajectories. Access to higher education, to jobs and to lifeworlds beyond the township that many parents desire for their children intersect to a significant extent with this socially very real linguistic construct. I suggest that unsettling the common-sense assumption that Standard English can only be tested within its own confines without pushing for a complete 'transcendence' of linguistic fixity would be a viable compromise that would inevitably also unsettle the construct itself in a productive way. A more flexible and linguistically more adequate concept of what constitutes a standard language and different suggestions of how to test for it might be statist enough to allow administrators to see it and flexible enough to appreciate the linguistic heterogeneity that lies at the heart of many South African language classrooms.

7.5 Outlook

7.5.1 On linguistics

I have argued that part of what made the experiment of this book possible was that I retained a certain naivety towards the discipline of linguistics. I therefore was not too deeply entangled in its established categories of sense-making and could provide a fresh perspective on the data (Section 3.1). Nevertheless, the tools of the discipline have been invaluable in this endeavour. Even though linguistics is so entangled with the nomolanguage ideology and with seeing like a state (Section 2.1), a disentanglement and the development of new vocabulary is possible – as I have tried to show – without having to throw the baby (linguistics) out with the bathwater (the essentialised statist lens). Therefore, once we know better how to detect and unsettle the statist vision, all the findings of the seminal work done with the descriptors that I refused to use in this experiment must not be discarded but rather turned towards and engaged with from a critical but curious perspective. Then we can ask: How could an inchoative languaging-and-space paradigm profit from insights from translation studies or dialectology? What do we find when we are (a) tracing 'train' through townships or (b) looking for 'loanwords' and 'borrowing'? What would a code-switching paper read like if relanguaged into languaging vocabulary? How could our understanding of languaging in turn be enriched by findings from code-switching research if we disentangled them from the nomolanguage ideology? And what would change for – but also what could be learned from – studies in the field of second language acquisition if the notion of first language (L1) were replaced with the idea of unsorted spatial repertoires?

There is a rich repertoire of linguistics that – rather than being 'transcended' – can be handled and shaped to equip us with tools to illuminate the relationality of languaging and nomolanguages without essentialising one or the other. So, as much as radical leaps must be taken that break with established categories to develop new lenses, there is also a need to go back and look at old insights through such new lenses and see what answers can be found to the above questions and to many more that I couldn't address in this work.

7.5.2 On 'mother tongues'

Taking linguistic heterogeneity in Khayelitsha seriously doesn't only have implications for the teaching and testing of Standard English. Standard Xhosa, via which learners get tested in Grade 3, is just as much a statist repertoire in watchful adherence to which they have to sort out their Khayelitshan languaging so that they can Xhosa. Accordingly, we can hypothesise that the Xhosa classrooms in Khayelitshan primary schools also necessitate relanguaging to negotiate Khayelitshan languaging and Standard Xhosa. What constitutes the practice in these spaces? If relanguaging could be made visible there, this could have consequences for debates around 'mother tongue education'. In how far does this language policy model – often advertised as the panacea to (South) Africa's educational problems – also force Khayelitshan learners to sort out a variety of their familiar language resources? Systematically investigating the tension between Khayelitshan languaging and Standard Xhosa this way has the potential to complexify debates around 'mother tongue education' in productive ways.

7.5.3 On 'centres' and 'peripheries'

There is a tendency in South African discourse around education to construct township (and in fact all lower-quintile schools) as linguistically inherently different from, for example, ex-Model C schools (see Section 1.5). My hypothesis to be tested by future research is that if we really stop linguistically seeing like a state, we can probably find relanguaging and a didactics of explicitness in spaces that aren't known for linguistic heterogeneity in teacher talk – like ex-Model C school classrooms, for example. But because there the relanguaging mechanism would produce combinations of forms that comply with the conflation of linguistic features and nomolanguages (Section 2.1.2), no statist boundaries between nomolanguages would be violated. At the moment, what surfaces through the statist lens in these spaces is not code-switching or translanguaging but *rephrasing, explaining* or *annotating* – all no threat to the linguistic ordering principles of the nation state and therefore neither seen as deficient nor as subversive practices. But when the very same relanguaging mechanism in Khayelitsha produces combinations of forms that *do* violate the conflation of linguistic features and nomolanguages that is constitutive of statist homogenisation and categorisation, then teachers are seen as 'code-switching' or 'translanguaging'. Accordingly, it is township teachers who are officially urged to 'reduce the amount of code-switching' (Western Cape Government, 2017), while what ex-Model C school teachers do with language is deemed fine.

My argument at this point is that classroom repertoires probably get ordered via relanguaging far beyond Khayelitsha and that it is the power of the statist lens that erases this common linguistic sorting mechanism. Through this lens, what township teachers do with language looks different from – and in fact less valuable than – what teachers in more affluent schools might be doing just as well. Positing heterogeneity as the norm and training the spotlight on the linguistic sorting mechanism provide an alternative perspective. If further substantiated and refined, this new lens and the relanguaging model might not only help to systematically unsettle the binary between linguistic heterogeneity and homogeneity but also that between township and ex-Model C schools and, by extension, that between constructed 'centres' and 'peripheries' in (South African) education. This is then a call to look for relanguaging in educational spaces that currently seem to be linguistically homogeneous – because they might not be.

7.5.4 Beyond linguistics, education and South Africa

The more inclusive conceptualisations of homogenised linguistic fixity and fluid, unsorted heterogeneity I propose here have relevance beyond education and beyond South Africa. Linguistic heterogeneity and diversity is increasing globally but stands in tension with simultaneously intensifying nationalist tendencies pushing for a fixation rather than a transcendence of borders and boundaries. Standardised language tests are becoming more rather than less important and the fixity of standard nomolanguages intensifies. Reflections presented here about unsettling and questioning standards without doing away with them – making fixity more flexible – and about testing for nomolanguages within languaging, could therefore be important far beyond Khayelitsha. Questions that emerge from this inquiry are: (1) How much linguistic homogeneity and fixity does the state need so that it can still see? and (2) What can linguists, educational administrators and policymakers in different spaces globally learn in this regard from South African township teachers and learners?

Notes

Chapter 1

(1) The verb 'to language' will be used throughout this book interchangeably with 'to use language'.
(2) Englished: The language of the township is *'mixed with the language of the Coloured people, [that] of the Xhosa people and [that] of the White people'*.
(3) As the opening quote shows, terms like 'Coloured' and 'White' reflect local language use with reference to South Africa's different population groups. I use such terms in this book without racist intention. 'Black' is used for persons of African descent, 'Coloured' for persons of KhoiSan or Cape Malay descent or mixed race and 'White' indicates European descent.
(4) https://www.etymonline.com/search?q=nominal (accessed 19 January 2021).
(5) 'Statist' is used throughout this book as an adjective derived from 'the state'. 'Statist' expresses a concern with simplification, homogenisation and categorisation for the purposes of promoting administrative legibility and control of the population.
(6) Unless specifically stated that Xhosa identity or ethnic affiliation is meant, I generally use the term Xhosa in this book to refer to the nomolanguage Xhosa.
(7) Personal communication Rose Marie Beck.
(8) Vast informal conglomerates of shacks and high degrees of informality make the population very difficult to count.
(9) These language practices are designated by their speakers with various names such as 'Tsotsitaal' or 'Iscamto' and scholars have analysed urban language practices under such labels as well – in South Africa (Deumert, 2013; Mesthrie & Hurst, 2013) and in other African urban settings (Beck, 2010; Kießling & Mous, 2004).
(10) Xhosa, Zulu, Tswana, Ndebele, Venda, Sotho, Northern Sotho, Swati, Tsonga, Afrikaans and English. Admittedly, these nomolanguages have different purchase in the structuring of that space as their ethnic and regional connotations are different.
(11) Primary schooling in South Africa is split into three phases: Foundation Phase (Grade R [preschool grade]–Grade 3), Intermediate Phase (Grades 4–6) and Senior Phase (Grade 7).
(12) In the South African context this code is often called 'Standard South African English' (SSAE). I am making general points about standardised nomolanguages versus non-codified languagING in this book and therefore I will not focus on differentiating between different standardised versions of 'a language'. Accordingly, I use 'Standard English' throughout.
(13) Classroom spaces, depending on the activity, can be structured by different linguistic constellations where, for example, only one of the standard nomolanguages is a relevant ordering principle. I will explain this further in Chapter 2, where I elaborate on languaging as a spatial practice, as well as at the relevant points of my data analyses.

(14) This particular quote is part of the unpublished data from my MA research project at Khayelitsha Primary that I will elaborate on in Section 3.1.
(15) The Bua-lit Collective is a collective of language and literacy researchers, activists, educators and teacher educators committed to addressing the inequality reproduced in the South African education system through sharing knowledge and resources on effective language and literacy teaching. https://bua-lit.org.za/.
(16) 'The English Language Skills Assessment (ELSA) Listening and Reading Tests measure general English language competence using work, home, social and travel settings; they test a person's ability to understand and communicate in the real world. ELSA tests are available in both British English and American English to meet all client requirements, and cover all levels of English language ability from very low to very high on a single scale for each skill. ELSA Listening and Reading Tests provide the precision, speed and convenience of multiple-choice tests' (LCCI Examinations Board, n.d.: 4).
(17) Here, the measurements are scaled in grade levels. Grade 12+ means English competencies that exceed those of a learner who mastered English in Grade 12.
(18) The CAPS, introduced in 2012, is the outcome of South Africa's most recent curriculum reform. For a discussion of the various reforms in the country since the end of apartheid, see for example Gumede and Biyase (2016).
(19) In this book, I am not engaging closely with the theory of sociolinguistic scales. See Prinsloo and Krause (2019b) for a theoretical discussion based on data from this PhD project.
(20) 'Nomolanguage ideology' is an adaptation of Sabino's (2018) 'languages ideology'.

Chapter 2

(1) I am aware of the complex debate around the topic of voice, especially in subaltern theory (cf. Spivak). A detailed account is beyond the scope and focus of this book and I therefore chose a rather simple and pragmatic definition of the concept at this point.
(2) Statements by the principal of Khayelitsha Primary that give insight into his nomolanguage ideology are discussed more extensively in Krause (2014), Krause and Prinsloo (2016) and Dowling and Krause (2018).
(3) In García's (2009) work, the bi- in bilingualism is not intended to stand for a repertoire made up of resources associated with two nomolanguages but bilingual speakers are those whose individual repertoire features resources associated with any number of named nomolanguages.
(4) Most scholars of translanguaging use the adjective 'pedagogical' for concrete teaching strategies. I find it useful, however, to use the term 'didactic' for those concrete classroom strategies and I reserve 'pedagogical' for all encompassing approaches to education that include, for example, a particular positioning and attitude towards learners. The introduction of 'didactic' also helps in discerning that translanguaging is indeed being used to describe three different things: language practices, didactic strategies and pedagogies.
(5) Sometimes Standard Xhosa is relevant as well, as I will show later.
(6) De Certeau's definition of spatial order describes what I will refer to merely as space throughout this work.
(7) De Certeau himself also draws a parallel between the act of walking and 'speech acts'. In his language comparison, however, he focuses on points different to those I want to make here. Nevertheless, it was his comparison of walking and speech acts that inspired me to try the same with walking and languaging.
(8) Somewhat more sedimented elements of the Khayelitshan repertoire include morphological resources for noun class agreement and other semantically rich

morphology that are not available in Standard English. While such morphology has been usefully described by Bantu linguists and is under that paradigm associated with Standard Xhosa, we have already seen in the opening quote that Khayelitshan languaging constantly thwarts the logic that entangles this morphology with a set of Standard Xhosa lexical items and grammar rules (e.g. ilanguage).

(9) I adopt the idea of 'foldedness' from Actor Network Theory (see, for example, Latour, 2005).

(10) I argue that Standard Xhosa is not a relevant ordering principle during the oral classroom activities in the English classroom, because adherence to this code is not policed or consistently approximated by teachers or learners. I will illustrate this point with empirical findings as I go along (e.g. in Sections 4.2.1, 4.4.2 and 4.5.5). When the classroom becomes a writing space, however, Standard Xhosa does become relevant as a linguistic ordering principle, as I will explain in Section 6.1.2.

(11) Instead of always talking about 'classroom languaging' and 'classroom englishing', I will sometimes just use 'languaging' and 'englishing'. These verbs in this context, however, always refer to actualisations of linguistic resources in the classroom, unless otherwise indicated.

(12) I take the idea that spatial repertoires can be differently 'balanced' from Baynham and Lee (2019: 111). They talk about the spatial repertoire during a capoeira dance session being sometimes balanced predominantly towards the verbal when the instructor explains or sings, and other times more towards 'a greater use of communication through physical movement' when the instructor demonstrates capoeira moves. In my case, I use the picture of balancing to illustrate how the teacher sometimes creates a more linguistically homogeneous and sometimes a more heterogeneous space through relanguaging.

(13) I am not positing that Khayelitshan languaging is 'unsorted'. Even though its ordering principles are mostly not nomolanguages, speakers certainly have shared ideas about what works and what doesn't, what combinations of linguistic features are and are not established. Even though those combinatory rules are highly flexible and non-codified and constantly transformed through languaging. With 'unsorted', I here refer to the state of the classroom repertoire that is contingent upon the particular resources present in a particular lesson. Depending, for example, on what story from the textbook is being read, there will be completely new languaging possibilities there compared to, for example, the day before and their combinatory possibilities are established by teachers and learners *in situ* rather than being 'presorted'.

Chapter 3

(1) Based on this manuscript but with a different focus on qualitative classroom research in cross-cultural contexts, a chapter with the title 'From Taxis to Classrooms in Khayelitsha: The Researcher as a Learner' is published in Hallitzky *et al.* (in press).

(2) 'The National Housing Subsidy Scheme, established in 1994, provides eligible households with a one-off housing subsidy that effectively gives ownership of a newly built house, colloquially known as RDP (Reconstruction and Development Programme) housing' (Lemanski, 2008: 394).

(3) Grade R is the pre-school grade with learners between 5 and 6 years of age.

(4) Information retrieved from the Education Management Information System (EMIS), accessed 19 July 2019.

(5) Data from the MA research project is also discussed in Krause and Prinsloo (2016) and Collins and Krause (2019).

(6) The name has been changed.

(7) A landmark close to Khayelitsha Primary, name changed here.

(8) The name has been changed.

(9) This is not an exact transcript of such an exchange as I didn't record informal interactions. Rather, it is based on memory protocols from my field notes.
(10) This issue is also discussed for the South African context in Setati (2005).
(11) This research is documented in Krause (2014), Krause and Prinsloo (2016) and Collins and Krause (2019).
(12) 'Achwayitile' is the Xhosa name I was given early on at the school.
(13) I am not an English teacher. I think sometimes the boundaries between me being interested in English teaching and teaching English myself became blurred, especially because 'doing research' is a rather intangible or unfamiliar activity for most participants.
(14) This is not to say that teachers speak more authoritatively because they comment on their own practices. Nevertheless, their skills and experiences as teachers and as witnesses of the situations in focus make them particular kinds of experts, whose voices help me in making sense of situated languaging.

Chapter 4

(1) The relanguaging circles in the data analyses are hyperlinked, so that when I refer to relanguaging moves (steps) further in the chapter, the reader can jump back to the relevant circle. Hyperlinked, clickable 'Steps' will be underlined.
(2) Interview excerpts are numbered with lower-case letters and transcripts of classroom data with capitals.
(3) For now, this describes any non-verbal, embodied resources actualised from the classroom repertoire. In Section 5.3.5, I discuss in more detail how such resources could also be described within the languaging vocabulary I develop in this book.
(4) Unpublished research obtained through personal communication with Tessa Dowling.
(5) In this case, Standard Xhosa would here briefly pop up as a relevant linguistic ordering principle in the classroom as well. In general, however, the animal examples illustrate that what is folded into each other in the English classroom as ordering principles during oral activities like this one is normally Standard English and Khayelitshan languaging, and not Standard Xhosa (see Section 2.3.2).
(6) In the negative (B7) the subjunctive is marked by -*nga*- in tense aspect (T(A)) position after the subject marker, and by the final vowel -*i* (e.g. in*ga*bi).
(7) To trace how this agreement morphology works together in reference tracking, see Appendix B and the tables with the noun class agreement morphology.
(8) ukuqeqesha = to train/ndiyiqeqeshile = I have trained it. It is common for speakers to include the infinitive in their own glosses of words, even if the infinitive morpheme uku- is not there.
(9) Gugulethu is a township directly adjacent to Khayelitsha, somewhat smaller and slightly closer to Cape Town.
(10) The teacher here refers to the morpheme as '-sha' while from a grammarian's point of view it includes 'i-' and the '-a', because the final vowel could change in different tenses and moods. Therefore, it is normally codified as 'ish-a'.
(11) This interview has also been reported on in Krause (2014), Krause and Prinsloo (2016) and Dowling and Krause (2018).
(12) Neither 'wobbled' nor 'flew' feature on the list of the 10,000 most used English words (last accessed on 25 July 2019).
(13) The learner's name has been changed.
(14) 'Ungabo' is short for 'ungahambi uyo-'.

Chapter 5

(1) According to the Curriculum Assessment and Policy document for Life Skills in the Intermediate Phase, 'the subject aims to develop learners through three different, but interrelated study areas, that is, Personal and Social Well-being, Physical Education and Creative Arts' (Department of Basic Education, 2011: 8).
(2) See Appendix C for a list of the dates on which each interview was conducted.
(3) This is a simplification as there are some consonant clusters, often for example with the letter 'h' that distinguishes some consonants to be either implosive or explosive (e.g. 'b' vs. 'bh'). The letter 'g' can indicate a voiced alveolar stop, or it can indicate voicing in clicks (e.g. 'gc', 'gx' or 'gq'). See, for example, Nurse and Philippson (2003) for more details on Bantu phonology.
(4) I reference here the Grade 5 teacher, who explained in Interview Excerpt a (p. 78) how she 'trains' her learners to read and speak in a particular rhythm.
(5) She identifies -ish-a here only as -*sha*, not including the -*i*- in her discussion of it.
(6) Although this is technically not a lesson transcript, I count it under the same category and use the capital letter referencing – we have arrived at 'I' at this point – for the lines as I refer to them throughout the analysis.
(7) The article 'the' doesn't appear in the original text but the teacher inserts it while reading.
(8) The expression 'each and every' is a typical feature of what scholars have described as 'Black South African English'. See de Klerk (2003) for a discussion.
(9) The verb '-bangel-' *(cause)* seems to be a useful resource for the teacher to relanguage cause-and-effect questions, as she uses it again in Question 1.6: 'Explain what the effect was of Oliver's request for more food?', which she relanguages into 'Ukucela kokunye ukutya kukaOliver kwaye kwa*bangela* ntoni?' *(What did Oliver's request for more food cause?).* This example is discussed in Prinsloo and Krause (2019b).

Chapter 6

(1) Teachers' writing on social media platforms and messenger services is often highly heterogeneous but in the classroom space writing is either in SWX (Foundation Phase) or beyond that in SWE.
(2) 'inye' = Standard Xhosa for 'one'.
(3) This quote is part of the unpublished data from my MA research project at Khayelitsha Primary. It was recently discussed in an article on 'The Conversation'. See https://theconversation.com/its-time-to-rethink-whats-meant-by-mother-tongue-education-96475, accessed 13 August 2019.
(4) There are many orthographic differences but also similarities between SWX and SWE, but discussing them in their entirety is not my interest here. Rather, I will discuss those that become relevant in the writing pieces I analyse in this chapter.
(5) At this point, I was still using the prefix 'isi-' to refer to Xhosa but I decided to drop the prefix when englishing further along in my research.
(6) My relanguaged language is not as heterogeneous as that of the teachers. I am quite strongly oriented towards Standard Xhosa as, for example, my use of 'ngesiNgesi' betrays – Khayelitshan languagers would mostly say 'ngeEnglish'.
(7) The exact percentage points are 43.6% because the total number of learners is 101, not 100. For ease of reference, I will round up all percentages to the next full point throughout.
(8) The learner writes this as 'uyabonaka kala ukuba' in A8 while the standard form would be 'uyabonakala'.

(9) The Standard Xhosa version of 'imntu' is 'ingumntu'.
(10) The SWX spelling of 'okaye' is 'okanye'.
(11) The SWX orthography for 'yoko kwabo' is 'yakokwabo'.
(12) Standard Xhosa orthography prescribes 'iingalo' *(arms)*.
(13) Standard Xhosa orthography prescribes 'yesithathu' to be written as one word.
(14) The 'u-' in 'uhis' is the same 'u-' from class 1a that I discussed with the example of 'uangry' in Section 5.2. The construction 'enguher' before that also includes the 'u-' in a relative construction: e (REL9) + ng (COP1a) + u (NPx1a) + her *(that is 'her')*.
(15) Again, the 'u-' in 'u-he-and-she' is the class 1a noun class prefix used as a metalanguaging device to talk *about* 'he and she' as one linguistic chunk while Englishing.
(16) SWX orthography prescribes 'iingalo' *(arms)*.
(17) 'uvuka' consists here of the subject marker 'u-' for class 1/class 1a plus the verb -vuka (wake up). Englished: he wakes up.
(18) This is not the same 'u-' as in 'uangry', where it was the noun class prefix for class 1a (NPx1a). In this case, in front of a verb (-vuka), the 'u-' is part of the noun class agreement morphology from class 1 or 1a. It is the subject marker (SM) that links the verb to 'the little boy' in this case.
(19) Standard English prepositions are also challenging for learners as they come from a languaging background where the form of a noun changes to indicate locatives, while prepositions 'aren't reconstructable word categories' (Nurse & Philippson, 2003: 188).
(20) Click here for the relevant Google search (last accessed on 13 August 2019).
(21) There are some exceptions if morpheme boundaries are involved. For example 'ndiyammamela' would feature two 'm', but the first one is an object marker for class 1/1a and the second one is the initial letter of the verb '-mamela' *(listen)*: ndi-ya-m-mamel-a *(I listen to her/him)*.
(22) By the way: Microsoft Word autocorrect clearly sees like a state, because it changes 'swiming' into 'swimming' each time I write it and then I have to go back and correct it to 'swiming'.

Appendix A

Glossing Conventions

1–15	Noun classes	LOC	Locative
1S	First-person singular	NEG	Negative
2S	Second-person singular	NEGSM	Negative subject marker
1Pl	First-person plural	NEUT	Neuter
2Pl	Second-person plural	NPx	Nominal prefix
ABS	Absolute pronoun	OM	Object marker
ANT	Anterior	PASS	Passive marker
ASS	Associative	PERF	Perfect
CAUS	Causative	PERS	Persistive
COP	Copula	POSS	Possessive
COMP	Completive	POSSSTEM	Possessive stem
COND	Conditional	PPx	Pronominal prefix
DEM	Demonstrative	PREP	Preposition
E	(Verbal) extension	PRES	Present
FUT	Future	PRO	Pronoun
FV	Final vowel	REL	Relative (pronoun)
HORT	Hortative	SM	Subject marker
INFIN	Infinitive	SUBJ	Subjunctive
INSTR	Instrumental	T(A)	Tense (aspect)
INTER	Interrogative	VR	Verb root

Appendix B

Noun Class Agreement Morphology (Positive and Negative)

Positive noun class table

Noun class	Nominal prefix (NPx)	Copulative concord (COP)	Subject marker (SM)	Possessive concord (POSS)	Possessive stem (POSSSTEM)	Object marker (OM)
1a	u-	ngu-	u-	wa-	-khe	-m-
2a	oo-	nga-	ba-	ba-	-bo	-ba-
1	um-	ngu-	u-	wa-	-khe	-m-
2	aba-	nga-	ba-	ba-	-bo	-ba-
3	um-	ngu-	u-	wa-	-wo	-wu-
4	imi-	yi-	i-	ya-	-yo	-yi-
5	ili-/i-	li-	li-	la-	-lo	-li-
6	ama-	nga-	a-	a-	-wo	-wa-
7	isi-/is-	si-	si-	sa-	-so	-si-
8	izi-/iz-	zi-	zi-	za-	-zo	-zi-
9	in-/i-	yi-	i-	ya-	-yo	-yi-
10	izin-/ii-	zi-	zi-	za-	-zo	-zi-
11	ulu-/ul-/ulw-/u-	lu-	lu-	lwa-	-lo	-lu-
14	ubu-/ub-/u-	bu-	bu-	ba-	-bo	-bu-
15	uku-/uk-/ukw-	ku-	ku-	kwa-	-ko	-ku-

Negative noun class table

Noun class			Negative copulative concord (NEGCOP)	Negative subject marker (NEGSM)			
1a			asingo-	aka-			
2a			asingo-	aba-			
1			asingo-	awu-			
2			asingo-	aba-			
3			asingo-	awu-			
4			asiyo-	ayi-			
5			asilo-	ali-			
6			asingo-	awa-			
7			asiso-	asi-			
8			asizo-	azi-			
9			asiyo-	ayi-			
10			asizo-	azi-			
11			asilo-	alu-			
14			asibo-	abu-			
15			asiko-	aku-			

Appendix C

Lists of Lesson Transcripts and Interviews

List of lesson transcripts

Lesson transcripts	Lesson date	Grade
A B C D E F	16.05.2016	5
G H	08.02.2016	4
I J K L M N	11.05.2016	5
O	30.05.2016	5
Lessons without full transcripts but with short excerpts quoted:		
	01.02.2016	4
	18.05.2016	5
	03.02.2016	6
	11.04.2016	7
	20.04.2016	5

List of interviews

Teacher in interview	Interview excerpt	Interview date
Grade 5	a b c d e i j +short citations throughout	14.09.2016
Grade 4	f g h +short citations throughout	19.05.2016
Grade 6/7	Short citations throughout	12.09.2016

List of main writing pieces discussed in Chapter 6

Writing piece	Grade
Example A Greaming abut sweeming in a betch	5
Example B I see the child engqengqe ngomqolo	6
Example C A tale of vuking, tshoning and swiming	6
Short citations of various other pieces throughout	

Appendix D

Table of Relanguaging Circles

Circle I: 'Sorting out' 43
Circle II: 'Bringing together' 45
Circle III: Two directions of relanguaging 46
Circle IV 65
Circle V 76
Circle VI 102
Circle VII 106
Circle VIII 109
Circle IX 115
Circle X 117
Circle XI 130
Circle XII 146
Circle XIII 148
Circle XIV 157
Circle XV 169

Appendix E

Excerpt from Formal Assessment Task Grade 5

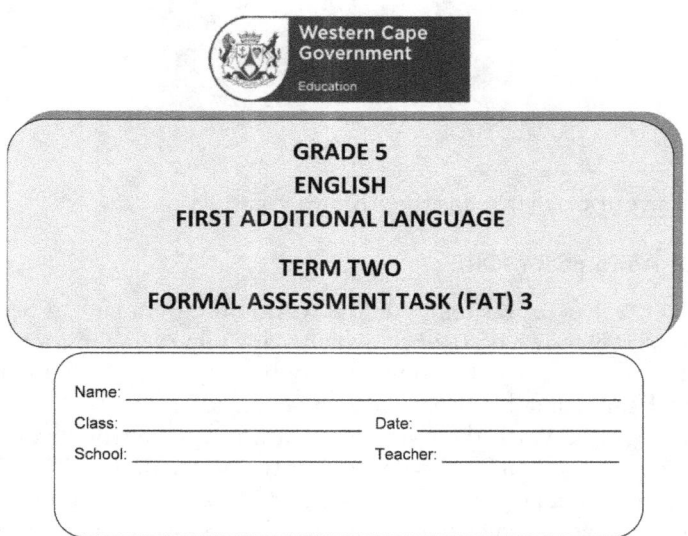

Please Note: Teachers are requested to review the contents of this FAT prior to implementation.

FAT	Activity	Learner's mark	Learner's %	%
Activity 1	Listens to and speaks about text			15
Activity 2	Reads aloud			10
Activity 3	Language structure and conventions			15
Activity 4	Reading comprehension			20
Activity 5	Reflects on stories/texts			10
Activity 6	Writing			30
Total				100

> **Activity 1.1 Listening & Speaking (15%)**

Instructions:

Listen as your teacher reads the story to you.

OLIVER ASKS FOR MORE

Oliver was even less happy in the workhouse than he had been with Mrs Mann. He now had to work, which made him even hungrier. He was only given three meals of thin watery soup a day, with an onion twice a week and half a small loaf of bread on Sundays.

The room in which the boys were fed was a large stone hall. At one end a servant stood and helped by one or two women, served the soup at meal times from a large pot. Each boy had one small bowl and no more. The bowls never needed washing. The boys polished them with their spoons till they shone. When they had done this, which never took very long, they would sit staring with wide eyes at the pot, as if they could have eaten even the metal of which it was made. They would also suck their fingers most carefully to catch any splashes of soup that might have fallen on them.

Oliver Twist and his companions suffered the pains of slow starvation for three months. At last they got so wild with hunger that one boy, who was tall for his age told the others that unless he had another bowl of soup daily, he was afraid he might eat the boy who slept next to him. He had a wild, hungry eye, and they fully believed him. A council was held and one boy was picked to walk up to the servant after supper and ask for more. The chosen boy was Oliver Twist.

The evening arrived and the boys took their places. The servant placed himself by the pot, his assistants stood behind him and the soup was served out. It soon disappeared. The boys whispered to each other and made signs at Oliver while his neighbours pushed him. Child though he was, his hunger gave him courage. He rose from the table and advanced towards the servant, bowl in hand.

'Please, sir, I want some more', he said.

The servant was a fat, healthy man but he turned very pale. He looked in astonishment on the small rebel for some seconds.

'What!' he said at length in a faint voice.

'Please, sir, I want some more'.

The servant aimed a blow at Oliver's head with his wooden spoon, then seized him in his arms and cried aloud for help.

Mr Bumble rushed into the room and was told of Oliver's crime.

'Asked for more!' he exclaimed. 'That boy will live to be hanged!'

Oliver was locked up at once. The workhouse officials discussed his case. As a result, a notice was next morning fixed outside of the gate, offering a reward of five pounds to anybody who would take Oliver Twist. In other words, five pounds and Oliver Twist would be given to any man or woman who wanted an apprentice to any trade or business.

Source: Charles Dickens – *Oliver Twist*

Instructions:
Answer the following questions to test your listening skills.

1.1 Who is the main character in this story? (1)

_____
_____

1.2 Rearrange the events in the correct order: Write the correct number in the block. (1)

1.	Oliver was locked up.	
2.	He rose from the table and advanced to the servant.	
3.	The chosen boy was Oliver Twist.	
4.	Oliver asked for more food.	

1.3 Explain why you think the boys did not get enough food. (2)

_____
_____
_____
_____

1.4 Why did the bowls never need washing? (1)

1.5 What plan did they make to get more food? (1)

1.6 Explain what the effect was of Oliver's request for more food? (2)

1.7 Explain how your life is different to Oliver's life. (2)

Total (10)

References

Alexander, N. (2009) Mother tongue based bilingual education in Africa: A cultural and intellectual imperative. In I. Gogolin and U. Neumann (eds) *Streitfall Zweisprachigkeit – The Bilingualism Controversy* (pp. 199–214). Wiesbaden: VS Verlag für Sozialwissenschaften.

Anderson, B. (1983) *Imagined Communities: Reflections on the Origin and Spread of Nationalism*. London: Verso Books.

Anthonissen, C. (2009) Bilingualism and language shift in Western Cape communities. *Stellenbosch Papers in Linguistics Plus* 38, 61–76.

Auer, P. (ed.) (1998) *Code-Switching in Conversation: Language, Interaction and Identity*. London/New York: Routledge.

Auer, P. (1999) From codeswitching via language mixing to fused lects: Toward a dynamic typology of bilingual speech. *International Journal of Bilingualism* 3 (4), 309–332.

Ayliff, J. (1846) *A Vocabulary of the Kaffir Language*. London: Wesleyan Mission House.

Baker, P., de Vos, J., Edwards, M., Ralenala, M. and Swanepoel, G. (2012a) *Platinum English First Additional Language: Grade 5*. Cape Town: Maskew Miller Longman.

Baker, P., Edwards, M., Ralenala, M., Swanepoel, G. and Townsend, B. (2012b) *Platinum English First Additional Language: Grade 4*. Cape Town: Maskew Miller Longman.

Banda, F. (2003) A survey of literacy practices in Black and Coloured communities in South Africa: Towards a pedagogy of multiliteracies. *Language, Culture and Curriculum* 16 (2), 106–129.

Banda, F. (2009) Critical perspectives on language planning and policy in Africa: Accounting for the notion of multilingualism. *Stellenbosch Papers in Linguistics Plus* 38, 1–11.

Banda, F. (2018) Translanguaging and English-African language mother tongues as linguistic dispensation in teaching and learning in a black township school in Cape Town. *Current Issues in Language Planning* 19 (2), 198–217.

Baynham, M. and Lee, T.-K. (2019) *Translation and Translanguaging*. New York: Routledge, Taylor & Francis Group.

Beck, R.M. (2003) Perceptions of gender in Swahili language and society. In H. Bussmann and M. Hellinger (eds) *Gender Across Languages: The Linguistic Representation of Women and Men* (pp. 311–337). Amsterdam: J. Benjamins.

Beck, R.M. (2010) Urban languages in Africa. *Africa Spectrum* 45 (3), 11–41.

Beck, R.M. (2015) Schweigen als Praxis: Praktiken des Schweigens. In M. Dobstadt, C. Fandrych and U.R. Riedner (eds) *Linguistik und Kulturwissenschaft: Zu ihrem Verhältnis aus der Perspektive des Faches Deutsch als Fremd-und Zweitsprache und anderer Disziplinen* (pp. 251–271). Bern: Peter Lang.

Beck, R.M. (2016) Tusidanganyane: Let's not fool ourselves! Knowledge production and HIV prevention in Nairobi (Kenya). *Sociolinguistic Studies* 10 (1/2), 15–44.

Beck, R.M. (2018) Language as apparatus: Entanglements of language, culture and territory and the invention of nation and ethnicity. *Postcolonial Studies* 21 (2), 231–253.

Bennie, J. (1826) *A Systematic Vocabulary of the Kaffrarian Language*. Alice: Lovedale Press.
Blackledge, A. and Creese, A. (2017) Translanguaging and the body. *International Journal of Multilingualism* 14 (3), 250–268.
Blommaert, J. (2007) On scope and depth in linguistic ethnography. *Journal of Sociolinguistics* 11 (5), 682–688.
Blommaert, J. (2008) Artefactual ideologies and the textual production of African languages. *Language & Communication* 28 (4), 291–307.
Blommaert, J. (2013) Writing as a sociolinguistic object. *Journal of Sociolinguistics* 17 (4), 440–459.
Blommaert, J. and Backus, A. (2013) Superdiverse repertoires and the individual. In I. de Saint-Georges and J.-J. Weber (eds) *Multilingualism and Multimodality: Current Challenges for Educational Studies* (pp. 11–32). Rotterdam: Sense Publishers.
Blommaert, J., Muyllaert, N., Huysmans, M. and Dyers, C. (2005) Peripheral normativity: Literacy and the production of locality in a South African township school. *Linguistics and Education* 16 (4), 378–403.
Böhm, A. (2003) Theoretisches Codieren: Textanalyse in der Grounded Theory. In U. Flick, E. von Kardorff and I. Steinke (eds) *Qualitative Forschung: Ein Handbuch* (pp. 475–487). Reinbeck: Rohwolt.
Bowker, G.C. and Star, S.L. (1999) *Sorting things out: Classification and Its Consequences*. Cambridge, MA: MIT Press.
Branford, W. and Claughton, J.S. (2002) Mutual lexical borrowings among some languages of southern Africa: Xhosa, Afrikaans and English. *Language in South Africa* 199–215.
Brereton Mathiesen, K. (2000) Learning South African languages: The historical origins of Xhosa and the usage to which the written form of the language was put c. 1770–1935. MA thesis, University of Cape Town.
Brock-Utne, B., Desai, Z. and Qorro, M.A.S. (2003) *Language of Instruction in Tanzania and South Africa (LOITASA)*. Dar es Salaam: E & D Limited.
Bua-Lit Collective (2018) How are we failing our children? Reconceptualizing language and literacy education. See www.bua-lit.org.za. (accessed 6 July 2019).
Busch, B. (2012) The linguistic repertoire revisited. *Applied Linguistics* 33 (5), 1–22.
Bylund, E. (2014) Unomathotholo or i-radio? Factors predicting the use of English loanwords among L1 isiXhosa–L2 English bilinguals. *Journal of Multilingual and Multicultural Development* 35 (2), 105–120.
Calderhead, J. (1981) Stimulated recall: A method for research on teaching. *British Journal of Educational Psychology* 51 (2), 211–217.
Canagarajah, A.S. (2006) The place of world Englishes in composition: Pluralization continued. *College Composition and Communication* 57 (4), 586–619.
Canagarajah, A.S. (2011) Translanguaging in the classroom: Emerging issues for research and pedagogy. *Applied Linguistics Review* 2, 1–28.
Canagarajah, A.S. (2013) Negotiating translingual literacy: An enactment. *Research in the Teaching of English* 48 (1), 40–67.
Canagarajah, A.S. (2015) Negotiating mobile codes and literacies at the contact zone: Another perspective on South African township schools. In C. Stroud and M. Prinsloo (eds) *Language, Literacy and Diversity: Moving Words* (pp. 34–54). New York: Routledge.
Canagarajah, A.S. (2018) Translingual practice as spatial repertoires: Expanding the paradigm beyond structuralist orientations. *Applied Linguistics* 39 (1), 31–54.
Casale, D. and Posel, D. (2011) English language proficiency and earnings in a developing country: The case of South Africa. *The Journal of Socio-Economics* 40 (4), 385–393.
Celic, C. and Seltzer, K. (2011) *Translanguaging: A CUNY-NYSIEB Guide for Educators*. New York: CUNY-NYSIEB.

Chick, J.K. (1996) Safe-talk: Collusion in apartheid education. In H. Coleman (ed.) *Society and the Language Classroom* (pp. 21–39). Cambridge: Cambridge University Press.
Chomsky, N. (1965) *Aspects of the Theory of Syntax*. Cambridge, MA: MIT Press.
Christie, P. (1995) Transition tricks? Policy models for school desegregation in South Africa, 1990–94. *Journal of Education Policy* 10 (1), 45–55.
Christie, P. and McKinney, C. (2017) Decoloniality and 'Model C' schools: Ethos, language and the protests of 2016. *Education as Change* 21 (3), 160–180.
Clark, P. and Crous, W. (2002) Public transport in metropolitan Cape Town: Past, present and future. *Transport Reviews* 22 (1), 77–101.
Collins, J. and Krause, L.-S. (2019) Register processes in contemporary South African schools: Dialectics of fixity and fluidity. In J. Jaspers and L.M. Madsen (eds) *Critical Perspectives on Linguistic Fixity and Fluidity: Languagised Lives* (pp. 241–265). New York: Routledge.
Comrie, B. (1999) Reference-tracking: Description and explanation. *STUF-Language Typology and Universals* 52 (3–4), 335–346.
Contini-Morava, E. (2002) (What) do noun class markers mean? In W. Reid, R. Otheguy and N. Stern (eds) *Signal, Meaning, and Message: Perspectives on Sign-Based Linguistics* (pp. 3–64). Amsterdam/Philadelphia: John Benjamins.
Contini-Morava, E. (2008) Human relationship terms, discourse prominence, and asymmetrical animacy in Swahili. *Journal of African Languages and Linguistics* 29 (2), 127–171.
Couldry, N. (2009) Rethinking the politics of voice: Commentary. *Continuum* 23 (4), 579–582.
Creese, A. (2010) Linguistic ethnography. In L. Litosseliti (ed.) *Research Methods in Linguistics* (pp. 138–154). London: Continuum.
Creese, A. and Blackledge, A. (2010) Translanguaging in the bilingual classroom: A pedagogy for learning and teaching? *The Modern Language Journal* 94 (1), 103–115.
Creswell, J.W. (2007) *Qualitative Inquiry and Research Design: Choosing Among Five Approaches*. Los Angeles, CA: SAGE Publications.
Davila, B. (2016) The inevitability of 'standard' English: Discursive constructions of standard language ideologies. *Written Communication* 33 (2), 127–148.
de Certeau, M. (1984) *The Practice of Everyday Life*. Berkeley, CA: University of California Press.
de Certeau, M. (1985) Practices of space. In M. Blonsky (ed.) *On Signs* (pp. 122–145). Baltimore, MD: The Johns Hopkins University Press.
de Klerk, V. (2003) Towards a norm in South African Englishes: The case for Xhosa English. *World Englishes* 22 (4), 463–481.
de Klerk, V. (2006) The features of 'teacher talk' in a corpus-based study of Xhosa English. *Language Matters* 37 (2), 125–140.
de los Ríos, C.V. and Seltzer, K. (2017) Translanguaging, coloniality, and English classrooms: An exploration of two bicoastal urban classrooms. *Research in the Teaching of English* 52 (1), 55–76.
Dempsey, N.P. (2010) Stimulated recall interviews in ethnography. *Qualitative Sociology* 33 (3), 349–367.
Demuth, K. (2000) Bantu noun class systems: Loan word and acquisition evidence of semantic productivity. In G. Senft and S.C. Levinson (eds) *Systems of Nominal Classification* (pp. 270–292). Cambridge: Cambridge University Press.
Department of Basic Education (2011) *Curriculum and Assessment Policy Statement (CAPS): Intermediate Phase, First Additional Language*. Pretoria.
Department of Education (2003) *Systemic Evaluation Foundation Phase Mainstream: National Report*. Pretoria.
Department of Education (2017) *Implementation Evaluation of the National Curriculum Statement Grade R to 12: Focusing on the Curriculum and Assessment Policy Statements (CAPS)*. Pretoria.

Deppermann, A. (2001) *Gespräche Analysieren*. Wiesbaden: VS Verlag für Sozialwissenschaften.
Deumert, A. (2010) Klk cc... Supporting indigenous literacies in the digital space. See https://m4lit.files.wordpress.com/2010/03/m4lit_indigenous_literacies_adeumert_2010.pdf (accessed 7 July 2019).
Deumert, A. (2013) Xhosa in town (revisited) – space, place and language. *International Journal of Sociolinguistics* 222, 51–75.
Ditsele, T. (2014) Why not use Sepitori to enrich the vocabularies of Setswana and Sepedi? *Southern African Linguistics and Applied Language Studies* 32 (2), 215–228.
Dowling, T. (2010) 'Akuchanywa apha please' No peeing here please: The language of signage in Cape Town. *South African Journal of African Languages* 30 (2), 192–208.
Dowling, T. (2011) 'Stressed and sexy': Lexical borrowing in Cape Town Xhosa. *International Journal of Multilingualism* 8 (4), 345–366.
Dowling, T. and Grier, L. (2015) 'Mnandi-licious!' trends in African language usage in South African television advertising. *Social Dynamics* 41 (3), 555–575.
Dowling, T. and Krause, L.-S. (2018) 'Ndifuna imeaning yakhe': Translingual morphology in English teaching in a South African township classroom. *International Journal of Multilingualism* 1–21.
Errington, J. (2008) *Linguistics in a Colonial World: A Story of Language, Meaning, and Power*. Malden, MA: Blackwell Publishing.
Fataar, A. (2009) Schooling subjectivities across the post-apartheid city. *Africa Education Review* 6 (1), 1–18.
Ferguson, G. (2003) Classroom code-switching in post-colonial contexts: Functions, attitudes and policies. *AILA Review* 16 (1), 38–51.
Ferguson, G. (2009) What next? Towards an agenda for classroom codeswitching research. *International Journal of Bilingual Education and Bilingualism* 12 (2), 231–241.
Frith, A. (n.d.) Census 2011: Khayelitsha. See https://census2011.adrianfrith.com/place/199038 (accessed 6 July 2019).
Futuse, L. (2018) An examination of how loanwords in a corpus of spoken and written contemporary isiXhosa are incorporated into the noun class system of isiXhosa. MA thesis, University of Cape Town.
García, O. (2009) *Bilingual Education in the 21st Century: A Global Perspective*. Oxford: Wiley-Blackwell.
García, O. and Leiva, C. (2014) Theorizing and enacting translanguaging for social justice. In A. Blackledge and A. Creese (eds) *Heteroglossia as Practice and Pedagogy* (pp. 199–216). Dordrecht: Springer.
García, O. and Wei, L. (2014) *Translanguaging: Language, Bilingualism and Education*. Basingstoke/New York: Palgrave Macmillan.
Garfinkel, H. (1967) *Studies in Ethnomethodology*. Englewood Cliffs, NJ: Prentice-Hall.
Goodwin, C. and Heritage, J. (1990) Conversation analysis. *Annual Review of Anthropology* 19 (1), 283–307.
Gough, D.H. (1993) A change of mood: Towards a re-analysis of the Dokean classification. In R.K. Herbert (ed.) *Not with One Mouth: Continuity and Change in Southern African Language Studies* (pp. 35–52). Johannesburg: Witwatersrand University Press.
Graves, M.F., August, D. and Mancilla-Martinez, J. (2013) *Teaching Vocabulary to English Language Learners*. New York: Teachers College Press.
Gumede, V. and Biyase, M. (2016) Educational reforms and curriculum transformation in post-apartheid South Africa. *Environmental Economics* 7 (2), 69–76.
Gumperz, J.J. (1964) Linguistic and social interaction in two communities. *American Anthropologist* 66 (6), 137–153.
Gumperz, J.J. (1965) Linguistic repertoires, grammars and second language instruction. In C.W. Kreidler (ed.) *Report of the Sixteenth Annual Roundtable Meeting on*

Linguistics and Language Studies (pp. 81–90). Washington, DC: Georgetown University Press.
Gumperz, J.J. (1977) The sociolinguistic significance of conversational code-switching. *RELC Journal* 8 (2), 1–34.
Guzula, X. (2018) Moving beyond artificial linguistic binaries in the education of African Language speaking children: A case for simultaneous biliteracy development. *Perspectives in Education* 36 (2), 1–14.
Guzula, X., McKinney, C. and Tyler, R. (2016) Languaging-for-learning: Legitimising translanguaging and enabling multimodal practices in third spaces. *Southern African Linguistics and Applied Language Studies* 34 (3), 211–226.
Halberstam, J. (2011) *The Queer Art of Failure*. Durham, NC: Duke University Press.
Hallitzky, M., Mulhanga, F. and Yoshida, N. (forthcoming) *Expanding Horizons and Local Connectedness. Challenges for Qualitative Teaching Research and Development in Intercultural Contexts*. Bad Heilbrunn: Verlag Julius Klinkhardt.
Harries, P. (1988) The roots of ethnicity: Discourse and the politics of language construction in South-East Africa. *African Affairs* 87 (346), 25–52.
Haspelmath, M. (2008) Loanword typology: Steps toward a systematic cross-linguistic study of lexical borrowability. *Empirical Approaches to Language Typology* 35, 43.
Haspelmath, M., König, E., Oesterreicher, W. and Raible, W. (eds) (2001) *Language Typology and Language Universals*. Berlin: Walter de Gruyter.
Heath, S.B. and Street, B.V. (2008) *On Ethnography: Approaches to Language and Literacy Research*. New York: Teachers College Press.
Heller, M. (2007) *Bilingualism: A Social Approach*. Basingstoke: Palgrave Macmillan.
Higgins, C. (2017) Space, place, and language. In A.S. Canagarajah (ed.) *The Routledge Handbook of Migration and Language* (pp. 102–116). London: Routledge, Taylor & Francis Group.
Horner, B., Lu, M., Royster, J.J. and Trimbur, J. (2011) Language difference in writing: Toward a translingual approach. *College English* 73 (3), 303–321.
Hymes, D. (1972) On communicative competence. In J.B. Pride and J. Holmes (eds) *Sociolinguistics: Selected Readings* (pp. 269–293). Harmondsworth: Penguin Books.
Jacobs, W. (2014) Migration patterns and migrant characteristics in the Western Cape through a differential urbanisation lens. MA thesis, University of Stellenbosch.
Jaspers, J. (2015) Modelling linguistic diversity at school: The excluding impact of inclusive multilingualism. *Language Policy* 14, 109–129.
Jaspers, J. (2019) Authority and morality in advocating heteroglossia. *Language, Culture and Society* 1 (1), 83–105.
Jaspers, J. and Madsen, L.M. (2019) Fixity and fluidity in sociolinguistic theory and practice. In J. Jaspers and L.M. Madsen (eds) *Critical Perspectives on Linguistic Fixity and Fluidity: Languagised Lives* (pp. 1–26). New York: Routledge.
Jewitt, C., Bezemer, J. and O'Halloran, K. (2016) *Introducing Multimodality*. London: Routledge.
Jørgensen, J.N. (2008) Polylingual languaging around and among children and adolescents. *International Journal of Multilingualism* 5 (3), 161–176.
Jørgensen, J.N., Karrebæk, M.S., Madsen, L.M. and Møller, J.S. (2011) Polylanguaging in superdiversity. *Diversities* 2, 23–37.
Kapp, R. (2004) 'Reading on the line': An analysis of literacy practices in ESL classes in a South African township school. *Language and Education* 18 (3), 246–263.
Kapp, R. (2006) Discourses of English and literacy in a Western Cape township school. In L. Thesen and E. van Pletzen (eds) *Academic Literacy and the Languages of Change* (pp. 30–52). London/New York: Continuum.
Katamba, F. (2003) Bantu nominal morphology. In D. Nurse and G. Philippson (eds) *The Bantu Languages* (pp. 103–120). London/New York: Routledge.

Kießling, R. and Mous, M. (2004) Urban youth languages in Africa. *Anthropological Linguistics* 46 (3), 303–341.
Koopman, A. (1999) *Zulu Language Change*. Howick: Brevitas.
Krause, L.-S. (2014) 'Xhosa is my identity English is my future': Complexities around language values and practices at a South African township school. MA thesis, Leipzig University.
Krause, L.-S. and Prinsloo, M. (2016) Translanguaging in a township primary school: Policy and practice. *Southern African Linguistics and Applied Language Studies* 34 (4), 347–357.
Kreutzer, T. (2009) Generation mobile: Online and digital media usage on mobile phones among low-income urban youth in South Africa See https://static1.squarespace.com/static/58128d055016e1a55790b035/t/58128fc1c534a556a5a95518/1477611459471/MobileOnlineMedia-SurveyResults-2009.pdf (accessed 7 July 2019).
Kropf, A. (1915) *Kafir–English Dictionary*. South Africa: Lovedale Mission Press.
Krugel, R. and Fourie, E. (2014) Concerns for the language skills of South African learners and their teachers. *International Journal of Educational Sciences* 7 (1), 219–228.
Kusters, A., Spotti, M., Swanwick, R. and Tapio, E. (2017) Beyond languages, beyond modalities: Transforming the study of semiotic repertoires. *International Journal of Multilingualism* 14 (3), 219–232.
Latour, B. (2005) *Reassembling the Social: An Introduction to Actor-Network-Theory*. New York: Oxford University Press.
Law, J. (2004) *After Method: Mess in Social Science Research*. Abington: Routledge.
LCCI Examinations Board (n.d.) English Language Skills Assessment: Listening/reading test. Information pack. See https://www.lccieb-germany.com/documents/ELSAInfo-Pack.pdf (accessed 7 July 2019).
Lemanski, C. (2008) Houses without community: Problems of community (in) capacity in Cape Town, South Africa. *Environment and Urbanization* 20 (2), 393–410.
Lewis, G., Jones, B. and Baker, C. (2012) Translanguaging: Origins and development from school to street and beyond. *Educational Research and Evaluation* 18 (7), 641–654.
Lin, A. (2013) Classroom code-switching: Three decades of research. *Applied Linguistics Review* 4 (1), 195–218.
Lombard, B.J.J. (2007) Reasons why educator-parents based at township schools transfer their own children from township schools to former Model C schools. *Education as Change* 11 (1), 43–57.
Madsen, L.M. (2018) Linguistic ethnography: Studying English language, cultures and practices. In P. Seargent, A. Hewings and S. Pihlaja (eds) *The Routledge Handbook of English Language Studies* (pp. 392–405). Abington/New York: Routledge.
Maile, S. (2004) School choice in South Africa. *Education and Urban Society* 37 (1), 94–116.
Makalela, L. (2013) Translanguaging in kasi-taal: Rethinking old language boundaries for new language planning. *Stellenbosch Papers in Linguistics Plus* 42, 111–125.
Makalela, L. (2016) Ubuntu translanguaging: An alternative framework for complex multilingual encounters. *Southern African Linguistics and Applied Language Studies* 34 (3), 187–196.
Makalela, L. (2018) Teaching African languages the ubuntu way: The effects of translanguaging among pre-service teachers in South Africa. In P. van Avermaet, S. Slembrouck, K. van Gorp, S. Sierens and K. Maryns (eds) *The Multilingual Edge of Education* (pp. 261–282). London: Palgrave Macmillan.
Makoni, S. and Mashiri, P. (2007) Critical historiography: Does language planning in Africa need a construct of language as part of its theoretical apparatus? In S. Makoni and A. Pennycook (eds) *Disinventing and Reconstituting Languages* (pp. 62–89). Clevedon: Multilingual Matters.

Makoni, S. and Pennycook, A. (2007a) Disinventing and reconstituting languages. In S. Makoni and A. Pennycook (eds) *Disinventing and Reconstituting Languages* (pp. 1–41). Clevedon: Multilingual Matters.

Makoni, S. and Pennycook, A. (eds) (2007b) *Disinventing and Reconstituting Languages*. Clevedon: Multilingual Matters.

Matlock, T. and Heredia, R.R. (2002) Understanding phrasal verbs in monolinguals and bilinguals. *Advances in Psychology* 134, 251–274.

McIntyre, D.J. (1980) Teacher evaluation and the observer effect. *NASSP Bulletin* 64 (434), 36–40.

McKinney, C., Carrim, H., Marshall, A. and Layton, L. (2015) What counts as language in South African schooling? Monoglossic ideologies and children's participation. *AILA Review* 28 (1), 103–126.

Meeuwis, M. and Blommaert, J. (1998) A monolectal view of code-switching: Layered code-switching among Zairians in Belgium. In P. Auer (ed.) *Code-Switching in Conversation: Language, Interaction and Identity* (pp. 76–100). London/New York: Routledge.

Mesthrie, R. (2005) Putting back the horse before the cart: The 'spelling form' fallacy in Second Language Acquisition studies, with special reference to the treatment of unstressed vowels in Black South African English. *English World-Wide* 26 (2), 127–151.

Mesthrie, R. and Hurst, E. (2013) Slang registers, code-switching and restructured urban varieties in South Africa: An analytic overview of tsotsitaals with special reference to the Cape Town variety. *Journal of Pidgin and Creole Languages* 28 (1), 103–130.

Michael-Luna, S. and Canagarajah, A.S. (2007) Multilingual academic literacies: Pedagogical foundations for code meshing in primary and higher education. *Journal of Applied Linguistics* 4 (1), 55–77.

Milroy, J. (1999) The consequences of standardisation in descriptive linguistics. In T. Bex and R.J. Watts (eds) *Standard English: The Widening Debate* (pp. 16–39). London/New York: Routledge.

Milroy, J. (2001) Language ideologies and the consequences of standardization. *Journal of Sociolinguistics* 5 (4), 530–555.

Morrison, M.E. (2018) Beyond derivation: Creative use of noun class prefixation for both semantic and reference tracking purposes. *Journal of Pragmatics* 123, 38–56.

Msila, V. (2009) School choice and intra-township migration: Black parents scrambling for quality education in South Africa. *Journal of Education* 46, 81–98.

Myers-Scotton, C. (1997) *Duelling Languages: Grammatical Structure in Codeswitching*. Oxford: Clarendon Press.

Nassenstein, N. (2016) The metrolingual use of Swahili in urban Ugandan landscapes and everyday conversation. *Voices from Around the World* 1, 2016.

Ndimande, B.S. (2012) Race and resources: Black parents' perspectives on post-apartheid South African schools. *Race Ethnicity and Education* 15 (4), 525–544.

Nel, N. and Müller, H. (2010) The impact of teachers' limited English proficiency on English second language learners in South African schools. *South African Journal of Education* 30, 635–650.

Ngcobo, M. (2013) Loan words classification in isiZulu: The need for a sociolinguistic approach. *Language Matters* 44 (1), 21–38.

Nkosi, M. (2016) Is South Africa's education system really 'in crisis'? BBC News, 29 January. See https://www.bbc.com/news/world-africa-35427853 (accessed 7 April 2019).

Nortier, J. and Svendsen, B.A. (2015) *Language, Youth and Identity in the 21st Century: Linguistic Practices across Urban Spaces*. Cambridge: Cambridge University Press.

Nurse, D. (2003) Aspect and tense in Bantu languages. In D. Nurse and G. Philippson (eds) *The Bantu Languages* (pp. 90–102). London/New York: Routledge.

Nurse, D. and Philippson, G. (eds) (2003) *The Bantu Languages*. London/New York: Routledge.

Oosthuysen, J.C. (2015) Extricating the description of the grammar of isiXhosa from a Eurocentric approach. *South African Journal of African Languages* 35 (1), 83–92.

Otheguy, R., García, O. and Reid, W. (2015) Clarifying translanguaging and deconstructing named languages: A perspective from linguistics. *Applied Linguistics Review* 6 (3), 281–307.

Otsuji, E. and Pennycook, A. (2010) Metrolingualism: Fixity, fluidity and language in flux. *International Journal of Multilingualism* 7 (3), 240–254.

Ouane, A. and Glanz, C. (eds) (2011) *Optimising Learning, Education and Publishing in Africa: The Language Factor – A Review and Analysis of Theory and Practice in Mother-Tongue and Bilingual Education in Sub-Saharan Africa*. New York: Mark Batty Publisher.

Pahl, H.W., Burns-Ncamashe, S.M. and Ntusi, D.M. (1971) *IsiXhosa: Sebanga Lematriki*. Johannesburg: Bona Press.

Pahl, H.W., Ntusi, D.M. and Burns-Ncamashe, S.M. (1978) *IsiXhosa*. King William's Town: Thandapers.

Pahl, H.W., Pienaar, A.M. and Ndungane, T.A. (eds) (1989) *The Greater Dictionary of Xhosa: Q to Z*. Alice: University of Fort Hare.

Pennycook, A. (2010) *Language as a Local Practice*. Abington: Routledge.

Pennycook, A. (2014) Principled polycentrism and resourceful speakers. *The Journal of ASIA TEFL* 11 (4), 1–19.

Pennycook, A. and Otsuji, E. (2015) *Metrolingualism: Language in the City*. London/New York: Routledge.

Poplack, S. (1988) Contrasting patterns of code-switching in two communities. In M. Heller (ed.) *Codeswitching: Anthropological and Sociolinguistic Perspectives* (pp. 215–244). Berlin: Mouton de Gruyter.

Posel, D. (2001) What's in a name: Racial categorisations under apartheid and their afterlife. *Transformation* 47, 59–82.

Prinsloo, M. and Krause, L.-S. (2019a) Testing practice in a Southern school. In D. Bloome, M.L. Castanheira, C. Leung and J. Rowsell (eds) *Re-Theorizing Literacy Practices: Complex Social and Cultural Contexts* (pp. 154–167). New York: Routledge.

Prinsloo, M. and Krause, L.-S. (2019b) Translanguaging, place and complexity. *Language and Education*, 1–16.

Probyn, M. (2001) Teachers voices: Teachers reflections on learning and teaching through the medium of English as an additional language in South Africa. *International Journal of Bilingual Education and Bilingualism* 4 (4), 249–266.

Probyn, M. (2009) 'Smuggling the vernacular into the classroom': Conflicts and tensions in classroom codeswitching in township/rural schools in South Africa. *International Journal of Bilingual Education and Bilingualism* 12 (2), 123–136.

Probyn, M. (2015) Pedagogical translanguaging: Bridging discourses in South African science classrooms. *Language and Education* 29 (3), 218–234.

Psathas, G. (1994) *Conversation Analysis: The Study of Talk-in-Interaction*. Thousand Oaks, CA: SAGE Publications.

Rampton, B. (2017) Interactional sociolinguistics. *Tilburg Papers in Culture Studies* (Paper 175), 1–15.

Rampton, B., Tusting, K., Maybin, J., Barwell, R., Creese, A. and Lytra, V. (2004) UK linguistic ethnography: A discussion paper. *Coordinating Committee UK Linguistic Ethnography Forum*.

Reckwitz, A. (2002) Toward a theory of social practices: A development in culturalist theorizing. *European Journal of Social Theory* 5 (2), 243–263.

Sabino, R. (2018) *Languaging Without Languages: Beyond Metro-, Multi-, Poly-, Pluri- and Translanguaging*. Leiden: Brill.

Saragih, H.F.S. (2008) The prefix re-: A study on its morphology and meanings. BA thesis, Sanatha Dharma University, Yogyakarta.
Schatzki, T.R. (2005) Practice mind-ed orders. In T.R. Schatzki, K. Knorr Cetina and E. von Savigny (eds) *The Practice Turn in Contemporary Theory* (pp. 50–63). London: Routledge.
Schegloff, E.A. (1996) Confirming allusions: Toward an empirical account of action. *American Journal of Sociology* 104, 161–216.
Schegloff, E.A. and Sacks, H. (1973) Opening up closings. *Semiotica* 8 (4), 289–327.
Schegloff, E.A., Koshik, I., Jacoby, S. and Olsher, D. (2002) Conversation analysis and applied linguistics. *Annual Review of Applied Linguistics* 22, 3–31.
Scott, J.C. (1998) *Seeing Like a State: How Certain Schemes to Improve the Human Condition Have Failed*. New Haven, CT/London: Yale University Press.
Seabe, D.S. (2014) Understanding volunteering in South Africa: A mixed methods approach. MA thesis, University of Stellenbosch.
Seekings, J. (2008) The continuing salience of race: Discrimination and diversity in South Africa. *Journal of Contemporary African Studies* 26 (1), 1–25.
Setati, M. (2005) Researching teaching and learning in school from 'with' or 'on' teachers to 'with' and 'on' teachers: Conversations. *Perspectives in Education* 23 (1), 91–101.
Setati, M., Adler, J., Reed, Y. and Bapoo, A. (2002) Incomplete journeys: Code-switching and other language practices in mathematics, science and English language classrooms in South Africa. *Language and Education* 16 (2), 128–149.
Sibanda, R. (2019) Mother-tongue education in a multilingual township: Possibilities for recognising lok'shin lingua in South Africa. *Reading & Writing* 10 (1), 1–10.
Silverstein, M. (1998) Contemporary transformations of local linguistic communities. *Annual Review of Anthropology* 27, 401–426.
Silverstein, M. (2010) Society, polity, and language community: An enlightenment trinity in anthropological perspective. *Journal of Language and Politics* 9 (3), 339–363.
Silverstein, M. (2014) How language communities intersect: Is 'superdiversity' an incremental or transformative condition? *Tilburg Papers in Culture Studies* (Paper 107), 1–36.
Slabbert, S. and Finlayson, R. (2002) Code-switching in South African townships. *Language in South Africa*, 235–257.
Smith, W.C. (2016) *The Global Testing Culture: Shaping Education Policy, Perceptions and Practice*. Didcot: Symposium Books.
Stein, P. (2008) *Multimodal Pedagogies in Diverse Classrooms: Representation, Rights and Resources*. London/New York: Routledge.
Streeck, J. (2009) *Gesturecraft: The Manu-Facture of Meaning*. Amsterdam: John Benjamins.
Stroud, C. and Mpendukana, S. (2009) Towards a material ethnography of linguistic landscape: Multilingualism, mobility and space in a South African township. *Journal of Sociolinguistics* 13 (3), 363–386.
Ten Have, P. (1999) *Doing Conversation Analysis: A Practical Guide*. London: Sage Publications Ltd.
Twidle, H. (2017) N2: Reading, writing, walking the South African highway. *Social Dynamics* 43 (1), 59–81.
van der Berg, S. and Spaull, N. (2011) SA education: The poorest choice. *Mail & Guardian*, 4 August. See https://mg.co.za/rticle/2011-04-08-sa-education-the-poorest-choice/ (accessed 7 December 2020).
Velasco, P. and García, O. (2014) Translanguaging and the writing of bilingual learners. *Bilingual Research Journal* 37 (1), 6–23.
Velghe, F. (2014) 'I wanna go in the phone': Literacy acquisition, informal learning processes, 'voice' and mobile phone appropriation in a South African township. *Ethnography and Education* 9 (1), 111–126.

Western Cape Government (2017) Curriculum FET minute: DCF 0016/2017 Retention of language compensation until 2022. See https://wcedonline.westerncape.gov.za/circulars/minutes17/CMminutes/edcf16_17.html (accessed 25 June 2019).

Williams, C. (1996) Secondary education: Teaching in the bilingual situation. In C. Williams, G. Lewis and C. Baker (eds) *The Language Policy: Taking Stock*. Llangefni: CAI Language Studies Centre.

Wolfersberger, M. (2003) L1 to L2 writing process and strategy transfer: A look at lower proficiency writers. *The Electronic Journal for English as a Second Language (TESL EJ)* 7 (2), 1–12.

Zentella, A.C. (1981) Tá bien, you could answer me en cualquier idioma: Puerto Rican codeswitching in bilingual classrooms. *Latino Language and Communicative Behavior* 6, 109–132.

Index

Actor Network Theory (ANT), 20, 21, 61, 62
adjective(s), 102, 103, 106, 134, 136, 148, 151
administrative(ly), 8, 9, 25, 33, 37, 70, 71, 96, 163, 192, 205
administrators, 7, 23, 25, 66, 99, 107, 159, 204, 209, 210, 212
administration, 2, 6, 7, 24, 25, 120, 147, 166
African language(s), 6, 9, 24, 25, 55, 188
African Studies, 51, 55
agreement, 8, 58, 85, 86, 87, 88, 89, 119, 137, 140, 150, 152, 182, 189, 208
apartheid, 5, 8, 12, 24, 25, 48, 49, 50
applied linguistics, 4, 206
assemblage, 31, 32, 39, 107, 120, 129, 139, 158, 163, 170, 201
(re/dis)assemble(d,s), 1, 20, 38, 44, 45, 58, 66, 70, 74, 75, 97, 98, 99, 100, 107, 110, 115, 120, 155, 170, 171, 180, 182, 191, 192, 193, 195, 196, 208

Bantu, 8, 20, 55, 58, 60, 61, 78, 86, 103, 132, 140, 164, 184, 188, 208
boundary(ies), 6, 33, 36, 37, 42, 65, 66, 82, 90, 97, 99, 100, 105, 117, 122, 149, 164, 170, 185, 191, 196, 211, 212
bringing together, 44-46, 57, 66, 70, 75, 82, 102, 117, 120, 121, 139, 141, 148, 149, 160, 172, 201
brings/brought together, 107, 155, 171, 199

Cape Town, 1, 5, 6, 8, 14, 16, 48, 49, 50, 51, 52, 55, 67, 68, 73, 87, 95, 186
centre, 7, 15, 17, 205, 211, 212
children, 6, 8, 9, 12, 17, 22, 29, 48, 53, 71, 72, 93, 98, 104, 124, 141, 156, 166, 201, 207, 209

class 1, 137, 139, 182
class 1a, 130, 132, 133, 137, 139, 152, 161, 188
class 9, 8, 86, 88, 132, 137, 139, 152, 182, 189
class 10, 189
class 11. 83, 86, 88
classroom languaging, 20, 31, 42, 44-46, 54, 57, 64, 65, 73-75, 77, 87-116, 121, 122, 127, 129, 130, 135, 139-141, 146, 147, 165, 166, 170, 172, 174, 175, 178, 188, 192, 199-201, 207, 208
classroom englishing, 20, 42-46, 115, 121, 122, 136, 140, 147, 151, 158, 166, 169, 184, 199
code-switching, 4, 15, 16, 20, 26, 30-35, 52, 61, 89, 93, 94, 98, 118, 129, 131, 135, 149, 163, 164, 168-170, 176, 177, 198, 201, 205, 210, 211
(non-)codified/codification, 1, 5, 9, 23, 24-27, 31, 41, 58, 90, 110, 120, 134, 164, 174, 194
(post-)colonial(ism), 8, 23-26, 55, 67
competence(ies), 10, 12, 17, 21, 27-30, 38, 107, 163, 171, 180, 187, 191, 194-197, 205, 207
(un)convention(al), 25, 57, 67, 71, 78, 95, 104, 126, 127, 136, 139, 142, 149, 151, 156, 164, 168, 176, 180-194, 209
conversation analysis, 20, 55, 56, 59
copulative, 83, 137
curriculum, 7, 8, 10-14, 40, 42, 77, 107, 123, 125, 130, 142, 143, 162, 163, 167, 200-204

deficit, 1, 15-18, 28, 99, 179, 180, 193, 194, 198, 205
Department of (Basic) Education, 9, 10-14, 29, 48, 64, 124, 142, 163-167, 201, 202, 204

240 Index

departmental, 21, 32, 50, 52, 53, 107, 122, 123, 127, 138, 142-144, 162-167, 173, 195, 205
detour, 1, 3, 4, 11, 18-20, 32, 35, 42, 47, 135, 164, 175, 193, 194
dichotomy, 66, 117, 122, 197
didactic(s), 2, 14, 33-35, 90, 152, 163, 201
didactics of explicitness, 81, 82, 86, 91, 122, 149, 150, 200, 211

englishing, to english, 42, 44, 45, 64, 66, 68, 70, 90, 93, 100, 107, 111, 118, 121, 125, 171, 180, 195, 201, 208
englishing device, 21, 42, 129, 134, 138, 164, 198
ensemble of linguistic possibilities, 39, 41, 43, 46, 64, 87, 100, 174, 199
exam(ination), 7, 9, 45, 126, 143, 147, 149, 162, 200, 201
experiment(al), 3, 5, 12, 17-21, 46, 55-58, 64, 68, 122, 178, 198, 210
expertise, 40, 54, 62, 101, 114, 119, 140, 175, 208

fail(ing), 1, 144, 162-167, 193, 194, 202
fixity/fixed, 1, 4, 5, 9, 22, 31, 32, 41, 75, 82, 99, 105, 120, 129, 134, 173, 191, 202-204, 209, 212
flexible, 9, 24, 49, 111, 201, 206, 209-212
fluidity, 1, 2, 4, 6, 19, 23, 25, 32, 75, 82, 99, 105, 120, 173, 175, 203, 204
folded/folds, 41-45, 64, 89, 110, 118, 171, 174, 186, 194, 207

grammar, 15, 20-27, 32, 33, 51, 58, 79, 130, 132, 180, 190

heuristic, 4, 11, 20, 42

ideology, 18, 28, 56, 173
individual repertoire(s), 20, 37, 38, 44, 59, 113, 203
in situ, 31, 32, 38, 45, 59, 115, 120, 129, 158
invention, 24, 43,

Khayelitshan languaging, 1, 3-11, 17, 19, 42, 51-53, 72, 79, 80, 86, 88, 95, 104, 114, 127, 133, 135, 137, 140, 158, 160-162, 184, 186, 192, 193, 203, 208, 211
Khayelitshan resources, 43, 44, 57, 75, 89, 97, 99, 100, 104-111, 118-121, 128, 130, 134, 135, 146, 147, 152, 158-160, 165-174, 91, 208

(re)languager(s), 21, 39, 41, 50, 54, 63, 98, 100, 174, 194, 196, 203, 204
language policy, 7-9, 25, 68, 109-111, 125, 141, 159, 162, 168-173, 201, 206, 211
languaging resource(s), 31, 34, 51, 64, 74, 75, 93, 110, 114, 134-138, 146, 152-156, 160-165, 171, 172, 176
linguistics/linguists, 3, 4, 8, 20, 23-26, 31, 36, 55-62, 66, 78, 86, 132, 156, 164-167, 205-212
linguistic descriptor(s), 21, 34, 36, 122, 196, 200, 206
linguistic ethnography, 12, 48, 55-59, 62
linguistic features, 3, 4, 20, 25-27, 31, 33-39, 42, 47, 58-63, 68, 74, 83, 90-96, 101, 107, 111, 117, 118, 122, 125, 134-141, 147, 149, 164-168, 180, 192, 196, 198, 202, 206, 211
linguistic heterogeneity, 2, 5, 17, 18, 21, 31, 36, 44, 52, 57, 66, 75, 94, 99, 105, 107, 116, 117, 120-122, 140, 141, 171, 197-212
linguistic homogeneity, 17, 26, 75, 77, 91, 112, 117, 120, 129, 165, 197, 200-212
local, 7, 9, 11, 15, 16, 21, 24, 27, 30, 39-42, 58-62, 72, 93, 101, 107, 114, 119, 124, 140, 141, 162, 166, 167, 184-187, 196, 201-204

mechanism, 9, 90, 93, 121-123, 144, 149, 163-166, 172, 200, 207, 211
mediate, 30, 107, 112-116, 120, 121, 125-130, 138
mediation, 68, 93, 100, 111, 139, 158, 164, 166, 177
metrolingualism, 32, 82
monolingualism, 82, 99, 111, 124, 135, 141, 142, 147, 152, 166, 171-173, 177, 191, 201, 203

morpheme(s), 3, 21, 25, 42, 75, 83, 90, 97, 132-138, 152-155, 159, 164, 193, 196, 202
morphology, 8, 45, 51-54, 56, 58, 78-89, 97, 105, 115, 119, 120, 129, 131, 134, 149, 152, 158, 170, 181, 188, 191-199, 207, 208
mother tongue, 6, 8, 12, 13, 71, 72, 131, 210, 211

nomolanguage ideology, 18, 19, 57, 95, 210
noun class(es), 8, 51, 58, 61, 71, 83-89, 119, 130, 132, 137, 140, 150, 152, 161, 182, 189, 208

ordering, 2, 3, 6, 8, 9, 21, 23, 26, 31, 36-39, 41-46, 56, 66, 91, 109, 110, 115, 117, 128, 146, 149, 159, 174, 182, 188, 191, 196-203, 2011
orthography, 24, 126, 183-186, 192-196

parents, 12, 13, 28, 40, 48, 73, 82, 98, 123, 161, 162, 173, 181-183, 209
past (tense), 25, 79, 102, 112, 148, 149, 155, 158
perfect (tense), 77, 78, 148
periphery, 15, 17, 205, 208
phoneme(s), 126, 132, 185
possessive, 8, 139, 182, 183, 189, 190
potential, 1, 16, 17, 20, 99, 165, 179, 180, 183, 193, 194, 200, 206, 211,
prefix, 2, 8, 32, 36, 43, 61, 62, 71, 78, 83, 130-135, 140, 161, 164, 175
present (tense), 77, 79, 88, 133, 180, 194, 195
pronoun(s), 83-86, 113, 136, 139, 151, 165, 180, 182-195, 204, 208
pronunciation, 81, 97, 140, 184, 185

re-, 43, 44, 147, 150, 164, 197
referential device, 85, 86
reference tracking, 86, 87, 119, 151, 152, 161, 182-190, 195, 208, 209
relanguaging circle, 43-45, 65, 90, 99, 102-110, 115, 117, 138, 144-148, 152, 157, 166, 169, 200

schooling, 7-17, 25, 33, 40, 48, 72, 99, 125, 141, 162, 174, 178, 184, 186, 195, 202, 203, 209

seeing like a state, 2-6, 14, 18, 23, 31, 35, 36, 47, 57, 67, 91, 117, 120, 122, 141, 150, 172, 194, 199, 204, 210, 211
segregation, 5, 48-50
socioeconomic, 5, 7, 15, 48
sorts out, sorted out, sorting out, 18, 21, 43-46, 57, 65, 66, 97, 99, 100, 106-111, 116, 117, 120, 121, 128, 138, 140, 149, 154, 158, 162-166, 170, 172, 185-187, 190-199, 203, 204, 209
sorting practice, 20, 38, 42-44, 66, 118, 159, 186, 204-209
source of confusion, 84, 116, 138, 140, 187
spatial repertoire, 4, 20, 21, 32, 37-42, 52, 58, 64, 68, 71, 74, 82, 86, 91-97, 100, 107, 118-121, 149, 152, 154, 156, 165, 174, 186, 194, 196, 200, 203, 207, 210
spelling, 15, 51, 140, 180-187, 192-198, 204, 209,
statist repertoire(s), 27, 28, 36, 41-45, 64, 66, 68, 75, 86-90, 95, 100, 108, 110, 115, 117, 147, 148, 162, 171, 174, 185, 191, 196, 204-211
stumbling block, 84, 118, 122, 140, 165, 190, 191, 199,
subjunctive (mood), 78-83
subvert, subversive, 82, 125, 141, 144, 166, 167, 173, 177, 201, 211
suffix, 59, 61, 79, 98, 103, 131, 134, 194

target, 1, 41, 97-99, 112, 170, 171, 174, 196,
testing, 6, 9-12, 21, 22, 33, 41, 123, 125, 142, 144-147, 152, 156, 159, 160-165, 175, 197, 202, 208-212
township school(s), 5, 11-73, 17, 28, 34, 81, 93, 144, 186, 194, 205
trans-, 33, 36, 147, 150, 164, 175
translanguaging, 3, 4, 20, 22, 32-38, 44, 59, 61, 75, 82, 89, 91, 97, 99, 105, 118, 122, 129, 131, 135, 149, 150, 163, 164, 173, 175, 177, 194-198, 200-211
trick, 1, 3, 11, 18, 19
trust, 50-53

xhosing, to xhosa, 42, 51, 121, 186, 207,

For Product Safety Concerns and Information please contact our EU Authorised Representative:

Easy Access System Europe

Mustamäe tee 50

10621 Tallinn

Estonia

gpsr.requests@easproject.com